A Garland Series

DISSERTATIONS
ON FILM

Advisory Editor: Garth S. Jowett

David H. Mould

AMERICAN NEWSFILM
1914–1919
The Underexposed War

Garland Publishing, Inc.
New York & London 1983

All volumes in this series are printed on
acid-free, 250-year-life paper.

Library of Congress Cataloging in Publication Data

Mould, David H. (David Harley), 1949–
    American newsfilm, 1914–1919.

    (Dissertations on film)
    Originally presented as the author's thesis (M.A.,
1980)
    Bibliography: p.
    1. World War, 1914–1918—Motion pictures and the war.
I. Title. II. Series.
D522.23.M68 1983   791.43'09'09358   81-48349
ISBN 0-8240-5107-6

Design by Jonathan Billing

Printed in the United States of America

AMERICAN NEWSFILM, 1914-1919:

THE UNDEREXPOSED WAR

by

David H. Mould

This thesis was submitted to the
Department of Radio-Television-
Film in partial fulfillment of
the requirements for the Degree
of Master of Arts in June 1980.

CONTENTS

ACKNOWLEDGEMENTS

My thanks to the following--for their time, ideas, specialized knowledge and encouragement. It made my task a pleasure, instead of a chore!

Charles M. Berg, Radio-TV-Film Department, University of Kansas.

Kevin Brownlow, film historian, London.

Nancy Casey, Sherman Grinberg Film Libraries, New York.

Raymond Fielding, film historian, University of Houston.

Hal Himmelstein, Radio-TV Center, Ohio University.

Garth Jowett, University of Houston.

Bruce Linton, Chairman, Radio-TV-Film Department, University of Kansas.

Linda Loree, John E. Allen, Inc., Park Ridge, New Jersey.

William T. Murphy, Chief, Motion Picture and Sound Recording Branch, National Archives, Washington, D.C.

Calder M. Pickett, School of Journalism, University of Kansas.

Nicholas Pronay, School of History, The University of Leeds.

Emily Sieger, and the staff of the Motion Picture Division of the Library of Congress, Washington, D.C.

Charles Silver, Film Study Center, Museum of Modern Art, New York.

D. H. M.

Lawrence, Kansas   Spring, 1980

INTRODUCTION

War is news. It has the quintessential elements of the news story: it affects the lives and welfare of large numbers of people; it involves conflict--between nations, armies and ideals; and it is timely, continually offering fresh developments and perspectives for the journalist. The proximity of the action determines its news value: a civil war at home is more newsworthy than a border dispute on the other side of the world. And the nature of the fighting shapes the coverage: a planned battle between two armies is easier to follow than the hit-and-run actions of guerrilla forces. While the question of whether to cover a war is rarely in doubt, the issues of how to do it--and, in retrospect, how well it was done--are.

These issues will be treated in this study of the first major war to be covered by motion picture photographers--World War I. For the United States, the war had two distinct phases: from August 1914 to April 1917, America was officially a neutral country, although economic, cultural and spiritual ties brought it closer to the Allies than to the Central Powers; after April 1917, the United States was in the war, providing men, money and munitions for the Allies.

These two phases are mirrored in the newsreels and documentary films shown in the United States. In the early years, American cameramen worked on both sides of the lines; if the films showed more of the Allied war effort, it was because these countries produced more footage, and their naval blockade prevented some German films from reaching the United States. After America joined the Allies, most film was shot by Army cameramen, censored by the military authorities in Paris and Washington, and distributed by a government agency, the Committee on Public Information.

When World War I broke out, the American film industry was at a stage of precocious adolescence. More and more films were being produced every year, and there were more and more movie theaters to show them. At the beginning of the war, American motion picture production accounted for more than half the world's total movie production; by 1917, America was making almost all the world's motion pictures, as the demands of war took their toll on the film industries of France, Britain, Italy and Germany. "For American producers," writes Lewis Jacobs, "the European disaster was a stroke of fortune, since it gave them a virtual monopoly of the world movie market."[1] At the same time, the domestic market was expanding; few weeks passed without reports in the trade press of new production ventures, although some were short-lived. A relatively new feature, the newsreel, was growing in favor, and during the war it became an essential part of the standard movie package as support for the main feature. But the young business had developed few professional standards to guide its members.

The industry was singularly ill-prepared to provide comprehensive coverage of a conflict on the scale of World War I. Its development had made it a primarily commercial business: film producers and

[1]Lewis Jacobs, The Rise of the American Film: A Critical History (New York: Harcourt, Brace and Company, 1939), p. 159.

exhibitors were more concerned with presenting attention-grabbing, heart-warming, tear-jerking subjects than with providing an accurate and balanced account of the war; in the prevailing climate, the faking and restaging of scenes was prevalent, though rarely condoned. Most of the photographers who worked at the front had little or no experience of war coverage; they were hampered by heavy equipment, obstructive military officers, poor communications and over-zealous censors. Even after the United States entered the war, the supply of newsfilm was erratic, censorship capricious and exhibition unashamedly propagandistic.

The study will begin by examining the background to the war for the movie industry--the coverage of previous conflicts and the growth of the newsreel, the main vehicle for the presentation of war footage. The outbreak of war in Europe was the impetus for a flood of war movies-- some factual, some fictional--in the United States; the reaction of the industry and audiences to the war will be set against the backdrop of commercial motives and an official policy of neutrality that attempted to set limits on the content of war movies. The experiences of American cameramen who worked in the war zone will be recounted in detail: their efforts to gain access to the front, to overcome problems ranging from unreliable equipment to poor lighting conditions and to evade censorship shaped the coverage of the war. The difficulties in obtaining footage were compounded by the public clamor for war film, and some producers tried to fill the void by faking and restaging scenes; such practices often went unchecked because theater audiences had not developed the critical perception of film we have today.

World War I was the first conflict in which film became a

significant instrument of propaganda; the efforts of the Allies and
Central Powers to use film to shape American opinion will be examined in
the context of their general propaganda campaigns. The use of film as
propaganda was intensified after America entered the war as the Committee on Public Information used newsreels and longer fact films to convince audiences at home and abroad of the righteousness of the Allied
cause. But the U.S. government's first major venture into motion pictures was fraught with problems: Signal Corps cameramen in France
encountered many of the physical difficulties their civilian counterparts had experienced; coverage was often incomplete and censorship
rigorous; disputes between the Committee and the newsreel companies over
the distribution of footage and permits for filming created an uneasy,
and occasionally hostile, relationship between the film industry and the
government.

Our perceptions of the role and authenticity of newsfilm in
wartime have changed fundamentally in the past sixty years. Films received enthusiastically by early audiences are regarded with skepticism
by modern scholars; when compared with footage from World War II and
television reports from Vietnam, the World War I films seem fragmentary,
artless and often dull. But to judge the films of this period by modern
standards is to stumble into the trap of historical hindsight. A perspective is necessary: trends that went undetected by contemporaries
may become clear on later examination. But the historical perspective
should be used to pull together the strands of the subject rather than
to measure it against some preconception of the essential elements of
war coverage. It is easy to chide film producers for faking and

restaging scenes, and for injecting the perceived emotional values of the fiction film into their fact films; yet these practices were, at least in part, dictated by the demands of an industry that was growing, of news-reel producers who needed a regular supply of subjects, and of audiences that had not developed a critical awareness of the techniques of film-making. The footage obtained at the front may seem patchy and monoton-ous; yet in no other major war, before or since, have motion picture photographers faced such physical difficulties. The blatant use of film as propaganda may appear offensive to modern observers; yet it must be regarded as merely one strand in a larger campaign of opinion manage-ment.

To appreciate the significance of newsfilm in World War I, the historian must be both detached and involved: the detachment brings an understanding of the broad themes, and permits the building of evidence to suggest trends and relationships; involvement helps the historian to realize how contemporaries saw things, and makes the "holier than thou" attitude of hindsight seem irrelevant. The aim of this thesis is to examine the newsfilm of World War I from the outside in, and the inside out--to be both detached and involved.

CHAPTER 1

THE BACKGROUND: WAR COVERAGE BEFORE 1914

To the pioneers of the motion picture, military activities were an attractive subject. In peacetime and wartime, parades, reviews and maneuvers were a staple source of newsfilm, and a popular item with audiences. Few Americans had seen the armies and navies of Europe; motion pictures brought scenes from Britain, France, Germany, Austria and Russia, where great military machines were taking shape. News from across the ocean was given visual form as armies marched, supply trains moved forward, soldiers trained and generals struck poses with their staff officers.

Some motion picture producers were better prepared to cover military subjects than others. Thomas Edison's first camera was so large and unwieldy that it was rarely moved outside his studio in West Orange, New Jersey.[1] Louis Lumière's cinematographe, by contrast, was light and adaptable; hand-cranked, it did not depend, as did Edison's, on electricity.[2] Lumière's operators did not wait for the world to come to them; they went out to seek visually interesting subjects. Travelling abroad, these operators frequently filmed military scenes and made them an integral feature in their screenings; for a program at

---

[1]Erik Barnouw, Documentary: A History of the Non-Fiction Film (New York: Oxford University Press, 1974), p. 5.

[2]Ibid., p. 6.

6

Proctor's Pleasure Palace in New York in March 1897, Felix Mesguich included "The Charge of the Austrian Lancers" and "German Dragoons Leaping the Hurdles."[1] Such scenes became a predictable element in what film historian Erik Barnouw has characterized as the "ritual composite" of the early newsreels: the other elements were "a royal visit, . . . a sports event, a funny item, a disaster, and a native festival in costume."[2]

To photographers seeking visually compelling subjects, the spate of wars around the turn of the century was a boon. In the Sudan, the war artist Réné Bull built a rostrum of bamboo poles to film the famed charge of the Dervishes at the Battle of Omdurman.[3] In 1897, the London Times reported that the war correspondent, F. Villiars, was filming the fighting in Crete.[4]

The Spanish-American War was the first major conflict covered by American motion picture companies, and their films reflected the jingoistic spirit of the period. From the time the American battleship Maine exploded in Havana Harbor on 15 February 1898, public interest was at fever pitch, and film producers set out to exploit the market for film--any film--about the war. On 21 April, soon after the declaration of war, the Vitagraph company cashed in on patriotic fervor with its

---

[1]David Robinson, The History of World Cinema (New York: Stein and Day, 1973), p. 23, quoted in ibid., p. 13.

[2]Barnouw, Documentary, p. 26.

[3]Kenneth Gordon, "The Early Days of News-Reels," British Kinematography, August 1950, pp. 47-8.

[4]Ibid., p. 48.

<u>Tearing Down the Spanish Flag</u>, produced by Albert E. Smith and J. Stuart
Blackton in their studio on the roof of the Morse building in New York
City. This short, simple film showed a flagpole from which a Spanish
flag was flying; the flag was abruptly torn down, and in its place the
American flag was raised. In a lecture at the University of Southern
California in 1929, Blackton revealed how the film was made:

> It was taken in a 10-by-12 studio room, the background a
> building next door. We had a flag pole and two 18-inch flags.
> Smith operated the machine and I, with this very hand, grab-
> bed the Spanish flag and tore it down from the pole and pulled
> the Stars and Stripes to the top of the flag pole. That was
> our very first dramatic picture and it is surprising how much
> dramatic effect it created. . . . The people went wild.[1]

Modesty was not Blackton's strong suit, but the film historian
Terry Ramsaye agreed that <u>Tearing Down the Spanish Flag</u> had an immediate
impact on audiences. When it was shown, he wrote, " . . . cheers rocked
the vaudeville houses and hats were tossed into the orchestra pits when
the hand of righteous destiny reached out to tear down the Spanish
banner."[2] And, as Smith wrote later:

> Projected on a thirty-foot screen, the effect on audiences
> was sensational and sent us searching for similar subjects. .
> . . The people were on fire and eager for every line of news.
> The New York <u>Journal</u> sold a million copies in a single day.
> The circulation of Pulitzer's New York <u>World</u> rose to five
> million a week. . . .[3]

<u>Tearing Down the Spanish Flag</u> was not even an original idea.

---

[1]Quoted in Jacobs, <u>The American Film</u>, p. 11.

[2]Terry Ramsaye, <u>A Million And One Nights</u> (New York: Simon and
Schuster, 1926), p. 389.

[3]Albert E. Smith, <u>Two Reels and a Crank</u> (Garden City, N.Y.:
Doubleday, 1952), pp. 54-5.

Thomas A. Edison had made two similar films the month before, both of them entitled <u>Old Glory and the Cuban Flag</u>; Edison used stop motion to replace a Cuban flag with an American flag.[1] Biograph released <u>Changing the Flag at Puerto Rico</u>. And there were other more obscure imitations.

Edison appears to have provided the first footage from the war zone with scenes from Colón, Cuba, of the funeral procession for victims of the <u>Maine</u> explosion,[2] and shots of the half-submerged wreck of the ship.[3] Vitagraph covered the burials at Arlington Cemetery; when the film was shown in New York, the theater orchestra provided accompaniment, making, in Smith's words, "the most of the occasion with a soul-rending dirge."[4] Vitagraph and Edison were at Hoboken, New Jersey, to film the departure of the 71st National Guard Regiment for Tampa, the assembly point for the invasion of Cuba.[5] Vitagraph's film was processed within hours and screened that same evening at Tony Pastor's Theater in New York:

> That night at Pastor's the audience, enthralled with the idea of a war with Spain, saw their boys marching for the first time on any screen. They broke into a thunderous storm of shouting and foot stamping. Hats and coats filled the air. Never had Pastor's witnessed such a night.[6]

---

[1]Library of Congress Collection, copyright nos. 17706 and 18131.

[2]Copyright no. 25325. See also "Speaking of Pictures . . . Library of Congress Unearths First Newsreels," <u>Life</u>, 20 September 1943, p. 18.

[3]Copyright no. 25323.

[4]Smith, <u>Two Reels and a Crank</u>, p. 54.

[5]Copyright no. 38239.

[6]Smith, <u>Two Reels and a Crank</u>, p. 56.

While films of American troops in training and embarking for the war zone continued to thrill audiences, little of the war itself found its way onto motion picture screens. It was easier to work in Hoboken than in Havana; several cameramen reached Cuba and filmed the troops disembarking, but that was as far as most of them got. Terry Ramsaye questions the accounts of cameramen who claimed to have worked at the front:

> A few of the old timers of those expeditions survive, telling tales of photographic desperation and film making amid the shock of clashing battle lines and bursting shrapnel. But all these tales end with, "And then a big shell came along and blew up my camera and I never got back with any of the film.[1]

With access to the front difficult, and the fighting undramatic, many film companies resorted to the outright manufacture of war scenes. The Campaign in Cuba series included scenes of American sailors Landing Under Fire, The Battle of San Juan Hill and the ensuing victory, Our Flag Is There to Stay! These films were presented to the public as genuine, but cameraman F.L. Donoghue recalled later that almost all the war scenes were filmed on the shores of New Jersey.[2]

In his catalog of pre-1912 entries in the Library of Congress collection, Kemp Niver classifies some Edison films, purportedly taken in Cuba and the Philippines, as obvious fakes: the advance of the Kansas volunteers at Caloocan, the capture of trenches at Candaba, a Cuban ambush, the retreat of Filipinos from trenches, the raising of the American flag over Morro Castle, a rout of Filipino soldiers, the

[1]Ramsaye, A Million And One Nights, p. 390.

[2]The New York Journal, 29 January 1937, quoted in Jacobs, American Film, p. 14.

shooting of captured insurgents, a skirmish of Rough Riders, American infantry at El Caney, and troops and Red Cross workers in the trenches near Caloocan.[1] The Edison Catalog of 1901-1902 diplomatically informed exhibitors that

> We are indebted to the fearless activity of our artist, Mr. William Paley, for the following war views taken on Cuban soil. Under the protection of a special correspondent's pass given by the United States Government, he improved the occasions as they presented themselves with gratifying results, as shown in the excellent films we are now offering the public.[2]

The Edison Company was probably no more blameworthy than its rivals in this respect; however, Edison's practice of copyrighting films has left historians with more evidence about his company than any other.[3] Edison also produced some genuine films, most of them concerning the embarkation of troops. That Edison was not alone in faking footage is confirmed by a contemporary account of a Biograph film that purported to show American troops charging a force of rebels in the Philippines:

> . . . If it is what it is represented to be, the camera must have been stationed just in front of the Tagalog position and in the direct line of fire, when the picture was taken. A Drill at Van Cortland Park would probably correctly describe it.[4]

---

[1]Kemp Niver, Motion Pictures from the Library of Congress Paper Print Collection, 1894-1912 (Berkeley: University of California Press, 1967).

[2]Quoted in Jacobs, American Film, p. 14.

[3]Between 1896 and 1900, Edison copyrighted more than 250 newsfilm titles, while it appears neither Biograph nor Vitagraph copyrighted any news-films. See "Newsreel" categories in Niver's catalog.

[4]Review in the Rochester Democrat and Chronicle, May 1900, quoted in George Pratt, "No Magic, No Mystery, No Sleight of Hand," Image, December 1959, p. 206. Van Cortland Park is in the Bronx, New York City.

Edison wasn't reluctant to admit he had faked war scenes; indeed, his company wholeheartedly endorsed the practice, by claiming to have "improved the occasions."[1] Smith and Blackton of Vitagraph were more reticent about their methods.

In his autobiography, Smith claims that he and Blackton accompanied Theodore Roosevelt to Cuba,[2] and filmed the assault of his Rough Riders on San Juan Hill.[3]

Smith's account appears to be as much of a fabrication as some of his films. Blackton's unpublished autobiography admits that they never got to Cuba.[4] However, Vitagraph claimed to have exclusive footage of the campaign, and theaters were clamoring for it. So Smith and Blackton went to work on the Battle of Santiago Bay where American warships had destroyed the spanish fleet.

> At this time vendors in New York were selling large sturdy photographs of ships of the American and Spanish fleets. We bought a set of each and cut out the battleships. On a table, topside down, we placed one of Blackton's large canvas covered frames and filled it with water an inch deep. In order to stand the cutouts of the ships in the water, we nailed them to lengths of wood about an inch square. In this way a little "shelf" was provided behind each ship, and on this shelf we placed pinches of gunpowder--three pinches for each ship--not too many, we felt, for a major sea engagement of this sort.
>
> For a background, Blackton daubed a few white clouds on a blue-tinted cardboard. To each of the ships, now sitting placidly in our shallow "bay," we attached a fine thread to enable us to pull the ships past the camera at the proper

---

[1]Clyde Jeavons, A Pictorial History of War Films (Secaucus, N.J.: Citadel Press, 1974), p. 16.

[2]Smith, Two Reels and a Crank, pp. 56-65.

[3]Although the engagement was popularly known as the Battle of San Juan Hill, it took place at nearby Kettle Hill.

[4]Information supplied by film historian Kevin Brownlow.

moment and in the correct order.

     We needed someone to blow smoke into the scene, but we couldn't
go too far outside our circle if the secret was to be kept.
Mrs. Blackton was called in and she volunteered, in this day of
nonsmoking womanhood, to smoke a cigarette. A friendly office
boy said he would try a cigar. This was fine, as we needed the
volume.

     A piece of cotton was dipped in alcohol and attached to a
wire slender enough to escape the eye of the camera. Blackton,
concealed behind the side of the table farthermost from the
camera, touched off the mounds of gunpowder with his wire taper
--and the battle was on. Mrs. Blackton, smoking and coughing,
delivered a fine haze. Jim had worked out a timing arrangement
with her so that she blew the smoke into the scene at approxi-
mately the moment of explosion. . . .

     The film and lenses of that day were imperfect enough to
conceal the crudities of our miniature, and as the picture ran
only two minutes there was not time for anyone to study it
critically. . . . .

     Pastor's and both Proctor houses played to capacity audi-
ences for several weeks. Jim and I felt less and less remorse
of conscience when we saw how much excitement and enthusiasm
were aroused by The Battle of Santiago Bay.[1]

The film had cost just $1.98 to produce. It played to capacity
audiences in three New York theaters for several weeks, giving Smith
and Blackton an excellent return on their investment. Its authenticity
does not appear to have been questioned at the time. Since there was
no genuine film of the battle, nothing could be used for purposes of
comparison. The only other film purporting to show the battle was an
even more elaborate re-creation by Edwin H. Amet, working at Waukegan
near Chicago. Beside his Battle of Santiago Bay, the Vitagraph effort
would have looked decidedly amateurish. Terry Ramsaye described the
step-by-step production of the film:

     . . . In miniature he [Amet] constructed the Bay of Santiago
in a tub, with all the ships participating in the action, working them up with a great fineness of detail and equipping them

[1]Ibid., pp. 66-8.

with guns, all to fit exactly with the pictures and descriptions in the periodicals. The models were proportioned to the lens angle to create perspective with great accuracy. Electrically controlled devices supplied waves, and push buttons controlled the guns and ship movements.[1]

Amet operated the camera, giving cues to his assistant, William H. Howard, who pushed the buttons. The ships got up steam, and ploughed through the water with a curling bow wave. At Amet's signal,

. . . Every ship went into action with shells bursting about, splattering on the armor. A destroyer charged the U.S.S. Iowa and a twelve inch rifle lowered and fired point blank. The destroyer lurched under the impact, settled by the stern and sank with a mound of waves rising as the bow went out of sight. So the battle raged.[2]

Amet said he had filmed the battle from a dispatch boat six miles away by using a telescopic lens, and it appears that the fake was generally accepted. When he showed the film at the U.S. Naval Training Station at Lake Bluff, Illinois, one officer wanted to know how Amet had been able to film the experimental ship U.S.S. Vesuvius, which operated only at night. "Easy," Amet is reputed to have said, "you see we used moonlight film."[3] A legend survives that the Spanish Government was so convinced of the film's authenticity that it bought a print for its military archives.[4]

The Boxer Rebellion in China did not arouse the nationalistic passions of the Spanish-American War, but the film producers did their utmost to stimulate public interest. The Edison Catalog recommended its Boxer Massacres in Pekin on the grounds that the rebellion had ". . .

---

[1]Ramsaye, A Million And One Nights, p. 390.

[2]Ibid., p. 391.

[3]Ibid.   [4]Ibid.

turned the eyes of the civilized world toward China. Public interest was intensely aroused and people eagerly appreciate any pictures that relate to the locality in which the war in China was prosecuted."[1] Another Edison film, Street Scene in Pekin, included "scenes taken on the ground in front of the Legation showing British police dispersing a crowd of unruly citizens."[2]

The role of the motion picture in informing the American public of foreign conflicts was recognized by contemporary newspapers. Leslie's Weekly eulogized Biograph's coverage of the Boxer Rebellion and the Boer War:

> The American Biograph is taking a prominent part in the two wars now occupying the center of the world's stage, and the pictures which are being shown at Keith's Theatre in New York and other leading houses throughout the country, are of intense interest. . . . We are promised some vivid, soul-stirring pictures of actual, gruesome war. A written description is always the point of view of the correspondent. But the Biograph camera does not lie and we form our judgement of this and that as we watch the magic of the screen.[3]

Biograph's camera may not have lied, but others did. As Barnouw notes: "Film companies did not want to ignore catastrophes or other headline events merely because their cameramen could not get there; enterprise filled the gap."[4] The British producer James Williamson shot his Attack on a Chinese Mission Station (1898) in his back yard, and some of his Boer War scenes on a golf course.[5] "Japanese" and "Russian"

---

[1]Quoted in Jacobs, American Film, p. 13.   [2]Ibid.

[3]Leslie's Weekly, 6 January 1900, quoted in ibid., pp. 13-14.

[4]Barnouw, Documentary, p. 25.

[5]Leslie Wood, The Miracle of the Movies (London: Burke, 1947), p. 192.

soldiers fought in the snows of Long Island and New Jersey for Biograph's
<u>Battle of the Yalu</u> (1904) and a competing Edison film, <u>Skirmish between
Russian and Japanese Advance Guards</u>.[1] In the latter, soldiers surge
back and forth before the unmoving camera, many falling in their tracks.
To help the audience follow the action, the Russians are conveniently
dressed in white and the Japanese in dark colors. French audiences were
astonished by the spectacle of "Russian" and "Japanese" soldiers fighting
to the death in front of the Chantilly grandstand.[2]

The most intensive coverage of the Boer War was provided by
W. K. L. Dickson of the Biograph company, who spent more than a year
with the British forces. With two assistants he travelled around front-
line areas in a horse-drawn cart. His coverage has been described by
film historian Raymond Fielding as "surprisingly detailed and of good
quality, considering the conditions under which he and his assistants
. . . had to work."[3]

Dickson's problems foreshadowed many of the difficulties encountered by motion picture photographers in World War I. His camera was
cumbersome, and could be operated only from the cart or a heavy tripod;
this lack of mobility prevented him from obtaining the intimate war
coverage to which modern audiences are accustomed. By using a telephoto
lens, he was occasionally able to photograph Boer soldiers from the

---

[1]Barnouw, <u>Documentary</u>, p. 25.

[2]Maurice Bardèche and Robert Brasilliach, <u>The History of Motion
Pictures</u> (New York: W. W. Norton, 1938), p. 40.

[3]Raymond Fielding, <u>The American Newsreel, 1911-1967</u> (Norman,
Okla.: University of Oklahoma Press, 1977), p. 35.

British lines; but, more often than not, the haze and smoke obscured his line of sight, and made it difficult to focus properly. Living conditions were unpleasant, travel uncomfortable and disease rampant. As a non-combatant correspondent, Dickson had none of the accepted rights of the ordinary soldier; if he was taken prisoner by the Boers, he faced the firing squad--the usual treatment for suspected spies.

Dickson was fortunate enough to enjoy almost unimpeded access to high military officers, some of whom gave him advance notice of engagements so that he could set up his equipment before the battle began. On one occasion, telegraph operators held up a message from Lord Kitchener so that Dickson would be able to film them sending it.[1] When he wanted to film Lord Roberts, the British Commander in Chief, at work with his staff, his table was taken out into the sun "for the convenience of Mr. Dickson."[2] However, not every high-ranking officer was as accommodating, and Dickson complained that on some occasions he was denied access to front-line areas.[3]

Smith went to South Africa for Vitagraph, and experienced the same difficulties as Dickson. Forced to work at some distance from the fighting, he was unable to obtain any action footage. But the veteran of The Battle of Santiago Bay came up with a characteristic solution:

> . . . I asked a few of the British soldiers if they would put on Boer clothes and go through a few mock skirmishes, which they did. They fired a few volleys from behind boulders and went screaming past the camera in fine "forward charge" tech-

---

[1]William Kennedy Laurie Dickson, The Biograph in Battle (London: Unwin, 1901), p. 62.

[2]Ibid., p. xiii.   [3]Ibid., p. 63 ff.

nique.[1]

Ironically, when Smith later photographed a really extraordinary event, American audiences believed it was a fake. The British used railway freight engines, without tracks, to ferry loads across a river and to pull trucks and wagons out of the mud:

> Huge railway freight engines steamed into sight! Enormous traction machines with the wide and high wheels and tremendous boiler. . . . That they were moving on land and taking part in a war in the very heart of Africa was almost unbelievable.
> I photographed the snorting giants as they dragged huge loads across the ford and towed the mired wagons and guns out of the river. When the film was shown in New York, Vitagraph was accused of having faked the freight engine scenes. Our critics claimed it was not possible for engines to move without rails, much less on anything as rough as the African terrain at the Tugela.[2]

Audiences had some cause to be suspicious because other film companies that claimed to have "Boer War scenes" did not go to the trouble and expense of a trip to Africa. Edison, for example, preferred the veldt of New Jersey:

> . . . it is an open secret that for weeks during the Boer War regularly equipped British and Boer armies confronted each other on the peaceful hills of Orange, New Jersey, ready to enact before the camera the stirring events told by the cable from the heat of the hostilities.[3]

According to Terry Ramsaye, Edison's war was "conducted with several handsome stovepipe cannons mounted on carriage wheels and two armies of Bowery drifters arrayed in costumes from the Eaves establishment."[4] But, unfortunately for Edison, the campaign did not go as

---

[1]Smith, Two Reels and a Crank, p. 102.   [2]Ibid., p. 120.

[3]Frank Lewis Dyer and Thomas Commerford Martin, Edison--His Life and Inventions (New York: Harper and Brothers, 1910), p. 547.

[4]Ramsaye, A Million and One Nights, pp. 403-4.

planned:

> The Edison picture forces might have fought the Boer-British war indefinitely if it had not been abruptly terminated by a one-man strike. Charles Geoly, general utility and office boy for Eaves, grew unhappy because the Bowery armies left the uniforms inhabited by cooties. He packed up the war and sent it back to New York to be fumigated. When the armies appeared they had nothing to wear for the next battle. The war was over, for Edison.[1]

Vitagraph continued to fake films for several years, and occasionally landed in serious trouble. In December 1911, the company produced a fraudulent film that purported to show alleged atrocities committed by the Italians on the Turks at Tripoli. When the film was shown at the Dewey Theater in New York City, Albert Pecorini, the managing director of the Italian-American Civic League, leaped from his seat and denounced the picture as a fake. One offending scene, he claimed, had been shot at Coney Island. He and two other Italian-Americans were arrested and charged with inciting a riot, but they were released by the magistrate when it was established that the film was a fake.[2]

The incident caused such a stir in the Italian-American community, in official circles and in the trade press that Vitagraph was obligated to withdraw the film and apologize to the Italian consul. An editorial in Moving Picture News roundly condemned Vitagraph, calling the film "an abominable lie" and saying that its makers had brought shame on the industry:

> . . . It was a disgrace to the Vitagraph Company, for the sake of pocketing a few dirty dollars, to bring out such a film, and,

[1]Ibid., p. 404.

[2]"Disgraceful Fake Pictures," Moving Picture News, 16 December 1911, p. 5.

worse still, for the Patents Company to allow such a disgusting exhibition of disgraceful avariciousness to be released by the General Film Company.[1]

Two years later, another company, the Mutual Film Corporation, was the butt of equally forthright criticism--not for faking, but for interfering in a war for sheer commercial gain. The Mexican rebel leader, Pancho Villa, whose colorful personality and exciting campaign had captured public attention in the United States, hit on a way of turning media interest to financial profit. He invited bids for the exclusive motion picture rights to his war. When cameramen in El Paso wired Villa's proposal to their head offices in New York, there was a deafening silence--except from Mutual. The idea appealed to its president, Harry E. Aitken, who despatched Frank M. Thayer and Gunther Lessing to Juarez to talk terms with Villa. The agreement, signed on 3 January 1914, gave Villa an immediate payment of $25,000, which was deposited in an El Paso bank, and a 50 per cent royalty on the earnings of the pictures.[2] In return, Villa agreed to provide horses, food and escorts for the Mutual cameramen, and not to allow photographers from any other company on the battlefield.[3] Whenever possible, battles would be fought during daylight hours, and at times convenient for the cameramen.[4] As the New York Times put it,

[1]Ibid.

[2]Ramsaye, A Million And One Nights, p. 671.

[3]Kevin Brownlow, The War, The West, and The Wilderness (New York: Knopf, 1978), p. 91.

[4]Ramsaye, A Million And One Nights, p. 671, and Homer Croy, How Motion Pictures are Made (New York: Harper and Brothers, 1918), p. 258.

To be a useful partner in this business, Gen. Villa will have to do more than let the camera men get what they can; he must see to it that the really interesting charges are made when the light is good and that a satisfactory part of the killing and dying is done in focus.[1]

Mutual wanted to keep the deal secret, but the Times got onto the story, and called Aitken at one o'clock in the morning. After expressing surprise that the Times had learned of the agreement before his own staff, the Mutual president appeared to have some misgivings about the deal, telling the reporter:

. . . it is true. I am a partner of Gen. Villa. It's a new proposition, and it has been worrying me a lot all day. How would you feel to be a partner of a man engaged in killing people, and do you suspect that the fact that moving picture machines are in range to immortalize an act of daring or of cruel brutality will have any effect on the warfare itself? I have been thinking of a lot of things since I made this contract.[2]

But Mutual was not ready to sacrifice its $25,000 investment for such scruples. Aitken had already sent four cameramen to Villa's camp; they were equipped, said the Times, with "apparatus designed especially to take pictures on battlefields."[3] Their leader was an Italian cameraman who had covered the Balkan Wars and had a bullet in his body to prove it.[4] These cameramen were later joined by four more, despatched from San Antonio.[5] One of them was Charles Rosher, who later became Mary Pickford's cameraman. In an interview with film historian Kevin Brownlow, he described the conditions under which he and other cameramen

[1]"Warfare is Waged for the Movies," New York Times, 8 January 1914, p. 10.

[2]"Villa To War For Movies," New York Times, 7 January 1914, p. 1.

[3]Ibid.   [4]Ibid.   [5]Ibid.

worked:

> . . . Part of the time, we lived in a boxcar, but during field
> operations we just slept on the ground. Our food consisted
> mainly of dried goat meat and tortillas. . . . I had to film
> everything; men digging their own graves . . . executions . . .
> battles. . . . Pancho Villa tried hard to be a director. He
> told me to film the funeral of a general. Villa's enemies, the
> Federal forces, had executed him by lashing him to the tracks
> and driving a train over him. The funeral spread over three
> days. I didn't have enough film for half a day. So I cranked
> the camera without any film in it. It was all I could do. I
> didn't want to be shot myself.[1]

Villa kept his side of the bargain when he delayed the attack on
Ojinaga to allow Mutual's cameramen to reach the battlefront.[2] The
Federal troops took advantage of this breathing space to bring millions
of cartridges across the frontier from the United States, and to lay in
food stocks.[3] Then, with the cameramen in position, the battle began,
and Ojinaga fell to Villa. The Federal forces crossed the Rio Grande
and surrendered to General Pershing.

Although Villa had delayed the battle for Mutual's benefit,
Harry Aitken did not think he had got his money's worth. When he
screened the film at Mutual's headquarters in New York on 22 January, he
saw a lot of Villa, and not much of anything else. As the Times reported:
"The 'movies' showed General Villa leading his army to battle at Ojinaga
in the dusk of the evening. He wore a broad smile. Another film showed
him leading his forces away from the battlefield the next morning. He

---

[1]Kevin Brownlow, The Parade's Gone By (New York: Knopf, 1969),
p. 254.

[2]Ramsaye, A Million And One Nights, p. 672.

[3]"Ojinaga Federals Defy Villa," New York Times, 8 January 1914,
p. 2.

was still smiling."[1]

Villa's insatiable desire for personal publicity exasperated the cameramen, as well as some theater audiences. As the film historian Homer Croy remarked a few years later,

> . . . Villa wished to appear personally in the film to the exclusion of all else. The public was desirous of seeing the leader, but after a few different poses at his tent, on horseback, sweeping the field with his glasses, and conferring with his staff, the public was eager to see the sanguinary results of all this preparation; but this the photographer was not allowed to show, Villa requiring that he expose another picture of him in some new and unique pose.[2]

According to Terry Ramsaye, Villa became "one of the worst of that genus described in camera vernacular as a lens louse."[3] But his ego might not have been so inflated had it not been for the attentions of the film companies. Military leaders had always been a fairly accessible subject; battles were more difficult to record. And the pattern was to continue in World War I.

Villa also staged battle scenes for Mutual's cameramen. On one occasion, he brought up a battery of light field guns to shell a hillside, allowing the cameramen to take close-ups of the guns and telephoto shots of the shells exploding. The ugly rumor got around that the hillside had been planted with prisoners who were being used for target practice.[4]

Mutual's commercial motives came in for some criticism, particularly from the Times, whose editorial writer observed:

---

[1]New York Times, 23 January 1914, p. 2.

[2]Croy, How Motion Pictures Are Made, p. 258.

[3]Ramsaye, A Million And One Nights, p. 672.   [4]Ibid., p. 673.

No doubt the films thus secured would command the attention and the money of multitudes, but even the most morbid
seeker for horrors might be shocked, if not by the sight of
carnage, at least by the thought that it had been commer-
cialized in this particularly cynical way.[1]

Mutual released two films, both entitled Mexican War Pictures,
in February and June 1914. The blurb in the trade press belied the lack
of real action in the scenes:

. . . Since early in January daring camera men have carried
Mutual cameras into the thick of every fight and have made
thousands of feet of film amid the roar of artillery, the
deadly hum of machine guns and the vicious crackle of rifle
fire. . . . You can almost hear the whistle of bullets as you
see the spatters of dust in the picture, and the shriek of
the shells as rapid-fire guns on armored trains leap back in
recoil.
Much of this film had to be cut out because it was too
realistically horrible to be publicly shown.
Some because it was obscured by the smoke and dust of
battle.
Some was lost entirely by the shattering of cameras by
bullets.[2]

Shattered cameras, smoke-obscured scenes and Mutual's sense of
propriety prevented the company from showing much action--if indeed
there was much to show. New York may have expected too much from Mexico.

But this conflict lent itself to motion picture coverage much
better than the war in Europe. The Mexican war ranged over a large
area, offering a variety of scenery, while military engagements frequently involved exciting cavalry charges. However, the military
authorities were often hostile to cameramen. Fritz Wagner of Pathé
was seized by the rebels, and his equipment, film and money taken.

---

[1]New York Times, 8 January 1914, p. 10.

[2]"Mexican War Pictures," Motion Picture News, 18 July 1914, p. 10.

Escaping from prison on foot, he reached Mexico City half-starved and suffering from dysentery.[1] Securing another camera, he returned to the battle area, where he got short shrift from the Federal forces:

> I have seen four big battles. On each occasion I was threatened with arrest from the Federal general if I took any pictures. He also threatened on one occasion when he caught me turning the crank to smash the camera. He would have done so, too, but for the fact that the rebels came pretty close just then and he had to take it on the run to save his hide.[2]

Sherman Martin, a cameraman for Universal's Animated Weekly newsreel, was continuously under fire for twelve days at Bermejillo; he and the other correspondents lived on tortillas and water. The Literary Digest reported: "Martin for five days was helpless with mountain fever, and once, for a thirty-hour stretch, war correspondents and photographers were without food or water."[3]

The Mexican war was an important training ground for some cameramen who were to establish their reputations in World War I. Wagner was sent to Germany by the American Correspondent Film Company. The Hearst cameraman Ariel Varges worked with the British army in Mesopotamia. The Chicago Tribune photographer Edwin F. Weigle, who was to make his reputation in Europe, went to Vera Cruz to film the retaliatory raid by American marines; he obtained shots of the street fighting, in which a marine from Chicago was killed, narrowly escaped injury himself, and returned to the Tribune a hero with his first scoop.[4]

---

[1] Moving Picture World, 18 July 1914, p. 440.   [2] Ibid.

[3] "Capturing Mexico with a Camera," Literary Digest, 6 June 1914, p. 1390.

[4] Frank C. Waldrop, McCormick of Chicago (Englewood Cliffs, N.J.: Prentice-Hall, 1966), p. 125.

The cameramen experienced many of the difficulties they would encounter in Europe: living conditions were spartan, food and water sometimes in short supply, and disease never far away; they were obstructed by the military authorities and their film censored; and the battles they filmed usually turned out to be less spectacular than their bosses, and the theater audiences, expected.

Film companies frequently staged battle scenes or, as in the case of The Battle of Santiago Bay,[1] resorted to outright faking to spice up dull footage. The film historian Raymond Fielding has classified fake news film into four categories:[2]

1) Theatrically staged re-creations of famous events, based roughly upon the original but not intended or likely to fool audiences. The clever re-creations produced by the French film-maker Georges Méliès would be in this category.

2) Realistically staged re-creations of famous events, based upon reliable information and duplicating insofar as possible the location, participants, and circumstances of the original. These films were generally designed to deceive audiences. The Vera Cruz raid provides a good example. Victor Milner arrived after the American marines had stormed the Post Office, the bandits' last stronghold. He complained of his misfortune to an army friend who arranged a replay of the assault, and, as Milner later told Kevin Brownlow:

. . . it was far better than the real thing. . . . The pictures were a newsreel sensation and were shown as scoops in all the

[1]Supra, pp. 12-14.

[2]Fielding, The American Newsreel, pp. 37-39.

theaters before any of us got back to the States. To this day,
I don't think anyone in the States was aware that they were a
replay, and the shots were staged.[1]

3) Rough re-creations of famous events, made without attempting
to duplicate known particulars of the events. These films were generally
designed to deceive audiences. Smith and Blackton's Battle of Santiago
Bay belongs here, although Amet's more sophisticated fake could be
classed in the second category.

4) The outright manufacture of unverifiable activities alleged
to have been associated with famous events--always intended to deceive
audiences. The mock skirmish filmed by Smith in the Boer War and the
filming of alleged Italian atrocities on Coney Island are examples.

Why did contemporary audiences accept restaged scenes and faked
footage as genuine? For the most part, they knew nothing better. At
that time, the motion picture was a new and vivid medium, and public
confidence in its veracity was high. Film criticism, like the medium
itself, was still in its infancy, and the motion picture was widely
regarded as a reliable instrument of documentary truth. As one contemporary remarked: "Cinematography cannot be made to lie, it is a machine
that merely records what is happening."[2]

For early audiences, with little or no film-going experience to
guide them, there was no way of evaluating the content of news films
purporting to show war scenes. The films were so short that it was

---

[1]Letter from Victor Milner to Kevin Brownlow, quoted in Brownlow, The War, p. 101.

[2]"The Historian of the Future," Moving Picture World, 8 July
1911, p. 1565.

difficult to detect errors; without extensive pictorial coverage of events on the screen and in newspapers, audiences and critics could not make comparisons, and had no way of knowing how the original appeared. Lastly, some fakes were virtually impossible to detect without the testimony of those involved in the production. Audiences, as Kevin Brownlow has indicated, generally accepted what they saw on the screen as an accurate record of the event:

> Propaganda apart, it is hard to convey the ingenuousness of the motion picture audiences of 1914. Scientific miracles had appeared at such breakneck speed that the public abandoned its skepticism, and named such phenomena "white magic." Ordinary people accepted that pictures moved, just as we now accept that rockets reach the moon, without the slightest idea how. They knew all about trick pictures, such as photographs of ghosts, yet they believed that the camera could not lie, and that the photographic image represented undistorted reality.[1]

Photographers and film producers were not inclined to contribute to public enlightenment; it might be bad for business. And by the outbreak of World War I, business was looking very good indeed. Theater audiences were increasing every year; by 1914, it was estimated that there were 14,000 theatres in the United States.[2]

The newsreel had become an established part of the theatre program. The cameramen in the field pushed, shoved and occasionally

---

[1]Brownlow, The War, p. 6. Some of the film historians claim that the quality of camera registration, optics and film was so poor that even the most amateur re-creation could fool unsophisticated viewers. However, this judgement is often based on the viewing of modern dupes of nitrate films, where the fault may be in the copy, not the original; definition and contrast may deteriorate in the transfer from nitrate to safety stock. Brownlow says the early camera and film manufacturers achieved a high technical standard; cameras such as the 1912 Bell and Howell are still used when precise optical work is required.

[2]Jacobs, American Film, p. 56.

physically assaulted their rivals to secure a scoop; their editors and managers were equally ruthless in their pursuit of bookings. The newsreels were commercial concerns, and journalistic standards were frequently set aside as the companies went searching for sensational events that would compel the attention of audiences. They could not wait for the news to happen; they had a deadline to meet, and if reality had to be doctored to meet it, so be it. That was the newsreel business.

* * * * *

CHAPTER 2

THE NEWSREEL BUSINESS

The early news films appeared sporadically--as and when a newsworthy event occurred. Wars provided opportunities for the enterprising
film company or even the freelancer; public interest was high, and there
was a ready market for footage. Peacetime was not without its newsworthy events--natural disasters, pageants and ceremonies, international
celebrities, sports and novelty items were all covered. But until the
advent of the newsreel the newsgathering process was not organized; the
individual news films were frequent but unscheduled, highly topical,
local or regional in release and often unreliable in their coverage.
The newsreel institutionalized the newsfilm, but, in the process, tied
it to a medium where journalistic values were not all that counted.

The newsreel made its debut in Europe earlier than in the United
States. The French company Pathé Frères launched its first newsreel in
Paris in 1909 or 1910;[1] The Pathé Journal soon had competition from the
Gaumont Company.[2] Around 1910, Charles Pathé introduced his newsreel to
England under the title of The Animated Gazette or The Pathé Gazette.[3]

---

[1]"The Weekly News Reel," Moving Picture World, 21 July 1917, p.
419, and Earl Thiesen, "Story of the Newsreel," International Photographer, September 1933, p. 24.

[2]Peter Baechlin and Maurice Muller-Strauss, Newsreels Across the
World (Paris: UNESCO, 1952), p. 11.

[3]Ibid.

According to Raymond Fielding, Pathé launched a newsreel in the United States on 8 August 1911, although the company's European editions may have been shown in American theaters before this date.[1] At that time, Pathé was associated with the Motion Picture Patents Company, a trust that tried to license all motion picture production and exhibition in the United States through control of patents. Its films were distributed through the General Film Company. Pathé's American manager, Jacques A. Berst, believed there was a market for an American news weekly, and in 1911, he proposed to the other members of the General Film Company that

> . . . they should each furnish negative material for a news reel, these negatives to be printed, edited, titled and assembled at the Pathe offices in Jersey City, the finished product to be released through the General Film Company, and each manufacturer to be paid from the receipts according to the amount of negative received from him and incorporated into the weekly.[2]

Although most of the companies[3] favored the plan, Vitagraph held back, and made plans to launch its own newsreel.[4] Berst decided to go it alone and ordered the assembly and release of the first issue--a venture enthusiastically greeted by Moving Picture World in an editorial in July 1911:

> Beginning on the first of next month the moving picture

---

[1]Fielding, The American Newsreel, pp. 69-71, and "The Weekly News Reel," Moving Picture World, 21 July 1917, p. 419.

[2]"The Weekly News Reel," p. 419.

[3]At that time, the ten participating film producers were Edison, Pathé, Méliès, Selig, Essanay, Lubin, Biograph, Vitagraph, Kleine and Kalem.

[4]Advertisements, Moving Picture World, 29 July 1911, p. 180, and 19 August 1911, p. 432.

theaters of this country will go into active and, we believe,
successful competition with the illustrated periodicals and
magazines, for they will be able to show the important news of
the world, not in cold type or in still pictures, but in actual
moving reproduction. The exhibitors will give their patrons
no descriptions or photographs, but the things themselves,
"just as they moved and had their being." This novel idea,
which will revolutionize pictorial journalism the world over
is called "The Weekly Journal" (sic), is edited by the Pathé
Frères, and will appear on the screens of the moving picture
houses every Tuesday.[1]

The first edition of Pathé's Weekly, appearing not on 1 August
but a week later, consisted largely of European scenes with a royal and
military flavor: the unveiling of a monument to Queen Victoria in London, the presentation of colors to a French regiment, the visit of the
German Crown Prince and his wife to St. Petersburg, water jousts in
France and a German military review; American items included a warship
under repair, a horse show and a regatta.[2] Ceremonies, celebrities,
parades and sports--they had been the standbys of the news cameraman
since the days of Lumière, and wartime would not significantly change
the mix.

Two weeks later, Pathé had a competitor--The Vitagraph Monthly
of Current Events. The company that had torn down a Spanish flag, faked
a sea battle, arranged a mock skirmish in South Africa and portrayed
Italian atrocities at Coney Island could be expected to lean towards
the sensational in its choice of subject-matter. The first issue
featured "a head-on collision between two giant locomotives going 60
miles an hour. The iron steeds of the rail clash and tear into one

[1]Moving Picture World, 29 July 1911, p. 187.

[2]Review, Moving Picture World, 12 August 1911, pp. 359-60.

another like two furious combatants. A sight that surpasses all imagination."[1] The success of the item prompted Vitagraph to buy four old engines and rent a stretch of abandoned railroad track in New Jersey to stage more collisions.[2] The Vitagraph newsreel proved unprofitable, however, and was merged with another newsreel within a year.

The first supervising editor of Pathé's Weekly was Herbert C. Hoagland, who was also in charge of the company's advertising and publicity.[3] Victor Milner, Faxon Dean and Eddie Snyder were among his first cameramen.[4] At the outset, domestic coverage was confined to the New York area, but as the staff was enlarged, film from other parts of the country became available. The newsreel continued to draw on European footage, but during the first year of its release about 60 per cent of the subjects were American.[5] It was released through the Keith-Albee and Orpheum circuits, and by the end of the first year 95 prints of each issue were being distributed.

With its operations growing, Pathé needed a full-time supervising editor, and Leon Franconi, Charles Pathé's interpreter in the United States, replaced Hoagland.[6] In 1913, Franconi was apparently replaced by P. Allen Parsons, who was succeeded in the spring of 1914 by William

[1]Advertisement, Moving Picture World, 29 July 1911, p. 180.

[2]Smith, Two Reels and a Crank, pp. 223-24.

[3]"The Weekly News Reel," Moving Picture World, 21 July 1917, p. 420, and Thiesen, "Story of the Newsreel," p. 24.

[4]Ibid.

[5]"The Weekly News Reel," p. 420.

[6]Ibid.

Helms, a New York newspaper man.[1] He resigned that summer, and Franconi again took charge.[2] In 1915, he was assigned to other work, and was replaced by P.D. Hugon, the former editor of The Pathé Gazette in London.[3] He resigned the following year, and was succeeded by Eric Mayell, who had also worked for the Gazette.[4] In 1916, he too resigned, and was replaced by his assistant Emmanuel "Jack" Cohen, who remained in the job for several years.[5]

The newsreel was released once a week until June 1914, when Pathé introduced a daily service and changed the title to the Pathé Daily News.[6] The company was now using safety stock, which, unlike the inflammable nitrate film, could be sent through the mails. The daily service did not replace the weekly releases, which were still taken by many theaters; the new system was for exhibitors who wanted newsfilm more frequently, and were prepared to pay for it. But with the outbreak of World War I, the supply of safety film from Pathé's factory in France was cut off, and the company reverted to a weekly release under the new title of Pathé News.[7]

By 1914, the Pathé News faced competition from several other newsreels. Another French company, Gaumont, was already producing news-

---

[1]Ibid.   [2]Ibid.   [3]Ibid.   [4]Ibid.

[5]Ibid. For Cohen's work as the Pathé editor, see Stuart Mackenzie, "How the Movie News Man Gets Pictures of World Events," American Magazine, January 1924, p. 38 ff.

[6]"Pathé Putting Out News Daily," Moving Picture World, 13 June 1914, p. 1524, and "The Weekly News Reel," Moving Picture World, 21 July, 1917, p. 420.

[7]"The Weekly News Reel," p. 420.

reels in France and Britain; in 1912, it launched an American version, The Gaumont Animated Weekly, which was released by the Motion Picture Distributing and Sales Company.[1] Although it was discontinued only five months after its launching, Gaumont Weekly, an international edition produced in Paris, London and New York, was released in the United States until 1921, when it was merged with the Kinograms newsreel.[2]

In 1912-13, the Mutual Film Corporation began The Mutual Weekly.[3] Its first editor was Pell Mitchell, and the cameramen included Al Gold and Larry Darmour.[4] The Mutual Weekly was succeeded by the Screen Telegram, one of whose editors was Terry Ramsaye, the film historian.[5] In November 1918, the Screen Telegram was bought by the Hearst company, which at the same time acquired Universal's newsreel interests.[6]

William Randolph Hearst went into the newsreel business three years after Pathé's Weekly was launched, and his newsreels, despite changes in format and organization, were popular through the war years. As early as the fall of 1911, Edgar B. Hatrick, the head of photographic

---

[1]"Gaumont Weekly for Film Supply Company," Moving Picture World, 3 August 1912, p. 431.

[2]Fielding, American Newsreel, p. 83.

[3]Francis Collins, The Camera Man (New York: Century, 1916), p. 93 ff.

[4]For Darmour's career as a war cameraman, see infra, pp. 208-09.

[5]Ramsaye later edited Kinograms. His history of the silent-film era, A Million And One Nights, is a valuable source for this period.

[6]"Hearst Buys Universal News; Will Issue Daily Service," Variety, 8 November 1918, p. 36; "Hearst-Universal-Mutual in Big Deal," Motion Picture News, 16 November 1918, p. 2929.

services at the Hearst Corporation, had proposed that the company produce a newsreel, but the idea was not taken up at that time.[1] In 1913, Hatrick produced a one-reel news film on the inauguration of President Woodrow Wilson, and began talks with a pioneer motion picture producer in Chicago--Colonel William Selig.[2]

Selig had been producing short news films since 1903. Hearst had a large, professional newsgathering organization. Why not combine the two resources to produce a newsreel? Accordingly, early in 1914, the Hearst Group and the Selig Polyscope Company launched the Hearst-Selig News Pictorial, with Ray Hall as editor.[3] The newsreel was released twice weekly through the General Film Company, which also distributed Pathé's Weekly. The distributors tended to favor the former, and Pathé soon decided to handle its own releases.[4]

Hearst and Selig collaborated on other film projects too. In January 1915, they released a five-reel picture extravagantly billed as "A wonderfully spectacular history of the World's Greatest War." Exhibitors were offered a special line of four-color posters, and the film was vigorously promoted in trade-paper advertisements:

> These Marvelous Motion Pictures were made on Gruesome European Battlefields and in the Blood-running, fighting trenches by the bold and intrepid Selig Camera Men in co-operation with the fearless and efficient Hearst Newspaper Correspondents who risked their lives to obtain these authentic views.[5]

---

[1]Thiesen, "Story of the Newsreel," p. 24.   [2]Ibid.

[3]Ibid., and Advertisement, Moving Picture World, 7 March 1914, p. 1263.

[4]Moving Picture World, 16 May 1914, p. 975.

[5]Advertisement, Motion Picture News, 2 January 1915, p. 6.

A print of the film does not survive, but there is nothing in contemporary accounts to suggest that the Selig cameramen actually filmed the action so vividly portrayed by the publicity writers. Troop movements, supply trains, artillery barrages and military reviews were the standard fare.

The partnership with Selig was ended in December 1915, and the following month Hearst entered into a new agreement with the Vitagraph Company; The Vitagraph Monthly of Current Events was replaced by a new release entitled The Hearst-Vitagraph Weekly News, with two issues a week.[1] But it foundered after a short time, and was withdrawn. During the latter half of 1916, and early in 1917, the Hearst Group released its own newsreel, variously titled The International Weekly and Hearst International News Pictorial. In the competitive newsreel market, Hearst had to convince exhibitors that the company's newsreels were a cut above the rest. Trade press advertisements for the Hearst International News Pictorial stressed the professionalism of the Hearst operation; it had "the greatest news gathering organization in the world" and "the biggest and livest camera staff in the world."[2] And it would not be satisfied with covering the standard newsreel subjects:

> The local boat race and the firemen's parade are the old standbys of the ordinary news reel. There's no credit in that. Anybody with a camera and carfare can produce that kind of news reel.

But--

---

[1]"The Weekly News Reel," p. 420, and Alfred A. Cohn, "A Film Newspaper in the Making," Photoplay Magazine, April 1916, p. 46.

[2]Advertisement, Motion Picture News, 22 July 1916, p. 379.

When the big thing happens--when the battleship goes down--
when our troops meet the Mexicans--when faraway, startling news
flashes across the world--you'll find it in the HEARST INTERNA-
TIONAL NEWS PICTORIAL.[1]

Newsreels, like some other commercial products, did not always
live up to the claims of their publicity writers. But the Hearst hack
had a point: even in the middle of the war, editors often relied on a
weekly batch of scheduled events to make up their newsreels. These
events were generally pre-arranged, easily accessible, and visually
interesting; they might have little or no news value.[2] This bias in
subject matter was one of the reasons why newsreel coverage of World
War I was often incomplete and ineffective.

On 1 January 1917, the Hearst company allied itself with its
rival, Pathé, to produce and distribute a newsreel. Under the terms
of a contract signed by Edward A. MacManus of Hearst and Jacques A.
Berst of Pathé, the Pathé News and The International Weekly were merged
to form the Hearst-Pathé News, the first edition being released on
January 10.[3] Using cameramen from both organizations, Hearst Interna-

---

[1]Ibid.

[2]Daniel Boorstin's concept of the pseudo-event is a useful yard-
stick for measuring the news value of such items. According to Boorstin,
a pseudo-event has the following characteristics: it is not spontaneous,
but comes about because it is planned; it is planted primarily, but not
always exclusively, for the immediate purpose of being reported or reproduced; its significance is ambiguous; and usually it is intended to be a
self-fulfilling prophecy. Many of the subjects of the war newsreels appear to fall into this classification, meeting at least two of Boorstin's
criteria--examples are military parades, medal ceremonies, generals posing, sports events, the comings and goings of celebrities, the launching
of ships and fashion shows. See Boorstin, The Image: A Guide to Pseudo-
Events in America (New York: Harper, 1964), pp. 7-44.

[3]"The Weekly News Reel," p. 420, and "Pathé and International
Weeklies Combine," Motion Picture News, 20 January 1917, p. 386.

tional gathered the footage; Pathé assembled and titled the film at its plant in Jersey City, and the newsreels were booked through Pathé's exchanges. Berst told the trade press that the two partners were well matched:

> The Pathé News could not equal Mr. Hearst's news gathering facilities. The Hearst organization could not equal Pathé's splendid factory facilities. The new Weekly, with its force of cameramen carefully selected from the best men of the two forces, thus becomes stronger and better than either of the old Weeklies.[1]

Pathé cameramen were officially accredited by the French and Russian armies; Hearst had some men on the German side, and Ariel Varges was with the British. Hearst's newspapers carried large advertisements for the Hearst-Pathé News, and, according to Moving Picture World, ". . . the effect upon booking and theater attendance has been marked."[2] But the new association lasted for little more than a year; the companies then decided to go it alone, each with its own newsreel.

Hearst's first partner in film production, the Selig Polyscope Company of Chicago, continued to turn out newsreels after the split. Among the competing newsreels in the Chicago area was the Chicago Tribune Animated Weekly. In December 1915, Colonel Selig and the Chicago Tribune concluded an agreement to produce a new bi-weekly entitled the Selig-Tribune, extravagantly billed as "The World's Greatest News Film."[3] Herbert Hoagland left Pathé to become its general manager,

---

[1]"Pathé and International Weeklies Combine," p. 386.

[2]"The Weekly News Reel," p. 420.

[3]Advertisement, Motion Picture News, 25 December 1915, p. 130.

and Lucien C. "Jack" Wheeler was its first editor.[1] Motion Picture News
reported that for the first edition, released 3 January 1916, "John D.
McCutcheon and other war correspondents have rushed some timely films
from the European battle fields."[2] Staff cameramen were assigned to the
French, British, Russian, German, Austrian, Italian and Bulgarian
armies.[3] The staff grew quickly; within half a year, 75 film technicians were employed in Chicago; there were staff cameramen in ten American cities, and 50 freelancers in Europe.[4] But despite its early promise,
the Selig-Tribune was out of business by early 1917.

The other major newsreel in the market, besides those of Pathé,
Hearst and Mutual, was produced by the Universal Film Manufacturing
Company. The company had been founded in 1912, and its president, Carl
Laemmle, helped to launch the Universal Animated Weekly the following
year.[5] Jack Cohn was appointed editor, and the newsreel soon built up
a reputation for thorough coverage. As Motion Picture News remarked in
1918,

> Not a single news event of importance has escaped the click-
> ing shutters of the Universal men since the service got under
> headway. Great achievements, feats of daring and "scoops"
> punctuate the history of the weeklies.

---

[1]Alfred A. Cohn, "A Film Newspaper in the Making," Photoplay
Magazine, April 1916, p. 44.

[2]"First Selig-Tribune News Pictorial Makes Hit," Motion Picture
News, 15 January 1916, p. 247.

[3]Ibid.

[4]Fielding, American Newsreel, p. 105.

[5]"Hearst-Universal-Mutual in Big Deal," Motion Picture News, 16
November 1918, p. 2929, and Thiesen, "Story of the Newsreel," p. 24.

The record of these exploits in many cases reads like fiction. Cameras that served Universal poked their noses into the first scenes of the war, and later dared all its hurricane of hail, according to report.[1]

With the Animated Weekly firmly established, Universal Current Events was launched. By 1918, the combined photographic staff numbered over 200, and Universal was grossing about $18,000 a month from newsreels.[2]

The last months of World War I saw two major developments in the newsreel business: a split between Hearst and Pathé, and Hearst's takeover of its other major competitors. On 21 October 1918, Pathé announced that it was ending its agreement with Hearst and would issue its own newsreel after Christmas. The company claimed that it had always owned the Hearst-Pathé News, which at that time was grossing $85,000 a month; the Hearst organization, said Pathé, had acted merely as a news-gathering agency.[3] The general manager of Hearst International, C.F. Zittel, countered by saying that his organization had ". . . always been responsible, in my opinion, for the news in the news reel" and had supplied all the negatives.[4]

As the Hearst-Pathé agreement ended, Hearst announced the purchase of the two Universal newsreels--the Animated Weekly and Current Events--and of Mutual's Screen Telegram.[5] The reported cost of the deal

[1]Ibid.

[2]"Hearst Buys Universal News; Will Issue Daily Service," Variety, 8 November 1918, p. 36.

[3]Ibid.   [4]"Hearst-Universal-Mutual in Big Deal," p. 2929.

[5]Ibid., and "Hearst Buys Universal News," Variety, 8 November 1918, p. 36.

was $100,000; Hearst also took over most of the staff employed by these newsreels, adding about $30,000 to its weekly payroll.[1] The combined newsreels were released as the Hearst International News, the first edition appearing on Christmas Day, and the bookings were made through Universal's exchanges.[2] With an influenza epidemic hitting theater audiences in the winter of 1918, the Hearst organization decided to issue the newsreel only twice a week, and to change to a daily service when market conditions improved.[3]

Edgar B. Hatrick, the man who had first proposed a Hearst news-reel, was put in charge of the Hearst International News;[4] the long-serving Universal editor, Jack Cohn, refused an offer to join the staff.[5] As with its previous newsreels, the Hearst emphasis was on the news-worthy rather than the sensational. Mr. Zittel said the newsreel would be treated ". . . from a newspaper, rather than a showman's standpoint."[6]

Although the newsreel market was dominated by Pathé, Hearst, Universal and Mutual, there were other ventures--most of them short-lived. Many of these were local or regional in release. Before its association with Colonel Selig, the Chicago Tribune was distributing its Animated Weekly in the city and in parts of Illinois; the New York Weekly was a local newsreel exhibited by Marcus Loew in New York City around 1914;[7] on the West Coast, Sol Lesser's Golden Gate Film Exchange

---

[1]"Hearst Buys Universal News," p. 36.   [2]Ibid.

[3]"Hearst-Universal-Mutual," p. 2929.   [4]Ibid.   [5]Ibid.

[6]Ibid.

[7]Advertisement, Moving Picture World, 24 January 1914, p. 463.

released the <u>Golden Gate Weekly</u> in 1914.[1] Other newsreels claimed to

specialize in a particular area of news coverage. The <u>American War News</u>

<u>Weekly</u>, launched in April 1917 by the Cinema War News Syndicate,

promised exhibitors the American war news their audiences were demanding

following the entry of the United States into the European war. The

public, said the company's president, Frederick W. Brooker, wanted ". . .

only high-class and truthful war news pictures showing their own soldiers

and sailors in action."[2] But lack of action obliged the company to seek

other subjects, and, on at least one occasion, to invent a story.[3]

Some of the larger theaters subscribed to more than one newsreel,

edited the footage into a single reel, and showed it under the theater's

name. The New York theater manager Samuel L. Rothapfel--known in the

industry as "Roxy"--was an acknowledged expert at this art, using the

juxtaposition of scenes, titles and music to give his newsreels an im-

pact which the original footage lacked.[4] Audiences at his Rivoli

---

[1]<u>Moving Picture World</u>, 17 January 1914, p. 334, and 25 April
1914, p. 537.

[2]"Independent Producer to Put Out American War News Weekly,"
<u>Motion Picture News</u>, 21 April 1917, p. 2498. See also <u>Exhibitors Trade</u>
<u>Review</u>, 14 April 1917, p. 1302. The <u>American War News Weekly</u> is dis-
cussed in detail infra, pp. 151-2, 246-8.

[3]A memo in the files of the Committee on Public Information's
Division of Films claims that one reel of the <u>American War News Weekly</u>
contains a faked scene purporting to show a parade in honor of the official United States flagmaker. See infra, p. 154.

[4]Rothapfel was a frequent contributor to the trade press, giving
advice on exhibition and the use of music. See "Dramatizing Music for
the Pictures," <u>Reel Life</u>, 5 September 1914, p. 23, "Rothapfel Gives Some
Hints on Weeklies," <u>Motion Picture News</u>, 24 August 1918, p. 1220, "Rothapfel Tells of Advance of Weeklies," <u>Motion Picture News</u>, 31 August 1918,
p. 1374.

Theater in New York City saw the Rivoli Animated Pictorial, while the Rialto Animated Magazine ran at his other theater, the Rialto. Its namesake in San Francisco had the Rialto Topical Digest, and the California, in the same city, the California Theater Topical Digest.[1]

The newsreel had become an established and profitable part of the motion picture industry in the United States by the time World War I began. But its position as part of an entertainment package of feature films and shorts shaped its content. From the outset, it was not primarily a journalistic medium; the best news stories did not always make the best film stories, and vice versa. As the film historian Ernest Rose has remarked:

> . . . from its earliest days, the newsreel suffered from a kind of schizophrenia that still characterizes much of our news programming today. Was it in journalism or was it in show business? . . . With the growth of popularity of the feature entertainment film, the newsreel became something like a side show to the main circus events. As the novelty of seeing real people and events on screen wore thin, the theatrical newsreels, which were all owned by the large entertainment film companies, began drifting away from a purely journalistic posture, mixing the few newsworthy headlines with large amounts of feature material like bathing beauty contests, visits to the zoo, fashion previews, and heavy emphasis on sports.[2]

In 1924, Jack Cohen of Pathé, the most experienced newsreel editor in the business, was asked which subjects were most popular with audiences. "Soldiers, airplanes, battleships--and babies!" he replied,

---

[1] For examples of their programs, see articles in trade press such as Exhibitors Trade Review, 12 January 1918, p. 515.

[2] Ernest Rose, "The Newsreel on American Screens," in The American Cinema, ed. Donald E. Staples (Washington, D.C.: Voice of America Forum Series, 1973), pp. 303-4.

re-emphasizing the strength of the war motif in newsreels.[1] Cohen had
what journalists have called a nose for news; he recognized news values
in events that were generally ignored, anticipated breaking stories and
arranged speedy shipping and processing to beat his rivals. But he also
had a keen appreciation of the tastes of contemporary audiences; he was
not editing a newspaper that people chose to read but a newsreel that
was part of a larger entertainment program. "When the news reel is put
on in a theatre," said Cohen, "the people in the audience have to look
at it, or else shut their eyes and miss some of the entertainment they
have paid for."[2]

To keep as many eyes open as possible, newsreel editors and
cameramen sought visually interesting and entertaining items to blend
with the harder news. The newsreel historian Raymond Fielding claims
that the subject matter of newsreels falls into seven identifiable
categories: catastrophe, international celebrities, pageantry and ceremony, sports, political and military events, technology, and spectacle
and novelty.[3] But while the early newsreels had been free to record--
or fake--events as they occurred, the newsreels, appearing daily, weekly,
bi-weekly or monthly, had a deadline to meet; they had to provide interesting and visually compelling items to order--whether or not they had
any intrinsic news value. Newsworthy events were covered, but so were a
host of others that, by themselves, had little journalistic merit; their
role was to give the newsreel a blend of items, and a varied pace, that

---

[1]Stuart Mackenzie, "How the Movie News Man Gets Pictures of World
Events," American Magazine, January 1924, p. 120.

[2]Ibid.   [3]Fielding, American Newsreel, p. 48.

would appeal to the audience. The film historian Erik Barnouw claims that the newsreel eroded journalistic values, and institutionalized the decline of the documentary. The newsreels, he says, ". . . tended to turn the customary documentary items into a ritual composite: a royal visit, a military maneuver, a sports event, a funny item, a disaster, and a native festival in costume."[1]

The newsreel went into World War I with a clear idea of what its audiences wanted. However, the war was not often the exciting and visually compelling subject that cameramen and editors expected; the fighting was static, the military authorities obstructive, and the censors efficient. War news did not keep out the fashion previews, the beauty contests, and the sports events. Indeed, if you had been in the audience for Pathé News No. 93 in December 1915, you might have forgotten there was a war on at all. The accent was on the spectacular, the bizarre:

> Largest railway engine in the world goes into service at Susquehanna, New York; monster chrysanthemums are shown at Philadelphia exhibit; King Alphonso encourages preparedness among his subjects at Madrid; Grandma Moore, twenty miles from the nearest store, spins her own wool, and makes her own clothes at Walker Valley, Tenn.; monkeys are finger-printed at the New York Zoo, to help in tracing thefts by animals; largest ocean-going craft ever constructed is seen at San Diego; bumper crop of 150 tons of walnuts is gathered at El Monte, California; congestion caused by shortage of ships is shown at New York terminals.[2]

In that same month, Douglas Haig succeeded Sir John French as Commander-in-Chief of the British forces on the Western Front; the French also appointed a new commander--Joseph Joffre. The British were begin-

[1]Barnouw, Documentary, p. 26.

[2]Review in Motion Picture News, 11 December 1915.

ning their withdrawal from Gallipoli and Italy agreed not to make a
separate peace. The British war cabinet, from which Winston Churchill
had recently resigned, approved the principle of compulsory military
service. And monkeys were finger-printed at the New York Zoo.

* * * * *

CHAPTER 3

WAR, WAR, WAR:

PROFIT VERSUS NEUTRALITY

> War, War, War. Ramo Films, Inc., Announce The War of Wars or
> The Franco-German Invasion of 1915. 400 Stupendous Scenes
> taken on The Actual Battlefields of France will be released
> within a week. The First Authentic Events of the Reigning
> Sensation of the World. Wire for Territory or Bookings.[1]

So ran the advertising blurb in Motion Picture News on 15 August

1914--just eleven days after the outbreak of war in Europe. While that

same magazine remarked that "the idea of profiting by the afflictions

and misfortunes of others is abhorrent to the generous feelings of

Americans,"[2] the film companies were falling over one another to cash in

on public interest by providing war scenes. Any war scenes. While

Ramo's advertisement may have led some exhibitors to believe that The

War of Wars was a documentary account of the fighting in France and

Belgium, it was actually nothing of the kind. The company had commis-

sioned a screenplay on the German invasion by Paul M. Potter;[3] the "400

Stupendous Scenes," reportedly taken by a correspondent at Nancy, France,

would help to illustrate it. When the film eventually appeared--not in

---

[1]Advertisement, Motion Picture News, 15 August 1914, pp. 10-11.

[2]"The War Cloud and Its Silver Lining," Motion Picture News, 15 August 1914, p. 43.

[3]"Ramo Rushes to Launch European War Film," Motion Picture News, 15 August 1914, p. 24.

late August, but in late October--<u>Motion Picture News</u> noted that "the interpolation at strategic intervals of scenes of actual war maneuvers increases the realism to a noticeable extent."[1] But not enough to obscure the plot. Much of the action takes place in a large chateau, and the only battle scenes are staged. As the reviewer for <u>Motion Picture News</u> remarked: "In some of the battle scenes there is rather an excess of flag waving and standing about in exposed positions on the part of the soldiers, but actors were ever loath to seek cover when facing the fire of the camera man, and it all looks quite patriotic."[2]

The war had taken the United States, and its film companies, by surprise. While some Americans were inclined to support one side or the other, government policy was to remain neutral. President Wilson issued his first neutrality proclamation on 4 August, and 15 days later appealed to the American people "to be neutral in fact as well as in name."[3] He asked movie theater audiences to remain above partisan feeling. "The war," he said, "is one with which we have nothing to do, whose causes cannot touch us."[4]

Despite the heat wave that swept the country in August and September, theaters were packed with people eager to see the latest pictures from the front. From Cincinnati, it was reported that "those theaters whose patronage is drawn from the foreign element have been making

---

[1]Review, <u>Motion Picture News</u>, 24 October 1914, p. 48.   [2]Ibid.

[3]James Brown Scott, <u>A Survey of International Relations between the United States and Germany</u> (New York: Oxford University Press, 1917), pp. 43, 48.

[4]William Leuchtenberg, <u>Perils of Prosperity</u> (Chicago: University of Chicago Press, 1958), p. 14.

persistent demands for war pictures of any kind."[1] One enterprising

theater manager in the city, A.J. Bauman, posted war reports in the

lobby of the aptly named Dreamland Theater, and attracted "hundreds of

Cincinnati's Hungarian, Austrian, Roumanian, Servian [sic] and German

population."[2] Bauman's business almost doubled.

The only real war news in the Dreamland Theater was in the lobby;

the main feature, The Fall of France, was a historical war drama, having

only the remotest link to current events.[3] Desperate for war news, and

unable to produce new dramas at short notice, distributors and exhibitors

laid their hands on anything that they thought would satisfy public

demand. As W. Stephen Bush, a regular contributor to Moving Picture

World, remarked:

> . . . A series of old pictures showing the various armies of
> Europe in maneuvers have been taken from the shelves where they
> had been reposing in peace for many months or even years.
>
> Old copies of Pathe's weekly [sic] and of other kinema-
> tographic news service bureaus have been ransacked and often
> duplicated just to offer the public something that might pass
> for war pictures. Of course, the public know as well as the
> exhibitors themselves that actual pictures from the front are
> impossible, but they seem glad of pictures of mimic war if the
> real article cannot be obtained. In the big cities especially,
> where foreign-born inhabitants form a considerable part of the
> population, this demand for something that looks like war is
> undeniably great.[4]

The Eclectic Film Company, a subsidiary of Pathé, pulled out all

its war features, and took a full page in Motion Picture News to adver-

---

[1]"Cincinnatians Flock to War Pictures," Motion Picture News, 5
September 1914, p. 22.

[2]Ibid.   [3]Ibid.

[4]W. Stephen Bush, "War Films," Moving Picture World, 19 September 1914, p. 1617.

tise them.[1] There was <u>Faithful Unto Death</u>--a "breathing story of the
Franco-Prussian War in four parts;" <u>All Love Excelling</u>--Sisters of Mercy
work through the Crimean War; and <u>War Is Hell</u>, featuring an air battle,
the destruction of balloons and the blowing up of an old mill.[2] In <u>The
Last Volunteer</u>, "the relations of a Crown-prince to an Innkeeper's
daughter involve international affairs;"[3] a film on Napoleon included
". . . Significant scenes from the last great struggle for European
supremacy which may easily be compared with today's crucial events."[4]
The implausibly named Austro-Servian Film Company had an equally implaus-
ible version of the background to the conflict; in <u>With Serb and Aus-
trian</u>, an Austrian prince falls in love with a Serbian princess and
burns the secret plans he has stolen.[5] "It is obvious," wrote Peter
Milne in his review for <u>Motion Picture News</u>, "that some of the scenes
were filmed here in New York City, but these are few and by those unacquainted with New York will not be noticed."[6]

In keeping with President Wilson's call for neutrality, these
films had no winners or losers. The prince puts his love above his
country in <u>With Serb and Austrian</u>. In Ramo's <u>The War of Wars</u>, ". . .
fortune smiles alternately on the contending parties, and their German
and French principals are seen as heroes in a regular sequence. As a
final victory of non-partisanship the film closes with an impending

[1]<u>Motion Picture News</u>, 22 August 1914, p. 4. [2]Ibid.

[3]Ibid. [4]Ibid.

[5]"Drama That Thrills With War Spirit," <u>Motion Picture News</u>, 15 August 1914, p. 61.

[6]Review, <u>Motion Picture News</u>, 22 August 1914, p. 70.

Franco-German alliance between an officer from the Fatherland and a fair maid of la belle France."[1]

The film companies remained as neutral as business allowed; releases in the fall of 1914 had such unequivocal titles as Neutrality, War Is Hell and The Horrors of War; it was reported that Universal rushed out its short, Be Neutral, in 48 hours to support the President's plea.[2] Some foreign films were shown in American theaters: Harold Shaw's England's Menace, which depicted an imaginary invasion of the South Coast, had been released before the outbreak of war,[3] as had George Kleine's import When War Threatens.[4] But the predominant mood was non-partisan; some even believed that films could cure the Europeans of their warlike intentions. Said the Chicago Tribune: "If the Austrians and Servians and other craving war continentals could just drop into the Studebaker for a couple of hours to watch the unreeling of 'The Littlest Rebel,' they would get an optical dose of war horror sufficient to drive them to hang up their guns and take their plowshares and fall instantly to tilling the soil."[5]

A return to pastoral pursuits would have deprived the American film industry of what many producers regarded as a great business opportunity. War pictures were playing to large audiences in the United

---

[1]Review, Motion Picture News, 24 October 1914, p. 48.

[2]Jack Spears, Films in Review, June-July 1966, p. 274.

[3]Ivan Butler, The War Film (S. Brunswick: A. S. Barnes, 1974), pp. 14, 17.

[4]Brownlow, The War, p. 22.

[5]Quoted in Motion Picture News, 15 August 1914, p. 8.

States; at the same time, film imports were declining and American companies could exploit the markets in neutral countries which had previously been supplied by the warring nations. Under the title, "The War Cloud and Its Silver Lining," an editorial writer in Motion Picture News noted that ". . . the outlook for a continuation of good business is promising;" if imports were reduced, domestic production would be stimulated. "War pictures," added the editorial, "are sure to be in active demand."[1] Export manager Arthur J. Lang agreed. The war, he said, had turned the film producers' attention to foreign markets, and had made it easier to sell films abroad. "The great chance for the American film producer," he wrote, "lies in the fact that the neutral markets have been cut off from their usual sources of supply, or that these sources are now greatly hampered in meeting the demand."[2] Lest anyone missed the point of the article, it was unequivocally headlined "Cashing in on Europe's War." As Kevin Brownlow comments: "Examining the trade papers of the time, one is struck not by concern or alarm about the war, but by the callous glee with which exhibitors and producers greeted this threat to rival concerns."[3] "So far as this company is concerned," said Lewis J. Selznick, "the turmoil in Europe would not be at all for the worse."[4]

The industry's enthusiasm was tempered by President Wilson's

[1]"The War Cloud and Its Silver Lining," Motion Picture News, 15 August 1914, p. 43.

[2]Arthur J. Lang, "Cashing in on Europe's War," Motion Picture News, 28 November 1914, p. 25.

[3]Brownlow, The War, p. 22.

[4]Quoted in Moving Picture World, 15 August 1914, p. 963.

desire to keep the United States out of the conflict. Some theater
managers, fearing trouble between national groups in the audience,
refused to show any war films. Others screened the films, but did not
allow their musicians to accompany them with the national airs of the
European powers. Moving Picture World reported that the Federal government had issued a notice prohibiting the performance of such music;[1] in
Chicago, the president of the city's Federation of Musicians urged his
members not to incite trouble by playing national airs.[2] When a musi-
cian in a small town in the Northwest wrote to Moving Picture World to
ask whether his manager had been right to tell him not to play these
tunes, the magazine's film music columnist, Clarence E. Sinn, replied in
no uncertain terms:

> The interest of the picture is something on the same order as
> the interest of the newspaper; a little stronger, maybe; but
> different from the purely emotional feeling which is appealed
> to by familiar songs of the home countries. Your "sprinkling
> of the foreign element" might enthuse a little over some of the
> war pictures, but when--at the moment of tension--you inject
> Rule Britannia, Wacht am Rhein or Marseilles [sic] into the
> performance, there is a chance that some enthusiast will become
> over-demonstrative.[3]

Sinn's advice was: "Be neutral. Play marches."[4]

Producers and exhibitors whose films were considered controver-
sial were likely to invite the wrath of city officials. In September
1914, the municipal authorities in San Francisco, Los Angeles and New

[1]Clarence E. Sinn, "Music for the Picture," Moving Picture World,
7 November 1914, p. 776.

[2]Sinn, "Music for the Picture," Moving Picture World, 17 October
1914, p. 340.

[3]Ibid., p. 339.   [4]Ibid., p. 340.

York took action to suppress films which they thought would inflame
hatred among national and ethnic groups.[1] New York's License Commissioner George Bell sent 50 inspectors to investigate complaints about
offensive motion pictures, and ordered that pictures exhibited in the
city should not show favoritism toward any country.[2] Bell was also
concerned about the production of war dramas:

> From what I can learn . . . many of these pictures promise
> to be very one-sided. I cannot say just now which countries
> the film-makers are giving the best of the bloodless conflicts.
> At any rate, the pictures, if shown the way they are being
> prepared, will stir up a lot of feeling. . . .
>
> The German pictures will show the Kaiser's troops chasing
> the allies all over the lot. Those from France and England
> will demonstrate a bayonet charge by Highland, Irish and
> English troops, with coattails of German infantry for a back-
> ground. I believe this is against the spirit of neutrality
> as proclaimed by President Wilson.[3]

In November, the Los Angeles police banned the screening of all
war films at Long Beach, and censored lobby displays.[4] When Eclectic's
War Is Hell was shown at the American Theater in Los Angeles, the police
ordered the manager, A.A. Frist, to tone down the lobby pictures; he had
to paste over the pictures of guns and exploding bombs.[5]

There is some evidence that, once the novelty of war films wore
off, there was a reaction against them. Writing from London for Moving
Picture World, W. Stephen Bush warned that ". . . the showing of war

---

[1]"New York and Los Angeles Authorities Open Campaign Against War
Films," Motion Picture News, 26 September 1914, p. 19.

[2]Ibid.   [3]Quoted in Ibid.

[4]"Los Angeles Censors Object to 'Fake' War Films," Motion Picture News, 26 September 1914, p. 19.

[5]Motion Picture News, 14 November 1914, p. 25.

films may easily be overdone in spite of the present strong demand."[1]
Motion picture audiences, he noted, are composed largely of women and
children. "The women as a rule will be grateful to the manager for
leaving the war pictures out of the program or at least showing them but
rarely," he wrote.[2] As early as September 1914, Theodore Franklin, a
correspondent for Motion Picture News in Washington, D.C., reported that
"There is much sentiment here at present against the exhibition of war
films."[3] Theater managers had taken Wilson's neutrality plea seriously,
but were perhaps more concerned with keeping an orderly house. One
exhibitor admitted that while war films filled his theater and made a
profit, he was not going to risk trouble:

> They caused too much disturbance in my house. There were
> demonstrations of sympathy in different quarters as the differ-
> ent troops entered the screen. The usual silence of the screen
> exhibitions was utterly disregarded and one might almost have
> imagined that it was a baseball game.
>
> No, I can't afford that. It would spoil my house. No more
> war films for me.[4]

The manager's concerns were not shared by the newsreel companies;
they had a different problem--obtaining news film from the war zone. For
the August 15 edition of Pathé's Weekly, the editors spliced together
shots of the crowned heads of Europe;[5] two weeks later, Pathé obtained

---

[1]Bush, "War Films," Moving Picture World, 19 September 1914, p.
1617.

[2]Ibid.

[3]Franklin, "Reaction in Capital Against War Films," Motion Picture News, 19 September 1914, p. 20.

[4]Quoted in Ibid.

[5]Review, Motion Picture News, 15 August 1914.

its first troop reviews--by the Czar and Prince Henry of Prussia. Universal had the unenviable distinction of reversing chronology; on August 29, the <u>Animated Weekly</u> No. 126 showed King George and Queen Mary of Britain visiting President Poincaré in Paris;[1] on September 5, a month after Britain and Germany went to war, the royal couple were seen visiting the Kaiser.[2] "Rather out of date but interesting," said <u>Motion Picture News</u> charitably.[3]

The newsreel companies tried to capitalize on public interest in the war by putting out special editions--war extras--with the usual line in extravagant claims by the publicity writers:

> . . . Camera news is the only news which nobody in the world can contradict. . . . Pathé Daily News, the films which give you the service of a newspaper on the European War and the interest of an eye witness. Accurate too--happenings caught by the Pathé camera happened. We are issuing war extras of the happenings people want to see now. You make a patron out of every passerby--they leave their work to see the Pathé War Views. . . .[4]

Each company claimed that its coverage was the most complete and dramatic--this from Mutual:

> Our photographers were on the ground when the European war broke out. They are on the battlefields now and their pictures are already being received. Call it good luck or good management, we've got the pictures. The films of the hour are the war films. Order the Mutual Weekly at once and you have the jump on your competitor.[5]

The rhetoric of trade press advertisements was empty; with a few exceptions, none of the newsreel cameramen were getting anywhere near

[1]Review, <u>Motion Picture News</u>, 29 August 1914, p. 16.

[2]Review, <u>Motion Picture News</u>, 5 September 1914, p. 20.   [3]Ibid.

[4]Advertisement, <u>Motion Picture News</u>, 22 August 1914, p. 3.

[5]Advertisement, <u>Reel Life</u>, 15 August 1914, p. 31.

the front lines. Indeed, until cameramen were accredited by the military authorities, the newsreel companies relied largely on the standard behind-the-lines scenes--troop reviews, maneuvers, supply trains and visiting celebrities. While Motion Picture News credited Universal's Animated Weekly with ". . . the distinction of showing some of the first authentic pictures of the great European War that have been shown on this side of the Atlantic,"[1] they did not show any fighting--the scenes were of wounded German prisoners, the defenders of Liege and the Belgian Civil Guard moving up to the front lines.[2]

The Mutual Weekly No. 88, described in the trade press as a "war number," offered war scenes, but no action--the French fleet in the North Sea, artillery on the French border, the King of Italy inspecting his fleet, captured guns and ammunition, troops leaving for the front, the Kings of Denmark and Sweden discussing neutrality, and a British cruiser waiting outside New York harbor to surprise German ships.[3] The next edition featured scenes from London: crowds in front of Parliament, waiting for news, Territorials leaving for the front, and stranded American tourists.[4] In Mutual Weekly No. 90, the attention shifted to Canada with film of the mobilization of troops and their departure for Europe.[5]

Why were audiences seeing troop transports, inspections and

[1]Review, Motion Picture News, 26 September 1914, p. 56.   [2]Ibid.

[3]Review, Motion Picture News, 5 September 1914, p. 20.

[4]Review, Motion Picture News, 12 September 1914, p. 18.

[5]Review, Motion Picture News, 19 September 1914, p. 22.

maneuvers when there was fighting in Europe? What prevented the newsreel companies from obtaining footage at the front? There were several
reasons, but the principal cause was the downright hostility of the
military authorities of the warring powers, who actively stopped
photographic coverage of the war.

* * * * *

CHAPTER 4

THE WAR PHOTOGRAPHERS

The newsreel companies had gone into the war with high expectations. In the Franco-Prussian War of 1870, newspaper correspondents had
been allowed to move freely in the war zone;[1] cameramen had covered the
Spanish-American and Boer Wars, and, most recently, the Mexican Revolution. However, there were soon indications that the military authorities did not welcome cameramen at the front, and were prepared to censor
and confiscate their films.

When Austria-Hungary declared war on Serbia on 28 July 1914,
American companies instructed their European correspondents to cover
the fighting. However, they were halted by an order from Vienna; only
those photographers employed by the Austrian government would be allowed
at the front.[2] One cameraman who, by devious means, obtained some footage of the fighting, had to surrender these reels to the Austrian
government, which promptly confiscated the rest of his film.[3] The other
cameramen found themselves virtually confined to Vienna, and their
predicament was evident in the footage they sent to the United States:

_____

[1]Emmet Crozier, American Reporters on the Western Front, 1914-18
(New York: Oxford University Press, 1959), pp. 23-24.

[2]H. H. Van Loan, "Shooting the War: The Camera as a Modern
Weapon of War," Motion Picture Magazine, March 1918, p. 63.

[3]Ibid.

> . . . The result was that the American camera-men and their
> European colleagues had to be satisfied with such pictures
> as they could get showing the movement of troops, maneuvers,
> and other similar stuff, in and around the capital of the
> Dual Monarchy. But these pictures proved incapable of satis-
> fying the curious public, and the majority of the camera-men
> were soon recalled.[1]

Cameramen got the same treatment as newspaper correspondents. When American newspaper reporters arrived in London on August 11, the War Office refused them credentials to accompany the British Expeditionary Force.[2] The French claimed that during the Franco-Prussian War, correspondents wrote about military movements, the condition and morale of troops and the generals' plans, all of which made interesting reading in Germany.[3] They did not want any reporters and cameramen at the front --unless they could supervise them.

In those first uncertain months of the war, cameramen were as likely to be shot at as to shoot. Contemporary accounts record their experiences--captured and questioned as spies, their equipment and film confiscated. Politicians feared that film of conditions at the front would damage morale at home and confidence abroad, and hit recruiting. At the front, military officers feared, with some justification, that cameras would be regarded by the enemy as a new and fearsome weapon, and would draw fire. Charles Rosher, who had filmed Pancho Villa for Mutual, was one of the first to warn that World War I would be a tougher assignment for cameramen. Returning to New York from London, Rosher, at that time a British subject, told Moving Picture World:

---

[1]Ibid.   [2]Crozier, American Reporters, p. 20.

[3]Ibid., pp. 23-24.

. . . not only is it out of the question to get a motion picture camera out of England in the direction of any of the belligerent countries, but likewise it is not possible to get a motion picture camera into England and retain possession of it.[1]

Rosher said he had brought to the United States "several hundred feet of film that could not be shown in Britain."[2] Taken by a newsreel company, the footage showed the mobilization of British troops, and Rosher said he had to use "finesse to get it out of the country."[3]

Despite such warnings, the newsreel companies were determined to send their photographers to the front. On 22 August, Universal announced that it was sending eight cameramen to the war zone "armed with passports and letters of introduction."[4] Most of them were veteran war photographers, and some had covered the Balkan War; they would shoot footage for the Animated Weekly. Universal's London representative, John D. Tippett, considered the operation dangerous, and urged his superiors to think again. In a letter to Universal's president, Carl Laemmle, published in Moving Picture World, Tippett wrote:

> . . . It just means a man's life to take any pictures over there at present, and the chances are that it will be so in the future as well. You have no conception of the conditions across the channel [sic]--absolutely no conception. I do not care what the American papers print, it is twice as terrible. . . .
>
> You received a subject from me a short time ago of some prisoners at Bruges. Well, that cost us altogether between $700 and $800, for I have had two men in Belgium from the very first, and good men, too. They were half of the time in jail and finally managed to leave there the other day, lucky to escape with their lives, with the loss of a lot of film and I think a camera

---

[1]"No Cameras Going to the Front," Moving Picture World, 12 September 1914, p. 1487.

[2]Ibid.   [3]Ibid.

[4]Motion Picture News, 22 August 1914, p. 25.

as well. Cameramen are absolutely forbidden to go anywhere near the points of interest.

To get even small photographs is a most daring exploit. I understand some officers have given orders to kill every English correspondent, and many of them have made a practice of killing any person caught with a camera, irrespective of who he is. The story has never been told as to what has happened during the last few weeks in Belgium, and men from America, and people from other neutral governments, have disappeared, and will never be heard of again.[1]

Although Tippett may have exaggerated the dangers, he had read the situation correctly. Less than a month after Universal's announcement, Motion Picture News reported: "At present, the five[2] cameramen engaged by the Universal Film Manufacturing Company to cover events at the front, from all accounts are incarcerated at various points in the war zone."[3] At the start of the war, Universal had sent one million feet of film to its London office, with instructions to Tippett to obtain war pictures at any cost. So far, Motion Picture News added, only 200 feet of genuine war material had been received.[4]

The suspicion with which cameramen were regarded by all the belligerents is well illustrated by the story of one optimistic young American cameraman--unnamed in contemporary accounts[5]-- who set out from

---

[1]"All War Picture Fakes," Moving Picture World, 3 October 1914, p. 50.

[2]No explanation is given for the discrepancy in the number of cameramen between this report and that in Motion Picture News, 22 August 1914, p. 25, where Jack Cohn, the manager of the Animated Weekly, was quoted as saying that eight cameramen had been sent.

[3]"War Films Coming In Slowly," Motion Picture News, 19 September 1914, p. 52.

[4]Ibid.

[5]The original account by Leonora Raines in the New York Evening

Paris on a bicycle with a diary, a passport and his apparatus slung over

his shoulder. He passed several sentries, who did not stop him, but on

the afternoon of the second day, he ran into trouble:

> All day he had been hearing the sound of cannon and shot and
> had been dodging shrapnel. Then of a sudden he found himself
> riding in the midst of shot and saw lines of soldiers on the
> hills all about. So the soldiers called him to a halt . . . The
> men were all Germans, and he was in the wing of the army of the
> Kaiser. The officers laughed at his impudence, which they
> called "American brass," and after examining all papers, strip-
> ping him, reading his diary from start to finish, they at last
> turned over all his papers and ordered him away.[1]

The next morning, he set up his apparatus to film a line of

soldiers; as he began to turn the crank, the apparatus was knocked over

and he was arrested by a French sentry. He was hauled in front of offi-

cers for interrogation, and soldiers who spoke German tried to put him

off his guard, so that he would reply in German--and therefore reveal

himself to be a spy. But the young American, who spoke neither French

nor German, was simply bewildered. He was held for two days and nights

as a suspected spy, and was guarded by two soldiers. Soon the French

realized that he was just a foolhardy American; he was released, and

his camera and diary returned to him, but his bicycle was never found.[2]

The writer in the New York Evening Sun concluded that in the war zone,

> . . . the vocation of the war correspondent is lost, for no one
> is allowed within thirty miles of a battle. No influence can
> be brought to bear on the Minister of War to permit one not
> actively engaged in the battle to be near. Even French corres-

---

Sun did not name the cameraman, but Brownlow says it was probably Donald
Thompson. Brownlow, The War, p. 8.

[1]"Close Calls of American Cameramen," Moving Picture World, 24
October 1914, p. 498.

[2]Ibid.

pondents are kept away.[1]

The British cameramen had no more success than the Americans.
Writing in the British magazine Bioscope, Evan Strong, who had worked in
Belgium, gloomily admitted that anyone with a camera risked arrest and
possible execution. "The camera was the badge of a spy," he wrote, "and
the mob would tear a suspect limb from limb if the guards did not arrest
him first. A friend of mine was arrested twelve times in one day--and
he had left his apparatus at home!"[2]

Despite the risk of arrest and imprisonment, if not death, some
cameramen did reach the war zone, and obtained film of the armies, if
not of the fighting. But their problems did not end there; they had to
evade the censor, and ship their film to the United States. Universal
claimed to have some of the first authentic film in the September 9 edition of the Animated Weekly. It showed wounded German prisoners in
Brussels, the defenders of Liege, and the Belgian Civil Guard leaving
for the front. According to Motion Picture News, "[T]he films were
brought out of Belgium at great risk, and carried across the Atlantic in
the personal baggage of Mrs. J.C. Graham, wife of the general manager of
the Universal Film Manufacturing Company."[3]

The Strand Film Company of New York City claimed that its cameramen had evaded the ban on filming in Belgium to obtain scenes at the

---

[1]Quoted in ibid.

[2]The Bioscope, 20 August 1914, p. 737, quoted in Brownlow, The
War, p. 9. Strong's comments were also reported in the American trade
press. See "Real War Pictures Will Be Rarities," Motion Picture News,
12 September 1914, p. 22.

[3]Review, Motion Picture News, 26 September 1914, p. 56.

front and behind the lines; The War In Belgium also showed King Albert
reviewing troops and his Queen nursing the wounded in the royal palace.[1]
And the film producer Sigmund Lubin wrote to Moving Picture World, questioning Tippett's claim that it was impossible to obtain genuine war
footage:

> . . . The Lubin Manufacturing Company has since the commence-
> ment of the war had several photographers engaged in taking war
> pictures and admitting the risk of life, have succeeded in
> sending to the Philadelphia plant quite a number of reels de-
> picting actual fighting. To attempt to fake such pictures would
> be a matter of impossibility. The streets of Alost and Antwerp
> could not be duplicated here, neither could any artist reproduce
> the partially destroyed Rheims Cathedral. . . . Admitting it to
> be a hazardous job, the fact remains that war pictures are being
> filmed and will truthfully depict the horrors of the unfortunate
> situation.[2]

One of Lubin's cameramen was an Englishman, A. Radcliffe Dugmore,
whose brother, a captain in the British army, used his influence to let
him work at the front. It was reported that while Dugmore was filming
the siege of Alost, a German shell wrecked a house a few doors away, and
"[A]ll the time he was at work shells and bullets whizzed uncomfortably
by his ears."[3]

Universal also obtained film of the siege of Antwerp for the
Animated Weekly. The cameraman was a Scotsman, J.M. Downie, who, like
Dugmore, used his contacts to work in the war zone; as Moving Picture
World reported:

[1]Advertisement, Motion Picture News, 12 September 1914, p. 67.

[2]"Faking War Pictures," Moving Picture World, 28 November 1914,
p. 1249.

[3]Ernest A. Dench, "Preserving the Great War for Posterity by the
Movies," Motion Picture Magazine, July 1915, p. 91.

. . . Mr. Downie enjoys a wide circle of friends among the Belgium (sic) and French armies. He was not only allowed to move pretty much as he pleased, but some of the army officers even assisted him, at times, in moving his camera and securing passage through restricted districts.[1]

Downie stayed in the besieged city until a few hours before the Germans arrived, and escaped just before all the roads out were blocked. According to one account, he filmed bursting shells from the inside of a cart.[2]

Two other Universal cameramen did not share Downie's influence or luck. First, they were arrested as spies. After they were freed, they made their way to a battlefield and filmed a German cavalry charge on the Belgian lines. Then, one of their cameras was put out of action by a flying bullet. In changing their position, they exposed themselves, and had to flee the German cavalry, abandoning the damaged camera and its film. Carrying the other camera, they boarded a train which was so full that they had to ride on the engine. When they stepped down at a station, a policeman apprehended them and, despite their appeals, insisted on taking the undeveloped film out of the camera to inspect it under a bright light.[3]

Edwin Weigle had also been in Antwerp, filming for the Chicago Tribune. When war was declared, Joseph Medill Patterson, one of the

---

[1]"Siege of Antwerp Shown in Pictures," Moving Picture World, 28 November 1914, p. 1218.

[2]Ernest A. Dench, Making The Movies (New York: Macmillan, 1915), p. 160.

[3]Ibid., p. 161.

editor-owners of the Tribune, left for Europe, taking Weigle along.[1] The newspaper signed a deal with the Belgian government allowing Weigle to work in the war zone; he filmed the siege of Antwerp and the flight of refugees across the Dutch border.[2] The agreement with the Belgians set the pattern for many other deals between governments and film companies; half the profits from Weigle's film were to go to the Belgian Red Cross. The footage was edited into a single release--On The Belgian Battlefield--which, by the end of 1914, had already made more than $28,000 for the Red Cross.[3]

As a French-based company with French employees, Pathé Frères hoped to gain privileges which its competitors were denied. But the first effect of the war was to deprive it of some of its best photographers, who volunteered for military service. Short of staff, the company employed some women as camera operators; even Charles Pathé took on some newsreel assignments.[4]

Although Pathé cameramen were eventually given credentials to work with the French army, they were in as much danger as any American during the first months of the war. H.A. Sanders, a Pathé cameraman who had British papers, was in Ghent when the Germans began to occupy the city. He did not know whether the Germans would treat him as a non-

[1]Waldrop, McCormick of Chicago, p. 125.

[2]Dench, "Preserving the Great War," p. 91, and Ramsaye, A Million And One Nights, p. 685.

[3]Brownlow, The War, p. 11.

[4]Ernest Dench, "Camera Men At The Front," Picture-Play Magazine, 1 January 1916, p. 92. See also Bardèche and Brasillach, History of Motion Pictures, p. 93.

combatant if they captured him, and he was not going to wait to find
out. Accompanied by a Daily Sketch (London) reporter, he raced for his
car and ordered the chauffeur to drive to Ostend; two Belgian soldiers
jumped on board and refused to get off. On the hood fluttered a Union
Jack, which gave them cause for concern when they encountered a German
motor cycle patrol. "Again flight was the only thing to be done in the
circumstances," wrote Sanders, "and our chauffeur, who was in as great
a state of panic as a man could be, dashed by with total disregard for
brakes, ditches or humanity that only fear can engender."[1] When they
had shaken off the patrol, Sanders stopped the car and threw the Union
Jack, a German rifle and other souvenirs into a canal. On they went,
passing the retreating Belgian army, to Ostend, where the townspeople
were fearfully awaiting the approaching German army.[2]

While Sanders was fleeing, a cameraman for a rival French company, Éclair, was secretly filming the German occupation of Ghent. M.
Bizuel secured a second-floor room in a cafe facing the town hall, and
set up his camera so that the lens passed through a slightly opened
window, while the body of the camera, and Bizeul himself, were hidden.
From this position, he filmed the German troops marching into the square
for one and a quarter hours. Bizeul then obtained a milk-cart, in which
he hid his films, and set out for neutral Holland accompanied by a
Flemish-speaking guide. Bizeul, dressed in old clothes and with eight

---

[1]The Bioscope, 22 October 1914, p. 299, quoted in Brownlow, The
War, p. 12. See also Dench, Making The Movies, pp. 161-62, and "Camera
Men At The Front," p. 92.

[2]Ibid.

days growth of beard, did not arouse the suspicion of sentries who were mainly concerned with looking for weapons. At Mendonck, he changed to a dog-cart and, pretending to be a refugee, crossed into Holland, from where he sailed to London.[1]

The Eclectic Film Company, an American subsidiary of Pathé, also resorted to subterfuge to obtain film in the city of Louvain, which was sacked and burned by the Germans. Orders had been issued to arrest all persons found with cameras within 20 miles of the armies. Eclectic's cameraman concealed his 14-pound camera, an Aeroscope, beneath his coat; the machine's gyroscopic stabilizer kept it level while he operated it.[2] He shot 1500 feet showing Belgian troops in hastily made entrenchments, the retreat, refugees and the city in flames.[3]

Such enterprise was often necessary to obtain any worthwhile footage at the front. Cameramen climbed telephone poles, shinned up trees, and cadged rides in airplanes to get a panoramic view of the action. When the French army erected observation posts, some 50 to 75 feet high, so that spotters could direct artillery fire to the German lines, Pierre Cossette, of the Universal Animated Weekly, went up too. He filmed the shells in the air and the explosions when they landed.[4]

---

[1]Pictures and Picturegoer, 5 December 1914, p. 263, quoted in Brownlow, The War, pp. 11-12. See also Dench, Making The Movies, p. 163, and "Camera Men At The Front," p. 92.

[2]For a description of the equipment used by cameramen and technical advances during World War I, see Chapter 6.

[3]Charles I. Reid, "The Adventures of the 'Movie' Camera Man," The Photographic Times, June 1915, p. 236.

[4]"Universal Weekly Gets Shipment of War Films," Motion Picture News, 18 December 1915, p. 54.

J.C. Bee Mason, an English cameraman working for the Hearst-Selig News
Pictorial, also had a head for heights. On one occasion, he climbed a
telegraph pole and hoisted up his camera, which he had attached to a
coil of wire. Precariously perched, he filmed ". . . a set of remarkable panoramic views of the German army."[1] Mason travelled with the
Belgian army for six weeks, in which time he shot about 6,000 feet. To
keep his camera steady, he often strapped it to a tree trunk, which also
protected him from stray bullets.[2] When he wanted to film Belgian
soldiers fighting in the trenches, he lay down in the middle of the
street and held the camera up in front of him.[3] He had several narrow
escapes; a Belgian refugee pulled him away from a wall just before it
was hit by a shell;[4] German shells hit a farmhouse in Grembergen where
he was sleeping but he hid under the bed, clutching his precious camera,
and escaped unharmed.[5]

According to contemporary reports, Mason's most audacious feat
was to travel into German-occupied territory--a considerable risk since,
although he was a non-combatant working for a company in a neutral
country, he was a British citizen. Mason wanted to film a camp for
British prisoners of war, and, when permission was refused, he resorted
to subterfuge:

---

[1]Ernest A. Dench, "Methods by Which the European War Has Been
Filmed," Scientific American, 20 March 1915, p. 277.

[2]Ibid.   [3]Ibid.

[4]Dench, Making The Movies, pp. 162-63, and "Camera Men At The
Front," p. 92.

[5]Ibid.

. . . As calmly as anything, he placed his Aeroscope, which is
a tripodless contrivance, underneath the barrack gates. Our
hero used a stone to rest the machine in an upright position.
Lighting a cigaret, he sat on the camera as if it were a chair.
Then when the guards accosted him he offered each a cigaret
and asked them how long they thought the war would last. With
their vigilance relaxed in this way, they did not notice him
turning the camera crank with one hand, with which he recorded
a squad of soldiers who were exercising in the barrack yard.[1]

Even the most resourceful operator was not safe from inquisitive
sentries and over-zealous censors, so cameramen went to great lengths to
smuggle footage out of Europe to America. Tourists were persuaded to
carry it in their baggage; other film went out concealed as cargo. The
American Paul Rader filmed an artillery duel between the French and the
Germans and then hid the reels and his camera in the cellar of an abandoned house. A few days later, after the fighting had moved to another
area, he returned for his equipment, and smuggled the film out of the
country.[2]

The ban on filming at the front and the rigorous censorship infuriated the American film industry and commentators in the trade press.
"If the cinematographer were to obey the belligerents," wrote Ernest A.
Dench, "we would not get a single view of actual warfare."[3] Censorship
by military authorities, wrote H.H. Van Loan, ensured that all that
reached the United States ". . . was such scenes as might have been
photographed during the review or dress-parade of the armies then fight-

[1]Dench, "Preserving the Great War," pp. 91, 169.

[2]Dench, "Methods by Which the European War Has Been Filmed,"
p. 277.

[3]"Preserving the Great War," p. 89.

ing."[1] When cameramen obtained realistic pictures by subterfuge, they were cut out by the censors, with the result that ". . . even the best pictures which have been shown on Broadway recently could easily have been faked--just as some were faked."[2]

Writing in Moving Picture World, W. Stephen Bush considered the restrictions "nothing less than a loss to civilization and an additional hindrance to peace."[3] While newspapers were biased, Bush wrote, the film was accepted as conclusive evidence. "The only real and incorruptible neutral in this war is not the type but the film," he wrote.[4] A committee of prominent Belgians was on its way to the United States to tell President Wilson of alleged German atrocities. If they had films of these outrages, the allegations could be proved. "If, on the other hand," wrote Bush, "these reports . . . are false or greatly exaggerated it would be easy enough to disprove them by showing the actual conditions in the cities and villages where the wanton destruction is claimed to have occurred."[5]

Not all the countries at war took the attitude of the major powers towards cameramen. When Canadian troops embarked for England, they were accompanied by three cameramen, who filmed the soldiers on board ship, at their training camps in France, and at the front.[6] The films were to be shown to the Canadian public, and then preserved as a

[1]Van Loan, "Shooting the War," p. 64.   [2]Ibid., p. 65.

[3]Bush, "War Films," Moving Picture World, 19 September 1914, p. 1617.

[4]Ibid.   [5]Ibid.

[6]Dench, "Preserving the Great War," p. 90.

historical record.[1] The American Donald Thompson--of whom more in the
next chapter--had filmed mobilization work in Canada and travelled to
France on a freighter as a Canadian correspondent.[2]

Of the major powers, Germany was the first to grant facilities
to the cameramen of neutral countries. In its first edition of 1915,
the Hearst-Selig News Pictorial featured film taken inside Germany;
the cameraman was A.E. Wallace, who had experience in Mexico.[3] According to Motion Picture News: "These views were taken by special permission of the German government, and are intended to give an idea of
conditions within the Teutonic kingdom during the fighting. The training of troops is chiefly shown."[4] Kevin Brownlow argues that the Allies
sacrificed an enormous propaganda advantage by their extended ban on war
correspondents because it "drove the cameramen from neutral America into
the arms of the Central Powers, whose own ban was soon relaxed."[5]

The American Correspondent Film Company had at least two cameramen with the German armies--John Allen Everets and Albert K. Dawson. In
the summer of 1915, German and Austro-Hungarian forces launched a campaign in Galicia to recapture territory from the Russians. Their main

[1]Ibid.

[2]"Paramount Photo-News Man," Moving Picture World, 6 November
1915, p. 1114, and "Cameraman Thompson Off to War for Paramount," Motion
Picture News, 6 November 1915, p. 46.

[3]Brownlow, The War, p. 91. In this reference, Wallace's initials
are given as E.A., while a contemporary review--see next footnote--calls
him A.E. Wallace.

[4]Review, Motion Picture News, 23 January 1915, p. 58.

[5]Brownlow, The War, p. 13.

objective was the town of Przemysl, a railway junction of strategic importance, whose Austrian garrison of 120,000 had surrendered in March 1915 after a siege lasting six months. Both Everets and Dawson filmed the bombardment and recapture of the town, and both recounted their experiences later--one of the few battles in the war where accounts by two cameramen can be compared.

Everets travelled to the front by wagon train, and was there to see the mortars and heavy artillery arrive. The siege began at 5:30 a.m., and Everets, awakened by the first explosions, quickly found a wagon and set off for the forward positions:

> They were beginning to speed up, and I got some real pictures. The earth trembled. Leaves and branches of the trees were blown off by the pressure. Brick walls fell apart; the air was full of noise. Soon the first pieces, further forward, began to join the concert. I had no time to lose. I had to press forward where I could see the shells fall. My nerves were trembling with excitement. Above me, some shells howled like a dog, others like a tenor in grand opera.
>
> My way wound up a hill. I noticed another noise, much more unpleasant than any I had heard, and coming from the shells which were thrown toward us. Boom! boom! Two shells struck the road ahead of us. You could hear the devils coming thru [sic] the air, but you never knew where they were going to strike until it might be too late. Two more landed to the right of us. Every moment I expected to be hurled into the air, but at length I reached the field batteries in safety. Here the din was increased by the constant firing of fifty guns. I found an officer and succeeded in making him understand where I wanted to go. He just pointed ahead and said: "Up the hill."
>
> "Up the hill" seemed a million miles off and impossible to reach without being hit by the Russians, but I decided that having come so far I must go on, and I went thru [sic] barricades of wood, hiding myself as well as possible. . . .
>
> The road I followed wound zigzag up the hill. There was little to see. The mortar batteries behind me made such a noise at every shot that I thought my ears should burst. Further forward, the field batteries had raised their more fem-

inine voices, firing salvos like the beating of a drum. . . .
Occasionally, a shell would come uncomfortably close, making me
wince. A look at the driver, who calmly disregarded everything
except his horses, made me feel ashamed to be afraid.[1]

Eventually, Everets reached a clump of trees where a reserve am-

munition train was standing. An officer advised him to leave the wagon,

because the road ahead was under fire, and to proceed on foot. Two

soldiers were detailed to carry his equipment but they ". . . did not

come along fast enough to suit me, and it seemed an eternity before we

reached the crest of the first hill."[2]

A wooded valley still separated Everets from his objective--a

hill code-named Cote 404. Everets and his helpers came under fire again

as they descended and made their way up the other side, and they had to

take refuge in the woods. Finally, they reached an eight-cornered earth-

work which was being used as an observation post for the mortar batteries.

A glance at the nature of my post showed me that it was impossible for me to use my camera tripod. The only places per-
mitting the exposure of the camera were apertures dug in the dirt
wall for observation purposes. I built a crude stand of logs,
and set my camera upon it, bringing the lens as close as possible
to the narrow little window. The pictures were all made from
Oberst-Lieutenant Rittner's observation-hole, from which he had
been watching the breaking of the Austrian shells on the outer
works of Przemysl. This gave me a clear, unobstructed view.
For three hours I heard nothing but the ear-splitting yelps of
shells, but I had a chance to make dandy pictures, and ground
away until I had "shot" a thousand feet of good kodak film.

I don't think I was at all afraid when I was making the pictures; in fact, I never realized the danger I had been in until
after the fall of Przemysl and my visit to the wrecked fort.[3]

---

[1]John Allen Everets, "How I Got to Przemysl and Filmed the Bombardment," Motion Picture Magazine, February 1916, pp. 59-62.

[2]Ibid., p. 64.

[3]Ibid.

Everets said that the town itself had suffered little damage, but that the forts surrounding it had been pulverized by the barrage. "The dead lay in heaps," he wrote. "The men had tried to get their guns away, but had been caught in a rain of iron that had torn craters twenty meters wide in the landscape and scattered death everywhere."[1]

Dawson's briefer, and less vivid, account of the siege is contained in an interview with Francis Collins, the author of a contemporary book on motion picture photographers. Said Dawson:

I had spent ten days in traveling from the Carpathians to join the forces bombarding Przemysl. My army pass permitted me to ride on any means of conveyance as long as there was room. Sometimes I traveled by train, and at other times on the government automobiles rushing towards the front, but most of the distance was covered tediously in army wagons. My tent was finally pitched with the artillery shelling Przemysl. It was hardly a tent but rather a very crude shelter made with barrel hoops covered with blankets, but it kept the worst of the weather off for a couple of weeks.

The range was about four miles so that our camp was continuously under fire. I was able to make pictures of the men bringing up the great siege guns, the work of setting them up, and the actual bombardment. In this bombardment the work is done mainly by the great siege guns, and the infantry is brought up later to clean up. Some of the guns were only a few feet from my tent and the shock of the reports was deafening. Like all the soldiers, I had to go about with my ears stuffed with cotton. This lasted for days until the forts of Przemysl fell and we rushed forward to find that the great fortifications of steel and solid masonry had been turned upside down by the bombardment.[2]

Dawson's footage[3] was edited into a four-reel film, The Battle of Przemysl, which was released in August 1915. The American Corres-

---

[1]Ibid., p. 65.

[2]Francis Collins, The Camera Man (New York: Century, 1916), pp. 7-8.

[3]There is no mention of Everets' footage in contemporary reviews.

pondent Film Company played on American antipathy to Russia in its trade-press publicity: "Smashing the armies of the Czar, Showing Austro-Hungarian drive through Galicia, terminating in the Battle of Przemysl."[1] The company smugly remarked that "The NEUTRALITY [sic] of our feature is wholly evidenced by the cordial reception of A.K. Dawson, our Correspondent, at the American Embassy in Berlin, by U.S. Ambassador James W. Gerard."[2] Gerard had not, of course, seen the film, and extending a courtesy to visiting cameramen did not constitute approval; indeed, Gerard was to become one of Germany's harshest critics, and his account of his work, My Four Years in Germany, was made into a wildly sensational propaganda film in 1918.[3] Moving Picture World noted that while The Battle of Przemysl "tends to glorify the prowess of the Teutonic allies," even an audience that opposed Austria-Hungary ". . . may overlook the political significance of the operations and marvel at scenes that so graphically suggest human tragedy and military resourcefulness."[4]

The film showed the various phases of the campaign--the troop movements, supply trains, bridge-building, the arrival of the artillery, the bombardment and aeroplane spotters. The reviewer also had fulsome praise for the cameraman. "Dawson frequently risked his life in the making of this picture," he wrote, "and for a crowning achievement photographed an actual battle--the capture of a town. It seems safe to

---

[1]Quoted in review, Moving Picture World, 14 August 1915, p. 1175.

[2]Advertisement, Motion Picture News, 4 September 1915, p. 73.

[3]For an analysis of the film, see Brownlow, The War, pp. 135-39.

[4]Review by Lynde Denig, Moving Picture World, 14 August 1915, p. 1175.

suppose that these scenes in the concluding reel have never been equaled."[1] Keven Brownlow doubts the authenticity of the battle scene, of which only a frame enlargement survives. "It looks suspiciously like a staged scene," he writes, "for the camera is in a position commanding an excellent view of the assault, and the explosion appears to be simulated."[2] Dawson claimed he had anticipated the charge and set up his camera in the shelter of a heavy stone wall. When the Russian artillery found the range, the wall collapsed, and Dawson beat a hasty retreat.[3]

Dawson's next major assignment for the American Correspondent Film Company was in the Balkans, where he filmed activities on the front at Saloniki.[4] In 1916, Mutual signed a deal with the company to use his footage from the Eastern Front. It was released as a five-reel feature, The Fighting Germans, in May of that year. Motion Picture News reported that the film included shots of the Kaiser at the front, the Crown Prince in command of his regiment, and the storming of the fortified village of Ivangorod.[5] When America entered the war, the American Correspondent Film Company fell under suspicion for its alleged pro-German activities, and in May 1918, its president, Felix Malitz, and secretary Gustave Engler were convicted and sent to prison.[6]

The Chicago Tribune also obtained permission for its cameramen to accompany the German forces. Edwin F. Weigle, who had covered the

[1]Ibid.   [2]Brownlow, The War, p. 16.   [3]Ibid.

[4]Motion Picture News, 26 February 1916, p. 1136.

[5]Motion Picture News, 20 May 1916, p. 3042.

[6]Ramsaye, A Million And One Nights, p. 690.

siege of Antwerp,[1] returned to Europe, and, while staying with relatives in Germany, produced a film called Germany in Wartime (1915).[2] Film shot by Weigle, Donald Thompson and others was edited into The German Side of the War, which was a huge success. When it opened at the 44th Street Theater in New York on 20 September 1915, the lines extended for four blocks.[3] According to Terry Ramsaye, "[T]he mad rush to the German war pictures was so impatiently tense that ticket scalpers, unable to renew their supply from the box office, went down the long lines selling strip soda checks to the unsuspecting."[4] The film broke the box office record with a daily attendance of 8,555; receipts for the week totalled almost $15,000.[5] The company handling the release secured many bookings in other large cities, and the Tribune bought a full page in Motion Picture News to warn exhibitors against cheap imitations:

> You must give your patrons the real thing. Substitutes will not do. You cannot get away with it very long. There is no doubt that all others are cheaper. But the public is wise and knows that "The Chicago Tribune's German Side of the War Pictures" are a sensation everywhere they are shown.[6]

The Tribune said the film would appeal to all Americans, whichever side they supported. "If you have pro-German sympathies, you want to see what Germany is doing. If your sympathies are with the Allies these pictures show you the terrific war machine the Allies have to

---

[1]See supra, pp. 67-68.

[2]Brownlow, The War, p. 82.

[3]Ramsaye, A Million And One Nights, p. 686.   [4]Ibid.

[5]"German Side of the War Makes Record Run," Motion Picture News, 13 November 1915, p. 75.

[6]Advertisement, Motion Picture News, 13 November 1915, p. 113.

fight."[1] There was no claim to neutrality; the film was enthusiastically endorsed by the German ambassador to the United States, Count
Bernstorff.[2]

Only a handful of scenes from the film survive,[3] so it is difficult to judge its overall quality. One of the opening scenes, No. 4,
seems hackneyed to modern eyes; Weigle is pictured outside the Chicago
Tribune offices, loading his camera and tripod into a cab as he prepares
to leave for Germany; he smiles rather self-consciously at the camera.
The first part of the film is concerned principally with war preparations and military training inside Germany: Boy Scouts on drill practice and a corps of motorcycle couriers are shown; a field hospital is
erected and trenches are built; at Lubeck, 300 soup wagons are loaded to
feed troops at the front. Scenes 53 to 62 were shot at the siege of
Przemysl. According to the titles, Weigle filmed exploding shells with
a telephoto lens at a distance of 3,000 feet.[4] But most of the scenes
show the town after its capture by the German and Austrian forces.
Soldiers are pictured sitting among the ruins, and guarding captured
artillery pieces.[5] Some of the last scenes of the film, 93 through 96,
were taken on the Italian front, where the mountainous terrain made
fighting difficult. Soldiers struggle to move field guns and a machine

---

[1]Ibid.   [2]Ibid.

[3]Scenes 4, 16, 23, 25, 26, 28, 41, 53, 55, 56, 57, 59 and 62 are
in John E. Allen's collection (see Appendix), reel no. 4301. Scenes 93,
94, 95, 96 and 104 are in a reel entitled Newsreel Clips From Various
Newsreels No. 9 in the Library of Congress Collection (see Appendix).

[4]Scene 53.

[5]Scenes 55, 56 and 57.

gun platoon plods up a mountain.[1] The closing title is an unmemorable
sentiment from Weigle: "Having the horrors of war indeliby inscribed in
my memory . . . I sailed to America--glad, indeed, to return to my home,
the land of peace."[2]

    Official accreditation by the German army did not mean that
American cameramen could shoot what they wanted. Like other correspondents, they were constantly under the close watch of officers who
decided where they could go and what they could see. But occasionally a
cameraman defied authority to get the shot he wanted.

    On the Eastern Front in 1915, a group of fifteen correspondents
were covering the German advance. According to Harry C. Carr of the Los
Angeles Times, they were watched over by two German staff officers ". . .
who fussed over us like a couple of old hens with a brood of ducklings."[3]
From Warsaw, the correspondents travelled to the fortress of Nowo Georgi-
evsk. For several days, they watched the Austrian howitzers pounding
the fortress. When news of its fall came through, they set out for the
front line. In the party was a cameraman, Wilbur H. Durborough, who,
according to Carr, was prepared to take a risk to get a good shot:

> I never believe they intended us to see it; but we acciden-
> tally bumped into the most majestic of military ceremonies--a
> Kaiser review. The troops which had taken part in the battle
> were assembling on the battle field when we got there. It was
> a splendid picture. The fortress was on fire against the sky.
> Down one road filed a long procession of Russian prisoners
> marching to the rear. Down another road trundled the big guns
> that had driven the Czar out of Poland. They had finished one
> job and were on the way to the next battle. In the middle of

[1]Scenes 94 and 95.   [2]Scene 104.

[3]Harry C. Carr, "Capturing The Kaiser," Photoplay Magazine,
March 1916, p. 111.

a great hollow square of troops stood the War Lord leaning on a little cane addressing his soldiers. Behind him were his field marshals, Von Hindenburg, Von Baseler, Von Falkenhyn and his sons, Prince Eitel Fritz and Prince Joachim.

Of course this was perfectly miserable stuff for moving pictures!

Durborough begged our officer to let him slip in between the files and shoot a picture. The worthy captain looked as though he was going to faint at the suggestion. "Aw, just for a minute," pleaded Durborough pathetically, but the captain had turned from him to another correspondent who had lit a cigar. "One does not smoke at a Kaiser review," he said in a thunderous stage whisper. Which shows what kind of a thing a Kaiser review is.

Finally the ceremony came to a close. "Adieu, Comrades!" cried the Kaiser. "Adieu, Majesty!" they shouted back. The ranks fell back; the square opened. The Kaiser strode back to his auto and climbed in. Spying Dr. Sven Hedin, the famous Swedish explorer, in the crowd, the Emperor beckoned him to the car. This was more than Durborough could stand. He suddenly broke away and we saw him running full tilt across the cleared place that the awe of the soldiers had left around His Majesty. Our captain was too much overcome to follow. The captain just stood waiting for an offended heaven to strike dead the impious wretch.

To the frozen horror of the whole German army, Durborough set up his machine about thirty feet away from the Kaiser's car and began grinding away for dear life.

The Kaiser looked up and took in the whole situation with his quick, comprehending eyes. He laughed and lit a cigarette, taking a little while longer, we believe, to give the plucky Yankee boy a chance.

Finally the Emperor and Dr. Hedin shook hands; the chauffer of the car threw in the hop and the Imperial auto started with a leap.

As it went by him, Durborough took off his hat and said with honest sociability, "Much obliged!" The Kaiser straightened up and one gauntleted hand rose to the visor of his helmet in salute to the American boy who had the nerve to snap an Emperor without asking permission.[1]

---

[1]Ibid., pp. 111-12.

Working with another cameraman, R.G. Ries, Durborough spent seven months with the German army on the Eastern Front, and returned to the United States with 16,000 feet of film.[1] 9,000 feet were selected and edited into <u>On the German Firing Line</u>, released by the Industrial Moving Picture Company in November 1915.[2] The opening scenes were taken on board a ship in the English Channel, with the passengers looking for submarines; then come shots of the Kaiser and the campaign in Poland. The film was premiered at the Stoddard Theater in Milwaukee on 28 November 1915, and played to packed houses in that city and in Chicago.[3]

Cameramen travelled with the Austro-Hungarian armies, who fought beside the Germans on the Eastern Front. One cameraman was filming an Austrian battery shelling a Russian fort some six miles away. The soldiers thought they were out of range of the Russian guns, but suddenly shells began falling around them. Neither they, nor the cameraman, took cover, as the barrage intensified. As contemporary film historian Francis Collins reported:

> The gunners nevertheless stuck pluckily to their guns, and the movie man stuck no less bravely to his camera. When a shell struck within range of his lens, he swung his camera in position and turned the crank. His films show great masses of earth, tons of it, leaping into the air, in some cases to a height of

---

[1]"On the German Firing Line Packs Western Houses," <u>Motion Picture News</u>, 18 December 1915, p. 48.

[2]Ibid. This film should not be confused with another released about the same time with a similar title--<u>Germany On The Firing Line</u>. The latter, which opened at the Park Theater in New York in December 1915, was said to be "the only moving picture taken by the German government itself." Its distributors claimed it was the work of 106 enlisted cameramen. See "Germany On Firing Line Officially Approved," <u>Motion Picture News</u>, 22 January 1916, p. 1015.

[3]Ibid.

fully one hundred and fifty feet, and then gradually falling
back. So close were many of these shots that the camera man
was sprinkled with the falling earth.

The focus was so sharp that the films at times show the
dismembered bodies of the gunners hurled into the air. In one
film the picture is actually shaken by the explosion which occurred less than one hundred feet away. . . .[1]

The best documented account of an American working with the

Austrian army is that of Captain F.E. Kleinschmidt, the Arctic explorer

and pioneer film-maker. In a letter to Moving Picture World, he ex-

plained how he gained the confidence of the Austrian General Staff:

Upon my arrival at the Great Headquarters of the Austrian
Army I was invited by the Crown Prince to give a lecture on my
last Arctic expedition and show my moving pictures to the officers of the general staff. The Archduke, Field Marshal Frederick, highest commanding officer; his wife, daughters and all
generals and officers were present. This lecture gave me the
magic key that unlocked all doors and gave me privileges and
opportunities to accomplish things.[2]

An officer was detailed to act as Kleinschmidt's guide, and he

had two servants who soon learned how to set up and pack the camera; he

was given a car and chauffeur, and when he was travelling across country,

a wagon and horses were requisitioned. And he had other privileges:

. . . In Russian Poland I often had an Uhlan or a troop for my
guidance and protection. This makes quite a caravan to travel
with, but to travel in style means comfort, and you get there
quickly. I almost forgot our gendarm [sic], who gets our quarters ready, looks after our wagons, drivers and servants.[3]

Kleinschmidt wrote of "Austrian hospitality and the Austrian

readiness to help and favor you," and compared it to the welcome he

---

[1]Collins, The Camera Man, pp. 10, 13.

[2]W. Stephen Bush, "Genuine War Films," Moving Picture World, 14
August 1915, p. 1134.

[3]Ibid.

received from prospectors while he was working in Alaska.[1] The Austrians

did not, in the tradition of Pancho Villa, fight any battles for his

benefit, but they went to great lengths to help the cameraman:

> Last week while I was in the foremost trenches and took
> pictures of the Russian trenches only 300 yards away, a whole
> battery was ordered to cover the Russian trenches with shrapnel
> to enable me to take the pictures of the exploding bombs.
> Troops of cavalry have been alarmed for me, flyers have taken
> me up to take pictures from above; . . . even the huge siege
> mortars that destroyed the forts of Antwerp, Liege and Namur
> were ordered to be set in action for me, although even one
> single shot costs a pretty sum of money.[2]

The Austrians could provide some action for the camera, but they

could not provide film for it. Obtaining raw stock was a constant prob-

lem for Kleinschmidt:

> Films are a rare article here. The Eastman films for mov-
> ing pictures and for cameras have been out of the market for
> four months, and I have had much trouble getting the German
> Agfa material.[3]

Kleinschmidt found that he had to be on the move to keep up with

the shifting battle front. Travelling across country was not only un-

comfortable for the cameraman, but tough on his equipment:

> . . . The life of a camera is short; the strain is something
> terrible. The jolting over littered streets, on horseback or
> jumping ditches and kicking around in barbed-wire entanglements
> loosens every screw and breaks the bolts. When you ride with
> an Uhlan regiment, all young horses that shy at every shell and
> trench, and you succeed in getting out your camera at the psy-
> chological moment only to find it a pitiful ruin, you begin to
> realize the meaning of the phrase, "Swearing like a trooper."[4]

It appeared that Kleinschmidt enjoyed no special influence with

the Austrian censors. He told Moving Picture World that he had printed

---

[1]Ibid.   [2]Ibid.   [3]Ibid., p. 1135.

[4]Ibid.

10,000 feet, and was enclosing some pictures, ". . . but the censor will scarcely let the battle scenes go through."[1] He followed the Austrian army on its advance to Przemysl and Lemberg; later he travelled to the Balkans and the Italian Front.

Kleinschmidt returned to the United States in 1916 with film from the Russian, Italian and Serbian fronts. The film was released by Lewis J. Selznick under the title War on Three Fronts in February 1917[2] --just two months before America went to war with Germany and Austria. Kleinschmidt announced that the profits would go directly to the German-Austro-Hungarian Relief Association[3]--not the most tactful suggestion at that time.

A favorable review appeared in the Exhibitors Trade Review,[4] which picked out some scenes for special attention: Polish women and children trapped in cross-fire, the city of Brest-Litovsk in flames, shrapnel bursting near the cameraman's aeroplane, U-boats going on a raid, and men falling on the battlefield within 20 yards of the camera. Kleinschmidt described the dangers he faced:

> We were very fortunate, not only in obtaining these pic-
> tures, but many times in escaping with our lives. When the
> shrapnel burst near our aeroplane, the concussion deafened us
> for several days, although none of the flying fragments struck
> either the machine or ourselves. I believe that we have

---

[1] Ibid.

[2] After several showings in New York City. The Selznick release was nationwide, through the company's exchanges. See "War on Three Fronts," Moving Picture World, 21 April 1917, p. 447.

[3] Brownlow, The War, p. 21.

[4] Exhibitors Trade Review, 10 February 1917, p. 675.

pictures here which no other cinematographer has ever equalled.[1]

George Blaisdell, writing in Moving Picture World, agreed that such scenes were impressive, but felt that, with America now in the war, exhibitors would be foolish to show the film. He thought the content and titles would encourage what he called the professional pacifist and anti-recruiting propagandist:

> It is the conviction of the writer that had "War on Three Fronts" been shown in this country prior to the entrance of the United States into the European conflict there would have been opportunity for little adverse criticism. It is his conviction that if it is shown now many exhibitors who display the subject probably will be buying a riot.[2]

Kleinschmidt had said that by releasing the film, he hoped ". . . to bring home to the people all the awfulness of modern warfare."[3] It came home to him when he was arrested on 24 November 1917--not on the charge of distributing enemy propaganda, but on the weaker count of possessing a loaded revolver.[4] D.W. Griffith, who needed battle footage for Hearts of the World, purchased Kleinschmidt's film for $16,000, but he was advised not to use it for risk of damaging his reputation.[5]

Russia was the first of the Allied powers to grant facilities to cameramen. Pathé sent George Ercole, half Irish and half French, to the Eastern Front, where he won praise for filming a Russian cavalry charge, which was regarded as the finest achievement for a front-line

---

[1]Ibid.

[2]"War on Three Fronts," Moving Picture World, 21 April 1917, p. 447.

[3]Exhibitors Trade Review, 10 February 1917, p. 675.

[4]Brownlow, The War, p. 21.   [5]Ibid., p. 22.

cameraman.[1] He was at the first battle of Przemysl, when the Russians laid siege to the Austrian garrison for six months. While filming, he was hit by a piece of shrapnel, but he kept turning the crank; for his bravery, the Russian government decorated him with the Cross of the Order of St. George.[2] His films reached the United States via Pathé offices in Moscow, Stockholm and London,

> . . . so on the very day the newsboys were using their fifty-seven different ways of pronouncing Przemysl to tell the public that the Austrian fortress had fallen, in the Pathé "News" projecting rooms at Jersey City the editorial staff of the "News" was looking at some very fine pictures of the siege.[3]

The Chicago Tribune sent its editor and war correspondent, Robert R. McCormick, and cameraman Donald Thompson to Russia in 1915. The four-reel feature, With the Russians at the Front (also called Russian Battlefields)[4] had more fire in its publicity material than on the celluloid. The Tribune spent thousands of dollars on advertisements such as this:

> Russian Soldiers fighting in the trenches! Russian Big Guns in Action on the Battle Front! Russian Cossacks madly charging! Russian Warship Bombarding Turkish Villages on the Bosporus [sic] Front![5]

Exhibitors were urged to "make your money on them while the

---

[1]Ibid., p. 16.

[2]"Pathé Camera Man Decorated for Work at Przemysl," Motion Picture News, 17 April 1915, p. 38.

[3]Ibid.

[4]There is a print of the film in the Film Study Center at the Museum of Modern Art in New York (see Appendix).

[5]Advertisement, Motion Picture News, 13 November 1915, p. 117.

public interest is at its height. . . . Cash in on this publicity."[1]

If the film was a success, the viewing public must have been
easily excited. The film opens with Russian officers surveying Austrian
positions; Russian soldiers pose self-consciously beside field guns;
when they open fire on a plane, it seems more intent on pursuing its
course (for the benefit of the cameraman?) than on taking evasive action.
The front line at Lomza was apparently safe enough to allow Thompson to
take up a position in which the troops run towards his camera; soldiers
are seen firing from a parapet, and some fall back, apparently wounded.
The Czar and Grand Duke Nicholas are shown reviewing troops and the film
concludes with scenes on board a Russian destroyer shelling Turkish
villages. Edwin Weigle had appeared in the earlier Tribune film, The
German Side of the War;[2] not to be outdone, Thompson appears in the
Russian film, posing beside a Chicago Tribune sign on his car. The
cumbersome camera equipment, and restrictions on Thompson's activities
by the army, may partly account for the slow pace of the film; most of
the shots are long and static, as if the cameraman recorded merely what
happened in front of the lens. There is no attempt to compress time and
action by editing; as in many war films of the period, the impression is
of a series of unconnected scenes, linked only by the titles.

In May 1915, the French War Office gave permission for cameramen
from Pathé, Éclair, Gaumont and Eclipse to take and show films of
activities at the front.[3] Pathé cameramen were appointed cinematographers

---

[1]Ibid.   [2]See supra, pp. 80-81.

[3]Rachael Low, The History of the British Film, 1914-1918 (London:
Allen and Unwin, 1948), p. 152.

to the French government, to which the company had to present a copy of each completed film. The first official film to be shown in the United States was released in June 1915 in Pathé News No. 39.[1] The French government maintained a strict control over all stages of the shooting and editing; military officers supervised the cameramen, and a body called the French Cinematograph Chamber of Commerce edited and censored the footage.[2] Exhibitors seemed unconcerned that the film had been censored, and might give audiences an essentially French view of the war. They were more worried about faked war films, so the fact that the footage had been "approved and censored by the French military authorities"[3] increased, rather than diminished, its credibility. And there was no doubt that Pathé's agreement with the French government gave the company's cameramen the edge on their competitors. Cameramen from Britain got no favors from the ally, as Ernest Dench reported:

> . . . A big English company sent no less than ten operators to France and provided them with three automobiles. These the French authorities appropriated and calmly told the much annoyed operators to claim them when peace was declared. To pile up the agony, the British army authorities seized their cameras and supplies before they had proceeded much further.[4]

French cameramen working for American companies fared better. Leon Crabier of the Mutual Weekly was with the French forces during the advance through the Vesges Mountains in early 1915. His film showed the troops, knee-deep in snow, moving forward, an attack to clear woods of

---

[1]Motion Picture News, 5 June 1915, p. 30.

[2]Advertisement, Motion Picture News, 19 June 1915, p. 9.

[3]Ibid.

[4]Dench, "Preserving the Great War," pp. 90-91.

German scouts, the Germans entrenched on a hill, and the French artillery in action. Mutual's own publication, Reel Life, described what happened next:

> Of a sudden the air is alive with bursting shells. Men are falling, dead and dying, many of them within but a few rods of the lens, the undaunted photographer having brought his machine right into the heat of battle. Then comes the charge through the snow, where the men are mowed down by hundreds. Rescue of the dying and injured and recovery of as many of the dead as possible are clearly depicted in all their horror, together with scores of other thrilling scenes and incidents of battle, making this set of pictures by far the most wonderful of their kind ever obtained.[1]

Motion Picture News joined in the congratulations, saying that Crabier had secured ". . . what will go down in history as the most wonderful motion pictures of warfare ever filmed."[2] Sadly, a print does not survive to prove or disprove these claims. A Pathé cameraman was also in the Vosges; Pathé News No. 42 of June 1915 showed the Alpine Chasseurs before and after a battle.[3]

Another Frenchman, Pierre Cossette, represented the Universal Animated Weekly, and, according to Motion Picture News, was ". . . equipped with passes and credentials to follow the French and English troops to the firing line."[4] The writer did not believe that censorship prevented Cossette from obtaining realistic film--indeed, rather the reverse. "As Mr. Cossette is a native of France and his pictures are

---

[1]"Facts And Figures And Such," Reel Life, 8 May 1915, p. 6.

[2]"First Authentic Pictures of Vosges Battle," Motion Picture News, 15 May 1915, p. 57.

[3]Motion Picture News, 12 June 1915, p. 28.

[4]"Universal Weekly Gets Shipment of War Films," Motion Picture News, 18 December 1915, p. 54.

all submitted to the French Government before they leave the country, he
has succeeded in obtaining some excellent real war pictures . . ."[1]
Official help, rather than official censorship, enabled Cossette to film
a 12-inch field gun firing from a concealed trench and to obtain, from
an observation tower, the shots of shells exploding on the German lines.[2]

Merl LaVoy was from Minnesota, but his French-sounding name must
have helped him when he worked in France. A born adventurer, he had
worked in a lumber camp, hauled freight into Alaska and travelled around
the world photographing scenes for a Chicago mail order journal.[3] Armed
with letters of introduction from Josephus Daniels, the Secretary of the
Navy, and Lindley M. Garrison, Secretary of War, he set out for France
in the spring of 1915.[4] He managed to stay 22 months, with authority
from the American Relief Clearing House. He was attached to the First
Aid Corps, and had a green pass which meant "let him alone."[5] But his
life ". . . wasn't worth a pickayune to the first-aid corps, because he
was a mere adventurer, making pictures."[6]

At Verdun, he worked under fire to film the French artillery in
action and conditions in the trenches. The American pilots of the
Lafayette Escadrille--a volunteer unit that served in the French sector
from April 1916--took him up to photograph reserve encampments behind

---

[1]Ibid.   [2]See supra, p. 70.

[3]Ramsaye, A Million And One Nights, pp. 686-87.

[4]Ibid., pp. 687-88.

[5]Roger Packard, "The Movie Machine Gunner," Picture-Play Magazine, September 1917, p. 62.

[6]Ibid.

Verdun.[1] And, if his own account is to be believed, he was one of the first cameramen to film a tank in the Somme district in the fall of 1916:

> . . . It was the first I'd seen, and I made up my mind right there that I was just going to tuck away a few feet of it in my little camera. It was a magnificent sight, that great, lumbering machine forging ahead thru [sic] the deep mud without any apparent effort . . . Barbed-wire entanglements were nothing in its young life; it plodded thru them like a bear thru brambles.
>
> About this time my circulation was about as spry as it ever gets, and it was all I could do to keep my hands off that camera. I begged the officer in the car for permission to "shoot" the tank, but he said "No!" emphatically--couldn't even think of taking a picture of it, even a "still." But I pleaded and kept at him with every argument I could think of, until he finally gave in. "But quickly!" he commanded in French, and I didn't waste any time. I ground away until that tank was out of sight, and wanted to get some more of it farther on, but my officer wouldn't hear of it.[2]

LaVoy was broke when he returned to Paris and wired his backers in America for more funds, mentioning in the cable that he had filmed a tank. About a week later, he was visited by three men from the French War Office who produced a copy of his cable and told him that the filming of tanks was forbidden. LaVoy was allowed to go free, but without his film.[3]

LaVoy's footage was edited into an eight-reel film, Heroic France, which was released by Mutual.[4] There were the usual behind-the-

---

[1]Ibid., and Brownlow, The War, p. 58.

[2]Hi Sibley, "The Why of the Tankless Film," Motion Picture Magazine, August 1917, pp. 60-61.

[3]Ibid., pp. 61-63.

[4]Packard, "The Movie Machine Gunner," p. 62.

lines scenes: French and British military and political leaders, the
American aviators Raoul Lufbery and Kiffin Rockwell, and even the French
boxer Georges Carpentier; British cavalry waiting to move up to the
front, and the reserve encampments at Verdun.[1] However, his front-line
film brought favorable comment:

> In contrast to most war pictures shown in this country which
> have been taken rather remote from the firing line, these pic-
> tures were almost invariably taken under the muzzles of the guns.
> Here you see the French artillery batteries swinging into line
> for one of the big "punches" on the Verdun front. In another
> scene are shown the ambulance corps men tending wounded under
> fire. . . .[2]

In 1917, LaVoy accompanied the American Red Cross Mission to
Serbia, and returned with film for Serbia Victorious. In 1918, he joined
the travelogue pioneer Burton Holmes on a tour of the European battlefields. After serving with the Red Cross, LaVoy became a cameraman for
Pathé News.[3]

Of the Allied powers, the British were the last to allow cameramen to accompany their troops. In October 1915, the British newsreel
companies, frustrated by official prevarication, formed the Cinematograph Trade Topical Committee to campaign for access to the front. It
negotiated with the military authorities for permission to send cameramen to France and Belgium, agreeing to pay a royalty on the films to
military charities.[4] Similar arrangements were made with the Canadian
government in July 1916.[5]

---

[1] Ibid., and Brownlow, The War, p. 58.

[2] Packard, "The Movie Machine Gunner," p. 62.

[3] Brownlow, The War, p. 58.   [4] Low, British Film, p. 35.

[5] Ibid.

The official cinematographers were subject to the military chain
of command. They wore the uniform of war correspondents--a British army
officer's uniform without insignia.[1] Two of the most successful operators, Geoffrey Malins and J.B. McDowell, were commissioned as officers.
The British cameramen were no less restricted than their counterparts
with other armies; they were told when, where, who and what they could
shoot.

Most of the footage of the British forces at the front which
reached the United States came from these cameramen, and such films as
The Battle of the Somme--the first of four feature-length battle films
shot by Malins and McDowell--had some impact on American audiences.[2]
However, the work of these cameramen is not within the scope of this
thesis. Kevin Brownlow has an excellent section on them in The War, The
West and The Wilderness,[3] and Malins recounted his war experiences in
the egotistically-titled How I Filmed The War,[4] in which he depicted
himself as a kind of death-defying comic-book hero.

The British imposed a strict censorship on photographic coverage
of the war. The rules[5] sought not only to keep military information from
the enemy but attempted to shape the impressions of the war that audiences would receive. There were sound military grounds for prohibiting

---

[1]Brownlow, The War, p. 59.   [2]See infra, p. 172-3.   [3]pp. 59-68.

[4]Lieut. Geoffrey H. Malins, How I Filmed The War (London: Herbert Jenkins, 1920).

[5]A copy is kept in the records of the American Expeditionary
Force General Headquarters, now in the National Archives. See "Corres-
pondence of Signal Corps Laboratory," Box no. 6188 (Navy and Old Army
Branch, National Archives, Washington, D.C.).

the use of regimental and group names, and for not revealing the location of units. But other clauses specified that "[P]hotos showing fraternization of British and Germans should not be passed," and no pictures of troops billeted in churches or shrines should be released. German prisoners should be shown only on agricultural work, and Chinese laborers should not be pictured near the front or ". . . at work in what may well be supposed by their countrymen to be purely military work, such as handling ammunition etc." "It is not considered desirable," the memo added, "to publish the fact that we are forced to keep a quantity of shells on gun positions without cover."

Ariel Varges, who had worked for Hearst in Mexico,[1] was one of the few American cameramen to be accredited to the British army. He was commissioned as a captain, and most of his work was in the Middle East. He supplied most of the footage for the four-reel With the Forces in Mesopotamia, made for the British War Office Topical Committee and released in January 1918.[2]

With some exceptions--Captain Kleinschmidt is the obvious one-- American cameramen in the war zones lived the hard life of the armies they filmed. Merl LaVoy ". . . lived so close to the struggle, and for such a long time, that you would scarcely think of him as apart from the poilu[3] if it were not for his trusty camera and tripod, which he swings jauntily over his shoulder. The steel helmet, khaki uniform, and mud-besmattered puttees give him the bearing of a trench fighter--and,

---

[1]Ariel Varges, "Ace Newsreeler Gives Light on How He Films News of the World," American Cinematographer, July 1938, p. 275.

[2]Low, British Film, p. 155.   [3]A French infantryman.

indeed, he is, for most of his twenty-two months were spent in the first-line diggings."[1] Travel was uncertain and uncomfortable, the weather often foul, living conditions spartan, food and clothes in short supply, disease a constant threat. They risked being wounded, killed or captured by the enemy, or arrested and shot as spies by the troops they were filming.

There are no reliable casualty figures for cameramen who worked in the war zone; if they were commissioned officers or enlisted men, their injuries and deaths may have been listed as military casualties. They were in as much danger at the front as ordinary soldiers: burdened with heavy equipment, they could not move quickly around a battlefield; when shells or enemy soldiers came too close, the wisest course was to dump the equipment and run, as some cameramen did.[2] As one contemporary historian remarked:

> Many films are exposed with the bullets literally flying about the camera man's head. It is a common experience for the cameras to be shot away or smashed by the impact of an exploding shell. Several of the operators have fallen beside their instruments, and a number have been decorated for conspicuous bravery.[3]

Such a man was George Ercole, wounded at Przemysl and decorated by the Russian government.[4] Donald Thompson was wounded several times. One account tells of a battle in Northern France where six cameramen were wounded, one of them dying later.[5]

---

[1]Packard, "The Movie Machine Gunner," p. 62.

[2]See supra, p. 67.   [3]Collins, The Camera Man, pp. 8-9.

[4]See supra, pp. 88-89.

[5]Van Loan, "Shooting the War," pp. 68, 121.

But surely the most macabre incident involving a cameraman occurred at the Battle of Verdun. The French operator J.A. Dupré halted in the midst of an advance, and apparently sat down, supporting the camera on his knees. The camera was running when he was killed, either by a bullet or shrapnel. He fell back, but the camera, steadied by its gyroscopic attachment and powered by compressed air, recorded the battle for several minutes after his death.[1] This piece of film was used in a French compilation, Pour la Paix du Monde, which was dedicated to the six French cameramen killed in active service.[2]

Cameramen such as LaVoy and Thompson may have regarded the war as something of an adventure, but most of the time the work was frustrating and dangerous. As the British film historian Rachael Low has remarked:

> . . . The job was a new one, evolved by the initiative and courage of men with few precedents to guide them. It can hardly have seemed reasonable for non-combatants to risk their lives carrying heavy cameras into dangerous hiding places thirty yards or so from the German snipers, filming soldiers running out into no-man's land, falling, lying in heaps or returning with bleeding, limping prisoners. Development of the scope of the record film depended on their own sense of what was possible, and their capacity to convince or override the often incredulous people on whom they depended for information, transport and many other forms of help. The qualities needed were those of a journalist rather than of an artist . . .[3]

* * * * *

---

[1] Croy, How Motion Pictures Are Made, pp. 260-61, and Bela Belazs, Theory of the Film (London: Dobson, 1952), p. 169.

[2] Brownlow, The War, p. 60.

[3] Low, British Film, pp. 154-55.

CHAPTER 5

A CASE STUDY:

DONALD THOMPSON OF TOPEKA

To Motion Picture News, he was an "expert photographer and globe
trotter."[1] The war correspondent Edward Alexander Powell thought he had
"more chilled steel nerve than any man I know."[2] Robert R. McCormick of
the Chicago Tribune said he was "only too glad to risk his neck on the
Eastern Front."[3] To his hometown newspaper, the Topeka Daily Capital,
he was simply "the photographic hero of the war."[4]

Donald Thompson, whose exploits were touched on in the last
chapter, embodied some of the best and worst qualities of the World War
I cameraman. He was brave, but often to the point of recklessness; he
was hard-working and resourceful in dealing with officialdom; by the
not-too-demanding standards of contemporary war coverage, his films were
well shot, though tediously edited; like other cameramen, he was prone
to hyperbole when he described his war experiences. If Thompson had an
image of the war cameraman, it was that of a born adventurer, a maverick

[1]"Cameraman Thompson Off to War for Paramount," Motion Picture
News, 6 November 1915, p. 46.

[2]Edward Alexander Powell, Fighting in Flanders (New York:
Charles Scribner and Sons, 1916), p. 14.

[3]Waldrop, McCormick of Chicago, p. 125.

[4]Topeka Daily Capital, 21 December 1915, p. 14.

who defied danger, death and censorship to get the film, and to get it home to the audiences. It was an image that Thompson tried hard to emulate. In this chapter, his career will be examined in detail as a case study of the work of war cameramen.

Little is known of Thompson's early life in Topeka. He first attracted attention in 1912, when, at the age of 23, he covered the Democratic Convention in Baltimore.[1] He added a motion-picture camera to his equipment, and, according to Moving Picture World, ". . . freelanced to such good purpose that he became a charter member of the Unusual Angle Club and distinctly welcome in the offices of the editors."[2]

When war broke out in Europe, Thompson was in Canada, where he received permission from the Minister of Militia, General Sam Hughes, to film the Canadian contingent.[3] As a representative of a Montreal newspaper, he sailed to France on a troop ship, working his passage by doing odd jobs. The journey was not uneventful; off the French coast, a German bomb narrowly missed the ship.[4]

The war correspondent, Edward Alexander Powell, of the New York World worked with Thompson in Belgium, and was as impressed by his bravado as by his bravery. In his book Fighting in Flanders, Powell

---

[1]"Paramount Photo-News Man," Moving Picture World, 6 November 1915, p. 1114.

[2]Ibid., and Motion Picture News, 6 November 1915, p. 46.

[3]Motion Picture News, 6 November 1915, p. 46, Moving Picture World, 6 November 1915, p. 1114, and Louis Tenny, "Filming the Trail of the Serpent," Picture-Play Magazine, March 1918, p. 111.

[4]Ibid., and Ramsaye, A Million And One Nights, p. 685.

recalls his first meeting with the young Kansan, and his later impressions:

> . . . I met him first while paying a flying visit to Ostend.
> He blew into the Consulate there wearing an American army
> shirt, a pair of British officer's riding-breeches, French
> puttees, and a Highlander's forage-cap, and carrying a camera
> the size of a parlor phonograph. No one but an American could
> have accomplished what he did, and no American but one from
> Kansas. He had not only seen war, all military prohibitions
> to the contrary, but he had actually photographed it.
>
> Thompson is a little man, built like Harry Lauder;[1] hard as
> nails, tough as raw-hide, his skin tanned to the color of a
> well-smoked meerschaum, and his face perpetually wreathed in
> what he called his "sunflower smile." . . . He has more
> chilled-steel nerve than any man I know, and before he had
> been in Belgium a month his name became a synonym throughout
> the army for coolness and daring. . . ."[2]

Thompson told Powell that he had made nine attempts to reach the front from Paris. On eight of these he was arrested, and spent a night in a guardhouse before talking his way out of trouble.[3] On one occasion, he told the French officer who arrested him that he was trying to rescue his wife and children, who were in the hands of the Germans; the officer was so sympathetic that he took Thompson part of the way to the front in his car.[4]

General Hughes had provided Thompson with a letter, authorizing him to take pictures of Canadian troops. According to Powell, he used this to good purpose:

> . . . Whenever he was stopped by patrols he would display his
> letter from the Minister of Militia and explain that he was
> trying to overtake the Canadian troops. "Vive le Canada!" the

[1]Scottish music-hall performer and comedian.

[2]Powell, Fighting in Flanders, pp. 13-14.

[3]Ibid., p. 15.   [4]Ibid., pp. 15-16.

French would shout enthusiastically. "Hurrah for our brave allies, les Canadiens! They are doubtless with the British at the front"--and permit him to proceed.[1]

The last time he was arrested, he was escorted to Amiens by two gendarmes, who were under instructions to see that he boarded the first train for Boulogne, where he would pick up the cross-channel ferry. Thompson dutifully bought a through ticket to London. When a train carrying wounded prisoners pulled into the station shortly after midnight, Thompson caused a general panic by scrambling on top of another train to take a picture. His flashlight caused alarm--people on the station thought a German bomb had exploded. The police arrested him, but let him go after some British soldiers said he belonged to their regiment. Later that night, a train carrying artillery to the front pulled in; Thompson slipped under a tarpaulin covering a field gun and fell asleep. When he awoke the next morning, he was at Mons.[2]

Thompson fell in with a regiment of Highlanders and after a two-hour march they went into the trenches. They came under heavy fire almost immediately; Thompson braved the barrage for seven days and nights, taking what Moving Picture World described as "some of the most remarkable pictures of the entire war."[3] The magazine commended his bravery: "His one idea is to get the pictures just as the born reporter thinks of nothing but his story."[4]

Because cameramen were not permitted at the front by the British,

---

[1]Ibid., p. 16.   [2]Ibid., pp. 16-17.

[3]Moving Picture World, 6 November 1915, p. 1114. See also Motion Picture News, 6 November 1915, p. 46.

[4]Ibid.

Thompson realized that his films could be confiscated by the authorities.
He returned to Amiens, and boarded a refugee train bound for Boulogne.
He told Powell that he met a Russian countess who was returning to
Petrograd via England. The cameraman asked her to carry his films in
her baggage; she agreed, on condition that he gave her 1,000 francs as
a gesture of trust. Having only 250 francs, Thompson made up the difference with United Cigar Stores coupons which he claimed were American
war currency. Powell continues:

> . . . At Boulogne he was arrested, as he had foreseen, was
> stripped, searched, and his camera opened, but as nothing was
> found he was permitted to continue to London, where he went
> to the countess's hotel and received his films--and, I might
> add, his money and cigar coupons. Two hours later, having
> posted his films to America, he was on his way to Belgium.[1]

Landing at Ostend, he managed to reach Malines by train; from
there he ". . . started to walk the twenty-odd miles into Brussels,
carrying his huge camera, his overcoat, field-glasses, and three hundred
films."[2] When a Uhlan patrol surprised him, he pulled a small silk
American flag from his pocket and shouted "Hoch der Kaiser" and "Auf
wiedersehn"--the only German phrases he knew. He was brought before an
officer to whom he explained that his Canadian credentials were merely
a ruse to allow him to pass through the Allied lines; he claimed to
represent a syndicate of German newspapers in America. He was released,
and given a seat on an ambulance going into Brussels.[3]

The next day, he was arrested again outside a cafe. A German
officer smashed his camera with a sword; Thompson's films were destroyed

[1]Fighting in Flanders, pp. 18-20.

[2]Ibid., p. 20.   [3]Ibid.

and he was told to be out of the city by six that evening. He walked
the thirty miles to Ghent and caught a train to Ostend, where he had
stored his other cameras. Powell met him there, and they travelled
together to Antwerp. Although the Belgian authorities had prohibited
photographers at the front, Powell said that Thompson obtained permission from the Chief of the General Staff "to take pictures when and
where he pleased."[1]

Powell found the Belgian authorities cooperative, and he also
obtained a pass allowing him to travel freely. With the German army
besieging Antwerp, he, Thompson and Captain Raymond Briggs of the United
States Army drove out to see the German assault on the forts near Wille-
broeck. After less than half an hour at the front, they were arrested
by two gendarmes and brought to the divisional army headquarters at Boom.
Thompson infuriated the officer questioning them by smoking a large
cigar, and by grinning when told to look serious. Their papers were in
order, but they were not allowed to return to the front.[2]

Thompson was with Powell when the latter accepted an invitation
to meet the commander of the German 9th Army, General von Boehn; he
wanted the opportunity to deny allegations of atrocities which Powell
had repeated in his articles for the New York World. Accompanied by the
American vice-consul, Julius Van Hee, they set out from Ghent for the
German headquarters. On their way through the city, they rescued two
German soldiers who were being threatened by a mob; when a man leaped
onto the running board and levelled a revolver at the Germans, Thompson

---

[1]Ibid., pp. 21-22.   [2]Ibid., pp. 45-47.

knocked his hand upwards, Powell hit the accelerator, and the car sped

through the crowd.[1]

In the town of Sotteghem, they found some American tourists who

had been cut off by the German advance:

> . . . It was what might be termed a mixed assemblage, including
> several women of wealth and fashion who had been motoring on the
> Continent and had had their cars taken from them, two prim
> schoolteachers from Brooklyn, a mine owner from West Virginia, a
> Pennsylvania Quaker, and a quartet of professional tango dancers
> --artists, they called themselves--who had been doing a "turn"
> at a Brussels music hall when the war suddenly ended their
> engagement.[2]

Van Hee and Powell hired two farm carts to take the Americans to

Ghent, and then left Sotteghem themselves. Half a mile outside the town,

on the Lille to Paris road, they found themselves in the middle of the

German army:

> . . . It was a sight never to be forgotten. Far as the eye
> could see stretched solid columns of marching men, pressing
> westward, ever westward. The army was advancing in three
> mighty columns on parallel roads, the dense masses of men in
> their elusive gray-green uniforms looking for all the world
> like three monstrous serpents crawling across the countryside.
> . . . For five solid hours, travelling always at express-train
> speed, we motored between walls of marching men. . . . It
> seemed that the interminable ranks would never end . . .[3]

At the 9th Army headquarters, the three Americans dined with the

staff officers; afterwards, they assembled on the terrace while Thompson

took pictures. While Powell and von Boehn discussed the atrocity allega-

tions, Thompson, with a senior officer as guide, went off to film the

columns of troops they had passed on the journey.

. . . It seems that they stopped the car beside the road, in a

---

[1]Ibid., pp. 110-12.   [2]Ibid., pp. 113-14.

[3]Ibid., pp. 114-15.

place where the light was good, and when Thompson saw approaching a regiment or a battery or a squadron of which he wished a picture he would tell the officer, whereupon the officer would blow a whistle and the whole column would halt.

"Just wait a few minutes until the dust settles," Thompson would remark, lighting a cigar, and the Ninth Imperial Army, whose columns stretched over the countryside as far as the eye could see, would stand in its tracks until the air was sufficiently clear to get a good picture.[1]

When a field battery passed by, Thompson made a remark about the accuracy of American gunners in the action at Vera Cruz in Mexico.

"Let us show you what our gunners can do," said the officer, and he gave an order. There were more orders--a perfect volley of them. A bugle shrilled, eight horses strained against their collars, the drivers cracked their whips, the cannoneers put their shoulders to the wheels, and a gun left the road and swung into position in an adjacent field. On a knoll three miles away an ancient windmill was beating the air with its huge wings. A shell hit the windmill and tore it into splinters.

"Good work," Thompson observed critically. "If those fellows of yours keep on they'll be able to get a job in the American navy when the war is over."

In all the annals of modern war I do not think there is a parallel to this little Kansas photographer halting, with peremptory hand, an advancing army and leisurely photographing it, regiment by regiment, and then having a field-gun of the Imperial Guard go into action solely to gratify his curiosity.[2]

"Le Capitaine Thompson" obviously enjoyed his reputation--

whether or not it was deserved. And it may have led him--in the manner

of the British official cinematographer, Lieutenant Geoffrey Malins--to

embroider accounts of his exploits for dramatic effect. Speaking to a

businessmen's luncheon in Topeka in December 1915, Thompson described

the battle for the town of Weerde near Malines, a strategic place on the

[1]Ibid., pp. 128-29.

[2]Ibid., pp. 129-30.

Antwerp-Brussels railroad.[1] If Thompson is to be believed, he was in-
directly responsible for the death of 7,000 Belgian soldiers.

Thompson and Powell had tried to reach the Belgian second line,
but their French driver got lost, and they suddenly found themselves
behind the front line. They left the car behind a convent and walked to
a farmhouse; they knocked a hole in the roof to provide themselves with
a vantage point for the battle. Thompson's account continues:

> . . . I had my cinematograph in good action, trained on a town
> in the wood where the Germans seemed the more strongly en-
> trenched, when some Belgian staff officers brought up some
> telephone instruments. Telling us that they were short of men,
> I was asked to direct the line of fire of the artillery. I
> consented, took up a receiver, and told the gunners in the rear
> how their shots were falling, particularly on the houses in the
> town. When the range was too short, I told them to lengthen
> out, on all but one house, a big white affair, I knew the girl
> who lived in that house, so I didn't direct any fire toward it.
>
> When the town was sufficiently in ruins, an attack was
> ordered. Powell and I followed the infantry. We got down into
> the ruined town and out of that big white house that I had
> spared poured German machine guns and pom pons and other pieces
> of artillery by the hundreds it seemed. The Belgians were over-
> whelmed and 7,000 died in a fifteen-minute battle in the wreck-
> strewn streets. The attackers retreated, first to the second
> line, which fell back on the third. Powell and I were left
> behind and immediately we got caught between two fires.[2]

Powell confirms Thompson's account in some respects, but on
several important points they differ. Powell writes that they observed
the battle from the roof of the farmhouse but does not say that Thompson
helped to direct the artillery fire.[3] He points out that the Belgian
infantry, firing from trenches, could not see the Germans, whose posi-

------

[1]"Thompson Tells Tales Of Battle," Topeka Daily Capital, 30
December 1915, p. 12.

[2]Ibid.   [3]Powell, Fighting in Flanders, pp. 160, 163.

tions were in the woods, and had no way of knowing how effective their
fire was. He agrees that when the Belgians advanced, they charged
straight into a trap:

> . . . Then hell itself broke loose. The whole German front,
> which for several hours past had replied but feebly to the
> Belgian fire, spat a continuous stream of lead and flame. The
> rolling crash of musketry and the ripping snarl of machine
> guns were stabbed by the vicious pom-pom-pom-pom-pom of the
> quick-firers. From every window of the three-storied chateau
> opposite us the lean muzzles of mitrailleuses poured out their
> hail of death. I have seen fighting on four continents, but I
> have never witnessed so deadly a fire as that which wiped out
> the head of a Belgian column as a sponge wipes out figures on
> a slate.[1]

Thompson claims that he and Powell followed the infantry; Powell
says they watched the massacre from the farmhouse roof. Thompson estimates that 7,000 soldiers were killed; Powell, an experienced observer,
offers no count. Powell goes into more detail on their escape; two
Belgian soldiers stopped them at gunpoint, but when they realized they
were Americans, they retreated as a group.[2] Powell says nothing about
the German officer who, according to Thompson, recognized him by his
riding trousers, and directed the fire away from them.[3]

According to Powell, Thompson was lucky to escape with his life
on another occasion when the German bombarded the village of Waelhem.
He had gone there with an American woman who was using her car to carry
wounded men to a British field hospital.[4] Thompson remained there to
film the action, and slept in a shop where Belgian soldiers were quar-

[1]Ibid., pp. 163-64.   [2]Ibid., pp. 166-67.

[3]Topeka Daily Capital, 30 December 1915, p. 12.

[4]Powell, Fighting in Flanders, pp. 174-75.

tered. Shortly after midnight, the building was struck by a 42-centimetre shell, and 24 of the soldiers were killed. Thompson told Powell that,

> . . . when the ceiling gave way and the mangled corpses came tumbling down upon him, he ran up the street with his hands above his head, screaming like a madman. He met an officer whom he knew and they ran down the street together, hoping to get out of the doomed town. Just then a projectile from one of the German siege-guns tore down the long straight street, a few yards above their heads. The blast of air which it created was so terrific that it threw them down.[1]

Thompson continued to work on the Belgian side of the lines and, like Edwin Weigle of the Chicago Tribune, was in Antwerp when the city fell to the Germans. According to the Topeka Daily Capital: "All about the hotel in which he was stopping flames were licking up business houses, while a few firemen fought hopelessly on. The waiter who had been serving Thompson's table, where the photographer, Medill McCormick, Jimmy Hare and English staff officers dined, appeared as the Germans entered, in the uniform of a captain of the Imperial Berlin Guard. As a spy, he doubtless got some information, Thompson believes."[2]

Allied propaganda in the United States in 1914 and 1915 had dwelt at length on alleged German atrocities in Belgium. Most American correspondents denied that all the atrocities had taken place;[3] Thompson

---

[1]Ibid., pp. 175-76.

[2]Topeka Daily Capital, 26 December 1915, p. 2B.

[3]American newspapermen who toured behind the German lines failed to find any evidence of atrocities. Their famous telegram to the Associated Press read: "In spirit fairness we unite in declaring German atrocities groundless as far as we were able to. After spending two weeks with German army accompanying troops upward hundred miles we unable report single instance unprovoked reprisal. Also unable confirm rumors mistreatment prisoners or non-combatants. . . . Numerous investigated

agreed,[1] and claimed that the worst atrocity he saw was committed on him during the German occupation of Antwerp:

> . . . I was walking down the street, a cigaret in my mouth, when I came to a party of Germans marching into the town. The Belgians immediately got down on their hands and knees, but I stood on the curb, calmly looking them over, when the officer in charge stepped up and barked at me in German. I didn't know what he was saying, but started to talk to him in English. Before I could get my mouth open he hit me over the head with the side of his sword, and knocked me down. I started to get up--and he knocked me down again. That made me pretty mad, and I began using some choice United States cuss words--from the ground--when he said in English, "What, are you an Englishman?" I yelled, "No, I am an American, and I am going to call the president's attention to this immediately." The officer apologized, and went on. I went to the American consulate. The consul had gone, and Powell installed himself as acting consul and myself as vice consul. Then I used the consulate automobile to get out of the country with some choice pictures which the Germans didn't want me to use.[2]

Thompson was wounded near Zeebrugge in Belgium.[3] He was sitting at a table with some German officers when a high-explosive shell struck the building. Two of the officers were killed outright, and everyone else in the room was wounded; shell splinters hit Thompson's nose and back. He awoke in an ambulance on the way to hospital, and on the operating table asked for a cigarette. "You can't have a cigaret," they told him. "Your nose is all shot away." Thompson reached up, felt his nose still there, and then said disgustedly, "Aw, hell, my nose's all

---

rumors proved groundless. . . . Discipline German soldiers excellent as observed. No drunkenness. To truth these statements we pledge personal professional word." Quoted in Horace C. Peterson, Propaganda For War: The Campaign Against American Neutrality, 1914-1917 (Norman: University of Oklahoma Press, 1939), p. 69. See also Crozier, American Reporters, pp. 41-42.

[1]"He also took occasion to deny, so far as he was able to speak, all reports of atrocities committed by the Germans on the Belgian people." Topeka Daily Capital, 30 December 1915, p. 12.

[2]Ibid.   [3]Ibid.

right. Give me a cigaret."[1]

Thompson had sailed to Europe as a representative of a Montreal newspaper, but once in the war zone he worked as a freelancer for American and British newspapers, including the Chicago Tribune, the New York World, the London Daily Mail and the Illustrated London News.[2] Kevin Brownlow notes that he became briefly notorious in English trade circles when two Belgians brought a court case against him. They had commissioned him to obtain front-line pictures; his camera was seized, but he held onto the film--5,000 feet--and conveniently disappeared. The King's Bench Division in London fined him 146 pounds 10s. plus costs.[3]

In London, he appears to have served as a correspondent for the New York World and the Daily Mail. Thompson said that the Mail's publisher, Lord Northcliffe, personally hired him to obtain pictures of the war, and authorized him to spend what he needed; he was not asked to itemize his expense account.

> . . . While Thompson wasn't extravagant, whenever he wanted to go any place he didn't let the cost deter him. One time he found it necessary to hire a special train to get across Holland, and special trains are expensive in Europe just now! When the business manager, a conservative Englishman, heard about that special train, he almost had apoplexy, and fired Thompson on the spot, only Thompson was under the personal hire of Northcliffe and the "fire" didn't stick.[4]

---

[1]Ibid.

[2]"Kane Gets War Films from Man in 38 Battles," Motion Picture News, 8 January 1916, p. 77. See also Ramsaye, A Million And One Nights, p. 685.

[3]The Bioscope, 20 May 1915, p. 761, quoted in Brownlow, The War, p. 685.

[4]Topeka Daily Capital, 27 December 1915, p. 6.

Thompson claimed that his expenses sometimes ran to a thousand dollars a week--and sometimes they were as little as 5 pounds. Journalists in London, he said, earned about 4 pounds a week while "I got something over a hundred times that amount."[1] Again, Thompson may have been stretching the truth for dramatic effect.

After leaving London, Thompson joined the Belgian army;[2] in 1915, he filmed inside Germany and with the Russian army. His footage was combined with that of Edwin Weigle and other cameramen in the successful Chicago Tribune film, The German Side of the War (1915).[3] He was with the Russians at the first siege of Przemysl, which ended with the surrender of the Austrian garrison in March 1915. He toured the city with the Tribune's war correspondent, Robert R. McCormick, who remarked that Thompson "was only too glad to risk his neck on the Eastern Front."[4] Later, they travelled to the forward positions below Gorlice in the Carpathians. "There, Thompson, the fearless cameraman, took what McCormick thought to be the first 360 degree panoramic sweep of a battle front ever put on film."[5]

Thompson supplied most of the footage for the Tribune's other major 1915 release, With the Russians at the Front.[6] And it was on the Russian front lines that Thompson, if we are to take him at his word,

---

[1]Ibid.

[2]Moving Picture World, 6 November 1915, p. 1114, and Motion Picture News, 6 November 1915, p. 46.

[3]See supra, pp. 80-82.

[4]Waldrop, McCormick of Chicago, p. 125.   [5]Ibid., p. 129.

[6]See supra, pp. 89-90.

acted as the catalyst for another battle. According to his account in
the Topeka Daily Capital:

> Everything was quiet, Thompson peeped through a periscope
> and could see nothing but a bank of dirt ahead. Turning to
> the Russian officer who had taken him into the trench, he said:
> "I thought I was going to get some action here." "Eh bien, it
> is action you want," ejaculated the Russian in a surprised
> tone, "well, you shall have it." He broke forth into a gut-
> teral [sic] order. Soon there was a sputtering of rifle fire
> from the trench, a reply from the Germans. Then the cannon
> in the rear of each line of entrenchments got into the game,
> and Thompson found himself the center of a hot fire. "And do
> you know, it was three days before I was able to get out of
> that trench? There were charges and counter charges from each
> side. The Germans got nearly to us. I got my action all
> right, and pretty nearly lost my life. I have been careful,
> very careful, in my requests with Russian officers since.
> They take a suggestion too much to heart.[1]

Thompson returned to the United States in late 1915 after more
than a year in Europe. On the crossing, his baggage was ransacked and
his American passport was stolen,[2] but his spirit was unsubdued. In his
time in the war zone, he told the trade press, he had worked with every
army in Europe--the Germans, the Austrians, the Turks, the French, the
British, the Serbians, the Russians, the Bulgarians, the Rumanians, the
Greeks, the Montenegrans, the Albanians and the Dutch;[3] tactfully, he
complimented them all. He had been in 38 battles, lost three cameras,
and bore the scar of his nose wound.[4]

---

[1]Topeka Daily Capital, 27 December 1915, p. 6.

[2]Topeka Daily Capital, 26 December 1915, p. 2B.

[3]Topeka Daily Capital, 27 December 1915, p. 6. See also Moving
Picture World, 6 November 1915, p. 1114, and Motion Picture News, 6
November 1915, p. 46.

[4]Motion Picture News, 8 January 1916, p. 77. See also Topeka
Daily Capital, 26 December 1915, p. 2B, 30 December 1915, p. 12.

There is some confusion over Thompson's movements from November 1915 to January 1916. On 6 November 1915, Moving Picture World and Motion Picture News reported that he was leaving New York on the liner St. Paul, bound for the Balkans.[1] Thompson was under contract to Leslie's Illustrated Weekly and the Paramount Pictures Corporation, which had acquired exclusive rights to his films. Thompson said he expected Greece to be in the war by the time he reached Athens.[2]

The Moving Picture World and Motion Picture News stories are almost word-for-word the same, and were probably filed by the same correspondent. However, it seems highly unlikely that Thompson left the United States in November 1915. His film, Somewhere in France, was about to be released, and in December he was back in his home town of Topeka to talk about his war experiences during the screening of the film.

Thompson's visit occupied many column inches in the Topeka Daily Capital. The newspaper might have given it less play had it not had a vested interest in the matter; it had secured exclusive rights to show the film in Topeka, and Thompson's talks would help to ensure a full house. On 19 December, the Capital brought its readers the thrilling news:

> Donald Thompson, Topekan globetrotter and daredevil war photographer, who has snapped his camera on the battlefields of Europe along every front and photographed some of the most stirring scenes of the great conflict, will be in Topeka the week of December 27 to vividly explain the pictures he has taken.[3]

---

[1]Moving Picture World, p. 1114, Motion Picture News, p. 46.

[2]Ibid.   [3]Topeka Daily Capital, 19 December 1915, p. 1.

. . . Two reels of film lasting 90 minutes will be shown and the Topeka war hero, the story of whose adventures in the battle-scarred countries reads like a romance, will describe the pictures just as he took them.

. . . By his utter fearlessness, his disregard for personal danger, his willingness to take a chance by prying where he was not supposed to go . . . Thompson, early in the war, became known, by name at least, to generals and officials of every country engaged in the conflict. And those qualities which gave him his initial success made it possible for him to secure better pictures than any man now working among the armies.[1]

Somewhere in France--the title is an allusion to the military censors' ban on revealing place-names--was scheduled for a five-day run at Topeka's Grand Theater after its premiere in Chicago.[2]

In the week preceding Thompson's visit, hardly a day went by without a story on the cameraman and his film in the Capital. On 21 December, Thompson's bravery was the angle; he would tell audiences ". . . just how it felt to be standing up turning a movie machine crank with the bullets whistling about him."[3] On December 23, the merits of the film were the topic. "In spite of the fact that Europe has been engaged in its greatest war for more than a year," said the Capital, "really good war pictures are unusually scarce. Of pictures that equal Thompson's there are none . . . They are hair-raising from start to finish and at times almost terrifying."[4] On 25 December, the Capital's readers learned that on one occasion, Thompson ". . . stood in the midst of a fusillade of bullets to photograph a trench engagement where the men stood only 30 yards apart."[5] The man himself arrived the same day:

---

[1]Ibid., pp. 1-2.   [2]Ibid., p. 1.   [3]p. 14.   [4]p. 11.
[5]p. 16.

A year ago Christmas, Donald C. Thompson, Topeka's war photographer famous the world over, watched Belgians and English soldiers come out of their trenches in Flanders to hobnob with German soldiers, swap buttons and tobacco and "kid" each other. Yesterday, Thompson sat down at the family table at 411 West 7th, to a real Christmas dinner of the "homey" sort, ate his favorite cake and related some of the thrilling experiences which have been his on this latest, the third trip to European battlefields.[1]

"No matter how long you are on the battle line during an engagement," Thompson told the reporter, "every day you must again accustom yourself to the firing."[2] Thompson thought his size was an advantage; the Capital said that ". . . had he been bigger countless bullets that passed him by unharmed would have written finis to his remarkable career."[3]

Monday was usually a poor day for theaters, but on Monday, 27 December 1915, the Grand had the largest matinee audience in its history for Somewhere in France and Thompson's lecture. The cameraman dressed in what he called his "working kit"--the khaki uniform he wore in Europe; he said he was ranked as a captain, and lived with the officers when not at work.[4] The Capital's reviewer was impressed by his nonchalance:

> When the film shows shells bursting near enough to the trenches to kill one man out of ten, Thompson casually explains that it is an 8-inch shell that spread death and maimed the living. Another scene showing the men hard at work firing toward the German trenches causes him to explain that in one engagement a million shells were fired from the French side against the Germans. Of a long line of wagons, bearing away hundreds of dead bodies, the young soldier of fortune remarks

[1]Topeka Daily Capital, 26 December 1915, p. 2B.   [2]Ibid.

[3]Ibid.   [4]Topeka Daily Capital, 27 December 1915, p. 6.

that in fifteen minutes Belgium lost 7,000 soldiers.[1] The
trenches, crowded with living and dead men, that held the
attention of the audience with an absorbing interest that at
times made them shudder, is to him an experience that he has
passed through so often that he regards it as an incident. .
. . Thompson does not "lecture" about his pictures. He talks
to the audience about them as casually as if he had wandered
into someone's office and were chatting with a friend. If
there is any criticism whatever to make of the exhibition, it
is because he does not talk enough.[2]

Although a print of Somewhere in France survives, it is on
nitrate stock and cannot be viewed;[3] the information on its content in
contemporary accounts is too incomplete to permit an analysis. The
first scenes were taken, not by Thompson, but by a Pathé cameraman;[4]
Topeka's war hero is shown filming at the front. This was not neces-
sarily vanity on Thompson's part; film companies were anxious to prove
that their footage was genuine, and a shot of the cameraman in the war
zone supported such claims. Thompson had appeared in the Chicago
Tribune's With the Russians at the Front,[5] and Edwin Weigle in the
Tribune's other 1915 release, The German Side of the War.[6]

Two scenes in Somewhere in France attracted specific comments
from reviewers. The trench engagement "where the men stood only 30
yards apart" was reportedly filmed at the Battle of Champagne and it

---

[1]Apparently a reference to the action at Weerde. See supra, pp.
107-09.

[2]Topeka Daily Capital, 28 December 1915, p. 10.

[3]In the Library of Congress collection (see Appendix).

[4]Topeka Daily Capital, 28 December 1915, p. 10.

[5]Supra, p. 90.

[6]Supra, p. 81.

showed French soldiers firing and hurling grenades;[1] by the middle of the week of December 27, the Capital had managed to reduce the distance between the trenches to 20 yards![2] The second is an aerial battle over the trenches in Flanders which Thompson filmed from a third machine, flying above. "Circling, darting, now the Frenchman, now the German above his opponent, the two huge birds fight to the finish, the German, defeated, finally forced to land behind the French lines."[3] Thompson also recalled another aerial battle over Belgrade when his machine was attacked. He estimated that 180 shells were fired at them, adding that "when the shells break too close to the machine, the suction will cause it to loop the loop."[4]

Another difficulty in judging Somewhere in France stems from Thompson's claim that he omitted or shortened some scenes because he thought they were too terrible to show in their entirety. "Dead lying in winnows as a result of charges and counter charges will be thrown on the screen," announced the Capital.[5] "I am going to cut those scenes rather short, however," said Thompson, "They are too awful to dwell upon."[6] However, he was not so restrained in describing his own narrow escapes, and was quick to compare his film to others which, in his view, showed little of real warfare:

> "You have all seen war pictures taken 10 miles from any actual fighting," laughed Thompson last night. "Well, I am going to show you the real thing." . . . One of the scenes in

[1]Topeka Daily Capital, 28 December 1915, p. 10.   [2]Ibid.

[3]Topeka Daily Capital, 30 December 1915, p. 12.

[4]Topeka Daily Capital, 27 December 1915, p. 6.

[5]Ibid.   [6]Ibid.

the exhibition . . . is of an explosion of a shell immediately
in front of the camera. A huge cloud of dust and broken trees
hurtling through the air are shown--then the picture abruptly
stops. "You see," explained Thompson, "it was just a little
close, only about 50 yards, and the concussion knocked me and
my camera down and put me to sleep for several minutes."[1]

The Capital's promotional efforts were not limited to the newspaper's columns. There was a display of Thompson's trophies, souvenirs
and baggage in the window of the Brunt-Martin drug company.[2] His passports, said the Capital, were "rather multitudinous documents, bearing
more seals than a suitcase of a transcontinental traveller,"[3] and they
"gave him carte blanche entrance at all times to the scenes of hostilities."[4]

The night of Thursday 30 December was billed as Military Night
at the Grand. Battery A of the Kansas National Guard, under the direction of Captain John Hite, was to give a 15-minute drill with two field
guns before the show. "Come and see how Uncle Sam manipulates his artillery as compared with the actual work of the French guns in the trenches,"
the Capital urged its readers.[5] The 22-piece Second Regiment Band gave
a concert and played patriotic numbers during the screening.[6] After the
show, Thompson complimented Battery A and its captain. "These fellows
are just as good as any battery in Europe," he said. "The way they
handle those guns would be a credit to any French, English, or German

---

[1]Ibid.   [2]Topeka Daily Capital, 28 December 1915, p. 1.

[3]Topeka Daily Capital, 27 December 1915, p. 6.

[4]Ibid.

[5]Advertisement, Topeka Daily Capital, 30 December 1915, p. 9.

[6]Ibid.

battery."[1]

That same day, Topeka's Commercial Club held a "Don Thompson luncheon," attended by 250 businessmen. According to the Capital, the cameraman "in plain, unaffected 'Kansas language' told in a clear, unassuming way, a tale of the war such as has never before been heard in Topeka."[2] Some of Thompson's tales, which perhaps should not be accepted absolutely, have already been mentioned in this chapter--the 15-minute battle in which he claims 7,000 Belgians died,[3] and his experiences during the German occupation of Antwerp.[4] He also told his audience of a remarkable escape from the German secret service--there is, unfortunately, no corrobrating account of the story.

When he returned to London from Belgium, Thompson heard that the Germans had posted notices calling for his arrest on sight. His employer, Lord Northcliffe of the Daily Mail, helped him to make up a fake newspaper clipping, from the non-existent Brooklyn Observer, which would re-establish his credibility with the Germans. The fake story purported to be an interview with Thompson in which he praised the German occupation of Belgium and the conduct of the German army.[5]

> With this clipping in his bill fold and with his cameras, Thompson invaded Germany with the assignment to get pictures showing the reported suffering, from lack of food, of the German people. No sooner had his train crossed the frontier than Thompson was set upon by two fellow passengers, beaten

---

[1]Topeka Daily Capital, 31 December 1915, p. 9.

[2]Topeka Daily Capital, 30 December 1915, p. 12.

[3]Supra, pp. 107-09.   [4]Supra, pp. 110-12.

[5]Topeka Daily Capital, 30 December 1915, p. 12.

and then thrown into jail. There, eventually, his effects were taken from him and the clipping found. This seemed to change the attitude of the authorities. Thompson was released and went on to Berlin. There, he stopped at the Kaiserhof. But while he was busy at work a spy in the office of the London Mail, who had helped set up the fake interview, advised the German secret service of the fact, and pointed as confirmation the English type in the advertisement. A chambermaid in the Kaiserhof "tipped" Thompson off, and with a five-minute lead on the German secret service, the young Topekan slid down a fire escape, hunted up a girl friend, proposed that they elope, got her consent and left town in her motor car, with a passport for the girl and her "brother," which she had hastily secured from her father, a prominent German officer. At the frontier Thompson was forced to tell the girl of his ruse, which he used only to save his own life, and the girl turned back home.[1]

Thompson's return to his home town was not an unmitigated personal success. His former wife, then living in New York City, returned to Kansas to settle some outstanding financial matters with him. The Topeka State Journal, which, unlike the Capital, had nothing tangible to gain from the cameraman's visit, could not resist this one:

> Donald C. Thompson, the daredevil war photographer, today discovered that matrimony is worse than war. Elizabeth E. Thompson, who secured a divorce from him in Jackson County in 1910, filed an affidavit and motion in the district court asking Thompson to show cause why he was not paying her $15 a month in alimony.[2]

She said Thompson was $990 in arrears, and asked for a warrant for his arrest. He was arrested, and released on bail. Within a month, he had left for Europe again, so it is not known whether his ex-wife got the money.

Such domestic inconveniences did not trouble the Capital, which regarded Thompson's visit as the most exciting event of the season. At times, the adulation seemed excessive:

---

[1] Ibid. [2] Topeka State Journal, 31 December 1915, p. 1.

Thompson is the photographic hero of the war. He is known
on every front and the reckless Kansan with his movie camera
is familiar to thousands of men who have stood in the trenches
and faced the fire of the enemy. Thompson they know because
he has been in the trenches with them while they were under
fire. They have seen him risk his life to get a good picture,
and come through every chance he took unscathed.[1] If Thompson
could talk freely, which he dares not do, he probably could
tell more of the inside story of the war than any other man in
America, because he has seen every phase of it.[2]

National distribution of Somewhere in France was handled by
Arthur S. Kane, who was able to obtain ample publicity and many bookings.[3]
Leslie's Illustrated Weekly carried a full page of enlargements from the
film. According to Motion Picture News, this was an important endorse-
ment for the film; Leslie's, it said, "has pictured many wars, consequently its staff comprises battle-photograph specialists. The selection of Thompson's film not only means that it is undeniably authentic,
but teems with interesting scenes."[4] Among the team of battle-photograph
specialists was Thompson himself, who was about to leave for Europe to
shoot stills for Leslie's and film for the Paramount Pictures Corporation. He was accompanied by Mrs. Florence Ann Harper, another member of
Leslie's staff.[5]

Thompson went to Saloniki in northern Greece, where the Allies

---

[1]He was wounded in the face by an exploding shell near Zeebrugge
in Belgium. See supra, p. 111.

[2]Topeka Daily Capital, 21 December 1915, p. 14.

[3]"Kane Gets War Films from Man in 38 Battles," Motion Picture
News, 8 January 1916, p. 77.

[4]"Kane-Thompson War Films Get Page in Leslie's," Motion Picture
News, 15 January 1916, p. 247.

[5]Motion Picture News, 2 December 1916, p. 3453.

had opened a new front in the Balkan campaign. Later, he worked with the French army; he was wounded at Verdun and was made an official cinematographer for the French government.[1] Although his official status was useful in gaining access to the front and assistance from the military authorities, it also meant that he had to submit his film to the French for censorship. He claimed they seized 70 per cent of his footage, and told him he would get it back after the war.[2]

Thompson returned to the United States in the fall of 1916, and his footage was edited into a seven-reel feature with the rather pretentious title of War As It Really Is.[3] It opens in predictable fashion, with a shot of Thompson reading telegrams. The next sequence shows a seaplane being launched at Saloniki; Thompson went up to take aerial views of the city, the harbor and the Allied fleet at anchor. The next sequence shows the launching of an observation balloon from a ship. The first scenes from the war zone are in the second reel, and the rest of the film was taken while Thompson was with the French army. There are the standard behind-the-lines scenes: troop reviews and medal ceremonies, artillery and supplies being moved up to the front, German prisoners in a stockade and soldiers washing their clothes in the River Meuse. But the film does shown something of trench warfare: soldiers are seen clearing gas from a trench, and infantry going over the top. In another

[1]Brownlow, The War, p. 55.

[2]"Real Thrills in Battle Pictures," Moving Picture World, 11 November 1916, p. 857.

[3]There is a copy on video-cassette in the National Archives collection (see Appendix).

sequence, French soldiers use compressed air drills to tunnel under the German lines, and they explode a mine under the trenches.

A reviewer for Moving Picture World singled out this scene for particular mention:

> One of the most impressive incidents is the complete obliter-
> ation of a portion of a trench and a number of soldiers by a
> shell. The men are seen hurling hand grenades in the direction
> of the enemy. The next instant the shell strikes squarely in
> the center of their ranks, the air is filled with flying debris,
> and nothing remains but a gaping hole in the ground.[1]

In other scenes, an observer parachutes from a balloon, anti-aircraft guns fire at German planes, French gunboats go into action on the River Yser, a gun mounted on a railroad car is fired, and a German officer is shot as a spy (the execution itself is not shown, for the film cuts from the German to his body).

Reporters and film critics saw a preview of War As It Really Is at the Wurlitzer Hall in New York City on Sunday, 22 October 1916; Thompson added comments during the screening.[2] Ten reels were shown, although when the film released to theaters, it had only seven. Two of the reels which the public did not see were hospital scenes. The third appears to have been taken from Somewhere in France; Moving Picture World mentions the aerial battle filmed from a French plane and the trench incident--the opposing sides, which, in the earliest reviews, were said to be 30 yards apart, were now only 40 feet from one another! The reviewer remarked that, "The most impressive feature of Mr. Thompson's

---

[1]"Real Thrills in Battle Pictures," Moving Picture World, 11 November 1916, p. 857.

[2]Ibid.

pictures is their authenticity. Nothing is faked. The photographer was under fire repeatedly, and scene after scene was taken at the risk of his life."[1]

The next month, Thompson arranged another preview--this time at the Army and Navy Club in Washington, D.C. According to Motion Picture News, "The officers were astounded when shown the pictures, as scenes never before exhibited were incorporated in the reels."[2] They made an agreement with Thompson to buy prints for government use.

The enthusiastic reception of War As It Really Is may have encouraged Thompson to handle the distribution himself. He arranged for the first public screening at the Rialto Theater in New York City, where he knew that the manager, Samuel L. Rothapfel, would do his best to give it a thoroughly professional presentation. He did--and it broke the Rialto's box office record.[3]

In late November, Thompson opened a suite of offices on the 21st floor of the Times Building in New York City. The Donald C. Thompson Film Company, said Motion Picture News, was set up to handle war and topical films. Thompson was named as president, Theodore Miller as vice-president, Mrs. Harper--who had accompanied him on his last European trip--as treasurer, and Captain Edwin Bower Hesser of Montreal as general sales manager and director of publicity.[4] Thompson appears to have main-

---

[1]Ibid.

[2]Motion Picture News, 18 November 1916, p. 3126.

[3]"War Films on State Rights from Thompson Company," Motion Picture News, 2 December 1916, p. 3453.

[4]Ibid.

tained his business links with <u>Leslie's Weekly</u>, where his pictures and
news from the war zone had been a regular feature. Bids were invited
for state rights to <u>War As It Really Is</u> and local contracts were handled
by newspapers which received syndicated material from <u>Leslie's</u>; Thompson
was therefore using <u>Leslie's</u> existing distribution chain. The magazine
also handled the publicity, and exhibitors were promised ". . . over 100
perfect stills, thirty kinds of ad plates in all sizes, and several
exhibition sets of priceless relics from the European battlefields, one
of which created so much comment at the Rialto theatre."[1] Thompson
clearly expected to leave the management of the business to his associ-
ates because he was already planning his next trip to the war zone.
"Captain Thompson and Mrs. Harper," reported <u>Motion Picture News</u>, ". . .
are having special Debrie cameras built; jeweled as if they were watches
and with many improvements for strenuous war service."[2]

In March 1917, Thompson left for Russia, travelling to Siberia
by way of Japan. As one magazine account later put it, he ". . . was
just getting nicely under way when the series of events which culminated
in the Russian dissolution began to take place under the eye of his
camera."[3] He was in Petrograd during the October Revolution, and filmed
Lenin and Trotsky.[4] And at the front he obtained what <u>Motion Picture
News</u> called "the most remarkable 'over the top' charges that have ever

---

[1]Ibid.   [2]Ibid.

[3]Louis Tenny, "Filming the Trail of the Serpent," <u>Picture-Play</u>
<u>Magazine</u>, March 1918, p. 112.

[4]<u>New York Times</u>, 10 December 1917, p. 15.

been photographed."[1] A contemporary account of Thompson's work in
Russia portrayed him as an idealist who wanted to bring home to his
fellow-Americans the tragedy of events, and the real reasons for the
revolution:

> . . . He saw that within his films lay concealed the pitiful
> story of how German intrigue had sapped a great nation. And
> he realized, too, that this story was needed in America as a
> timely warning.
>
> . . . There are scenes of the Russian troops marching erect
> to face their enemy, and of the same troops, their minds
> poisoned by German propaganda, running away.[2]

The theme is explicit in the title of Thompson's film, The
German Curse in Russia (also called Blood-stained Russia).[3] Its premiere was at the Strand Theater in New York City on 9 December 1917,
and it was enthusiastically reviewed by the New York Times, which said
it contained "some of the most vivid war scenes which have yet been
exhibited here."[4]

In the same month that The German Curse in Russia was released,
Russia withdrew from the war, and, under the terms of the Treaty of
Brest-Litovsk, the Germans occupied the Ukraine. American opinion
turned against the former ally, and films like Thompson's helped to
convince some Americans that the October Revolution was not a popular
rising against tyranny and the hardships of war, but a coup engineered

---

[1]"Pathé Shows Good War Films," Motion Picture News, 29 December
1917, p. 4535.

[2]"Filming the Trail," p. 113.

[3]The title used in the New York Times, 10 December 1917, p. 10.

[4]Ibid.

by German propaganda. As <u>Motion Picture News</u> remarked:

> . . . Every foot of the film that is shown helps, it is claimed,
> to visualize for the American people the means that the Germans
> utilized in Russia to bring about food riots, street fighting
> and the final overthrow of the government which had been estab-
> lished for them upon a foundation of freedom and liberty.[1]

<u>The German Curse in Russia</u> gave the argument more force by docu-
menting the gallant deeds of the revolutionary army while Russia continued to fight. Of particular interest were scenes of the Women's Death
Battalions led by Yasha Bochareva; they were shown in training and at
the front, "where, it is said, they not only took over two lines of
German trenches but captured hundreds of Germans and a number of officers."[2]

Again, it was Thompson's front-line footage that attracted most
attention. <u>Picture-Play Magazine</u> described his ingenious method for
obtaining shots "over the top" without exposing himself to danger. One
of his cameras was powered by an electric motor; Thompson attached it to
a pole, started the mechanism and raised it above the trench, using a
periscope to watch the action.[3] The magazine went on to describe some
of the scenes obtained in this way:

> One of these trench films shows the starting of a gas attack
> by the Germans--not for the purpose of a charge, but to enable
> them to place their barbed wire. A detachment of Russians is
> then shown going forth to cut the wire. This fails, and the
> artillery is called into play. At last the Russians charge.
> Men are seen to fall, wounded and killed. At the end a Russian
> soldier is shown crawling back toward the lines, carrying on

[1]"Pathé Shows Good War Films," <u>Motion Picture News</u>, 29 December
1917, p. 4535. Presumably the reference to the government is to the
Kerensky administration, not to that of the Tsar.

[2]Ibid.   [3]"Filming the Trail," p. 114.

his back a wounded officer. The officer dies the second time
he slips from the man's shoulders, and, after crossing himself,
the private hurries away to join his fighting comrades again.[1]

The German Curse in Russia was not distributed by Thompson's
own company (if it was still operating), but by Pathé, which had success-
fully handled the official French war films.[2] It was released in January 1918. If Thompson returned to the war zone before the Armistice,
the motion picture magazines, which had assiduously followed his progress through the war, did not report it.

In common with other war cameramen, Thompson had a tendency to
talk big when he discussed the war. Some of his stories can be fully
or partly corroborated from other sources, but most cannot; even the
most plausible tales may have gained a little more flavor in the telling. Yet Thompson's significance should not be underestimated. A
self-confessed adventurer, he embodied the essential qualities of the
successful war cameraman: stamina, courage, the ability to deal with
officialdom, technical ability, a sharp news sense and a taste for
danger. If the war films which led contemporaries to heap superlatives
on him seem slow and undramatic to modern eyes, it is because our expectations of the war film have been raised by World War II and later conflicts, particularly the television coverage of Vietnam. In Thompson's
day, it was a considerable achievement to reach the war zone and obtain
footage; to secure the front-line scenes of Somewhere in France, War As
It Really Is and The German Curse in Russia was a feat emulated by few

_____

[1]Ibid., pp. 114-15.

[2]Motion Picture News, 29 December 1917, p. 4535.

others. Thompson clearly revelled in the travel, excitement and fame that his films brought him; whether he was consciously trying to raise the awareness of the American public is more questionable. But, whatever his intentions, his films enabled American audiences to understand more about the war their country was to enter.

* * * * *

CHAPTER 6

EQUIPMENT:

THE CAMERAMAN'S BURDEN

When Donald Thompson squatted in a Russian trench, attached his camera to a pole, started the electric motor, and raised it above the edge of the trench, he was not only being resourceful; his action also demonstrated how far camera design had progressed in a quarter of a century. If war had been declared in New Jersey in the 1890s, Thomas Edison would have been unable to cover it from his studio in West Orange. His first camera was so large that several men were needed to move it; it could record anything that happened in the "Black Maria" studio, but was too unwieldy for work outside.[1] Louis Lumière's cinématographe, introduced in 1895, was much superior for field work. It weighed only twelve pounds, and could be carried as easily as a small suitcase; hand-cranked, it was not dependent on electricity, and was ideal for outside filming.[2] The cinématographe was the model for a number of other hand-cranked cameras: the Moy, the Williamson, the Eclair, the Prestwich and the Debrie.[3]

Many of these saw service in World War I and they had advantages;

_____

[1]Barnouw, Documentary, p. 5.   [2]Ibid., p. 6.

[3]Kenneth Gordon, "The Early Days of News-Reels," British Kinematography, August 1950, p. 48.

they were sturdily built and fairly easy to repair. Yet in another way they were not well suited to war coverage. The best results were obtained when a tripod was used; the operator stood behind the camera and cranked away. Such a procedure was fine for a peacetime parade or sports event, but in the trenches any cameraman foolhardy enough to set up a camera and tripod in full view of the enemy was destined for a short career. Indeed, cameras were often mistaken for new and fearsome weapons. John Tippett, writing two months after the outbreak of the war in Europe, said that even if a camera operator reached the front, ". . . the enemy would assume, with the aid of their glasses, that it was a new-fangled gun, and they would spot him with a big, fat shell before he could turn the crank a dozen times."[1] Another contributor to the motion picture magazine, Homer Croy, agreed: "A camera employing a tripod not only exposed the photographer to the attack of the enemy, but brought him to the particular attention of the marksmen by reason of the machine that he was turning, which as far as they were able to determine might be a new arrangement of rapid-fire gun."[2]

Military authorities often stopped cameramen from operating their machines for fear of drawing fire; any sign of activity might make that part of the front line the target for an artillery barrage. Film historian Francis Collins claimed that on one occasion the sight of a camera in a trench in France caused a serious engagement:

---

[1]Letter from John D. Tippett, Universal's London representative, to Universal's president, Carl Laemmle, quoted in "All War Pictures Fakes," Moving Picture World, 3 October 1914, p. 50.

[2]Croy, How Motion Pictures Are Made, pp. 259-60.

. . . All had been quiet for days and the movie man had ventured into a German trench where he secured some interesting
films. The watchful enemy noticed that something unusual was
going on, and jumped to the conclusion that a new gun was being
mounted or some important strategic move was about to be carried out. An advance was ordered, and the French and English
troops in great force charged the German position, resulting
in a serious loss of ground and of men.[1]

Camera equipment was bulky; even with an assistant to carry the
tripod, changing position was difficult and dangerous. One war cameraman described the problems to Kevin Brownlow: "Hand cranking came
naturally. Purely automatic, even under shellfire. . . . It was mobility that was lacking. You couldn't take a really satisfactory picture
without a hefty great tripod. Sometimes you felt like throwing it away."[2]
"Under the adverse conditions," wrote Austin Lescaboura in 1919, "the
conventional hand-cranked camera leaves much to be desired. It is
clumsy in the extreme, and much action is lost in shifting it about."[3]
Homer Croy put it more forcefully: "You've got that camera to take with
you wherever you go, and when you're packing a motion picture camera
across a chewed-up terrain you're just about as busy as a one-armed man
carrying a trunk up a back stairs. . . . A motion picture camera is not
light and airy. The man who designed it later turned his attention to
perfecting the steam hoist."[4]

---

[1]Collins, The Camera Man, p. 14.

[2]Interview with Bertram Brookes-Carrington, quoted in Brownlow,
The War, p. 67.

[3]Austin Lescaboura, Behind the Motion Picture Screen (New York:
Scientific American Publishing Company, 1919), p. 232.

[4]Croy, "Handing It Down To Posterity," Photoplay Magazine, September 1919, pp. 71-72.

To eliminate the need for hand-cranking, camera designers had to find an alternative source of power. Batteries were sometimes used. The camera was set up under cover of night or during a lull in the hostilities; the operator would shelter in the trench and start and stop the camera by using a push-button wired to the machine. The camera was usually staked to the ground and protected by a steel jacket; but even so the force of an explosion could overturn it, and it might be several hours before it was safe to right it. Because of its fixed position, it could record only one view of the battle area.[1]

The credit for designing the first truly automatic film camera goes to a man with the unlikely name of Kasimir de Proszynski. His Aeroscope camera, first used by the Warwick Trading Company in Britain,[2] did not require hand-cranking or a tripod; Raymond Fielding describes it as "the progenitor of all hand-held 'self-powered' motion picture cameras."[3] In the Aeroscope, a reservoir of compressed air moved the film; the reservoir was recharged with a foot pump, an operation which took about 10 minutes. Although the camera weighed less than twenty pounds, it was large enough to hold 400 feet of film, enough for seven minutes of continuous operation at the standard silent-film speed of 60 feet per minute. Another feature of the camera was its stabilizing gyroscope, which automatically maintained horizontal stability. The camera was well suited for war coverage because it could be operated at eye level or

[1]Croy, How Motion Pictures Are Made, p. 260.

[2]Gordon, "The Early Days Of News-Reels," p. 48.

[3]Fielding, American Newsreel, p. 121.

raised above the wall of the trench. And since it did not require a tripod, the operator could change position quickly, and follow advancing troops. "With the camera operated by compressed air and held stable by the gyroscope disk, the camera man had his right hand free for instant adjusting of his gas mask," wrote Croy.[1]

The French cameraman J.A. Dupré was using an Aeroscope when he was killed because it enabled him to follow the advance; the camera, automatically held level by the gyroscopic stabilizer, continued operating for several minutes.[2] According to P.J. (Jack) Smith, a soldier at the Battle of the Somme, and later a newsreel cameraman himself, most operators at the front used an Aeroscope:

> Certainly I saw cameramen from time to time, but I never saw one with a tripod in the trenches. The troops would probably curse it for getting in the way. The cameramen that I saw always used an Aeroscope, as this was the only automatic camera that could be hand-held, and it was very compact. The camera operator used to set the camera on top of the trench parapet in the dark, cover it with sandbags and turf, leaving only the lens showing, having pumped it up beforehand by means of a triple-pump. He would leave it until daylight and watch for action--shells bursting, troops going over the top, etc., and release the mechanism by remote control, at the same time watching through a periscope. Some of these cameramen went over the top with the rest of us, starting the camera as they went, perhaps running off the whole magazine without stopping. They had guts, did those chaps.[3]

While the Aeroscope was compact and portable, some cameramen considered it less reliable than the hand-cranked machines. Captain F. E. Kleinschmidt, the American cameraman with the Austrian army,[4] told

---

[1]Croy, <u>How Motion Pictures Are Made</u>, p. 261.   [2]See supra, p.

[3]Letter from P.J. Smith to Kevin Brownlow, quoted in Brownlow, <u>The War</u>, p. 59.

[4]See supra, pp. 85-88.

readers of <u>Moving Picture World</u> about his temperamental machine:

> . . . I have an aeroscope, worked with compressed air instead of a crank. It is a delicate and fine apparatus--whenever it works. I took some nice pictures from an aeroplane with it, but most of the time it has the habits and propensities of the automobile of twenty years ago. Last time I stuck it in a loophole to take the Russian trenches in front of me but it balked as usual and I had to expose myself with the big Erne-mann. A Russian sharpshooter tried to find the range with explosive bullets, but I got the pictures before he scored a hit.[1]

On the ground, cameramen were often frustrated in their efforts to obtain film of the enemy lines, so many, like Kleinschmidt, went up in aeroplanes to try to film the battle area. Merl LaVoy flew with the pilots of the Lafayette Escadrille to obtain footage for <u>Heroic France</u>;[2] an aerial battle was one of the highlights of Donald Thompson's <u>Some-where in France</u>;[3] <u>War As It Really Is</u> opens with an aerial view of Saloniki,[4] and Thompson told his Topeka audience about an air battle over Belgrade in which his plane was hit.[5] However, the problems of filming from the air were not easily overcome, as Croy noted:

> . . . it was soon found that the vibration of the flying-machine distorted the pictures by reason of the comparative slow shutter used by the motion-picture camera. The film must stay in place a certain length of time before it can be advanced for a further picture, so that the exposures must be slow; with a still camera the picture may be taken at an exposure of as high as one five-thousandth part of a second. As a result, after a few experiments it was seen that aero-plane pictures would have to be confined largely to still photography. Pictures of aeroplanes in flight could be taken by movie cameras in other machines, but still cameras were

---

[1]W. Stephen Bush, "Genuine War Films," <u>Moving Picture World</u>, 14 August 1915, p. 1135.

[2]See supra, pp. 93-94.   [3]See supra, p. 119.

[4]See supra, p. 124.   [5]See supra, p. 119.

best suited for ground views.[1]

If a cameraman was looking for a shaky ride, there was only one military vehicle less steady than the aeroplane--the tank. These new machines of war held a ready fascination for motion picture audiences, and cameramen would take considerable risks to film them.[2] But, as Croy remarked in another article, good tank pictures were few and far between:

> . . . You can get them deploying but to get a tank going over the top--ah, that is another matter. One photographer had the idea that he would get inside a tank, point his lens out of the porthole and get the real stuff. He got all he wanted. It took three mechanics a week to get his camera in shape again. His picture looked as if it was coming home on the night of June 30th. It simply can't be done. The vibration is too great. A tank shakes the filling out of your teeth and then goes back to see if it didn't overlook some of the amalgam. . . . Action tank pictures are as scarce as the well-known poultry bicuspids.[3]

When the United States entered the war in April 1917, the government decided that its official cameramen needed a machine that would stand up to the rigors of war coverage. The Society of Motion Picture Engineers, meeting at the Hotel Astor in New York in October 1917, considered a request for specifications for a war camera, and agreed that its president, C. Francis Jenkins, should inform Washington "what camera is best suited to stand the wear and tear on the filed of battle and and also can stand the gaff when also in operation on battleships."[4] Variety noted that,

[1]Croy, How Motion Pictures Are Made, p. 262.

[2]Merl LaVoy was one; see supra, p. 94.

[3]Croy, "Handing It Down to Posterity," pp. 72, 132.

[4]"Picture Engineers Devise War Camera For Government," Variety, 12 October 1917, p. 30.

In taking pictures of the war at close range very few film cameras have been able to stand the test, although there have been a number that have rendered yeoman service under direct war pressure.

The terrific noise concussion tears the average film camera to pieces. The Government, in having close-up war activities taken "over there," has asked the Society to O.K. the kind of specifications that will provide for the make of the strongest camera.[1]

I have been unable to find any evidence--either in government or military records, or in the motion picture magazines--that a special war camera was designed or adapted from an existing model; if the Society made recommendations, they were apparently not taken up. As late as June 1918, the Signal Corps, which was charged with motion-picture coverage of the war, was considering modifications to the Universal camera for use at the front.[2] Cameramen had complained that in the wet climate of France, their wooden cameras warped and split, the doors became stuck and the magazines swelled; it was difficult to reload in a hurry, and the cracks and swollen doors let light into the apparatus. An aluminum camera with aluminum magazines was recommended; it would be lighter to carry, and could stand rough use.[3] But again, there's no evidence that the idea was pursued. Most Signal Corps cameramen used hand-cranked machines with tripods such as the Debrie.

Cameramen in the Boer War had used long-focus lenses with mixed

---

[1] Ibid.

[2] Intra-office memo from Lieutenant S.G. Boernstein to Lieutenant J.M. Dawson, 4 June 1918, in "Correspondence of the Office of the Chief Signal Officer, 1917-40," Box no. 1378 (General Archives Division, National Archives, Washington, D.C.).

[3] Ibid.

success; W.K.L. Dickson tried to film the Boer lines, but found that the haze made it difficult to focus properly.[1] In trench warfare, the telephoto lens was particularly valuable; it could produce clear images at up to 600 yards while the normal lens was limited to 200 feet.[2] All the Pathé cameramen carried a telephoto lens, but, according to Brownlow, the British Official Cinematographers were generally limited to one ordinary lens, a 50 mm.[3] In the first year of the war, the British military authorities would not allow long-focus lenses--though some were used furtively--and prohibited cameramen from filming aircraft at closer than 40 yards.[4]

Military authorities took some interest in technical developments because film could be used for intelligence and training work. Motion and still picture cameras were used to take aerial reconaissance pictures, and telephoto lenses to record activity on the other side of the trenches. Training films showed soldiers how to shoot, use a bayonet, advance, retreat, and give first aid. And, according to Kevin Brownlow, one of the most remarkable technical advances of the war period--the development of a primitive form of sound-on-film--was made to meet a military need:

> . . . Artillery spotting by sound ranging had been a haphazard operation; observers armed with stopwatches were stationed along the front, and whenever they heard the report of an enemy

---

[1]See supra, pp. 16-17.

[2]Dench, "Methods by Which the European War Has Been Filmed," Scientific American, 20 March 1915, p. 277.

[3]Brownlow, The War, p. 59.

[4]Dench, "Preserving the Great War for Posterity," p. 89.

gun they pressed the button and sent their timings to a central station. This method proved inaccurate. The alternative was most sophisticated. Five-gallon gasoline cans were fitted up as microphones, which recorded the sound waves--six tracks, one above the other, on regular 35 mm film.[1]

The apparatus was invented by Dr. Lucien Bull of the Institut Marey near Paris, and was first used by the U.S. Army Signal Corps.[2]

It would be overstating the case to say that World War I caused certain technical advances--notably the use of batteries and compressed air to power cameras, and the gyroscopic stabilizer to replace the tripod. No doubt they would have been introduced in due course. But the special demands of war coverage may have acted as a catalyst, spurring designers to perfect equipment for use at the front. The Aeroscope camera, in particular, might have gained favor more slowly if it had not been widely used by war cameramen. They knew that the tripod-mounted, hand-cranked camera was awkward, bulky and, above all, an easy target. In this case, necessity may not have been the mother of invention, but it was certainly a constant companion.

* * * * *

[1]Brownlow, The War, p. 126.   [2]Ibid.

CHAPTER 7

FAKING THE WAR FILMS

. . . The only real and incorruptible neutral in this war is
not the type but the film. The moving picture camera is convincing beyond the peradventure of a doubt. . . . It is utterly
without bias and records and reports but does not color or dis-
tort.

W. Stephen Bush, Moving Picture
World, 1914.[1]

. . . Real battles do not lend themselves to dramatic struc-
turing, nor to coverage by dozens of cameras from all the right
angles and action points. Combat cameramen are no more immor-
tal, nor are they braver, than their fellow humans on both
sides of the battle line. And so it should come as no great
surprise to know that deceit, sham and mockery are as much a
tradition in war film coverage as they are in the strategy of
war itself.

Ernest Rose, The American Cinema,
1973.[2]

Our perceptions of the authenticity and role of the newsfilm in

wartime have changed fundamentally over the past 60 years. Films re-

ceived uncritically by early audiences are regarded with scepticism by

modern scholars. To filmgoers in World War I, the motion picture was

still a thing of wonder; they had little or no understanding of how films

were shot, processed, edited, and screened; the images on the screen were

normally accepted for what they purported to be. The medium was still

_____

[1]W. Stephen Bush, "War Films," Moving Picture World, 19 September 1914, p. 1617.

[2]Ernest Rose, "The Newsreel on the American Screens," in The
American Cinema, ed. Donald E. Staples (Washington, D.C.: Voice of
America, 1973), p. 305.

new, and they had little experience on which to judge the content of a film. The poor technical quality of some films made analysis difficult; in any case, most were so short that it was difficult for theater audiences to spot errors. As Ariel Varges, whose war assignments took him to Mexico and Mesopotamia, wrote later: "Luckily, newsreel editors and newsreel audiences were not so critical then. If we were there when important events happened even a blurred or shadowy ghost record of the scenes would get us by--provided no competitor popped up with a crisp, properly-exposed record of the same scene!"[1] Faked films did not always pass muster: the volume of film and still photographs increased during the war, so it was sometimes possible to compare two pictorial records of the same event. But many fakes went undetected.

"Of all the things which a newsreel editor hates, war is first. It is expensive, it is dangerous for the cameraman, and it seldom if ever produces pictures worth looking at."[2] Thomas Sugrue said that in 1937, but it was just as true in World War I. Pictorial coverage was hampered by the obduracy of the military authorities, the physical dangers of filming at the front, the cumbersome and temperamental camera equipment, the static nature of the fighting, official censorship and the uncertainties of shipping. It was no surprise that many cameramen found it more rewarding to work behind the lines--filming the predictable troop reviews, medal ceremonies, supply trains, hospitals and field

---

[1]Ariel Varges, "Ace Newsreeler Gives Light on How He Films News of the World," American Cinematographer, July 1938, p. 275.

[2]Thomas Sugrue, "The Newsreels," Scribner's Magazine, April 1937, p. 17.

kitchens. But the audiences demanded--or at least the exhibitors thought
they demanded--front-line scenes, with as much action as possible. To
oblige, cameramen and film companies resorted to restaging the action,
or to the outright faking of battles.

The war was hardly six weeks old when the first rumors of faking
reached the trade press. Inspectors in New York City's License Department learned that ". . . film makers, having sounded public sentiment,
are now staging mimic battles, which will be ready for the nickelettes
and theatres in a few weeks."[1] The films, it was reported, were supposed
to represent the front lines in France, Belgium and East Prussia.[2] The
Los Angeles board of censors voted unanimously to condemn all faked pictures of the war.[3] The theater manager, A.P. Tugwell, president of the
Exhibitors' League of Southern California and vice-president of the
National Association of Motion Picture Exhibitors, said the "So-called
war pictures are likely to inflame the minds of some of the people making up the motion picture audience, . . . The President has advised
against discussing the war, and I do not believe any make-believe European war picture can be shown that will not favor one or the other side
of the great conflict."[4] The board stressed that genuine war films,
made under the supervision of military authorities and exported with

[1]"New York and Los Angeles Authorities Open Campaign Against War
Films," Motion Picture News, 26 September 1914, p. 19.

[2]Ibid.

[3]"Los Angeles Censors Object to 'Fake' War Films," Motion Picture News, 26 September 1914, p. 19.

[4]Quoted in ibid.

their permission, could be shown.

The concern of exhibitors and producers was not without an element of self-interest; whatever their opinions on the ethics of faking
and President Wilson's call for neutrality, they were anxious to pre-
serve their credibility. Mr. M. Sausby, the manager of Ramo's Minnea-
polis office, may have spoken for many in the industry in October 1914
when he told Motion Picture News: "When the pictures of the war really
come to us we don't want the patrons saying, 'Oh, that film was made in
New Jersey or New York.' We know the trouble newspapers have with
scoffers, even when they do their utmost to get authentic news, and we
want to keep scoffing and doubt away from our news films, if possible."[1]
His company was not exactly blameless in this regard; in the same month,
it released The War of Wars--a blatant attempt to cash in on the public
appetite for war film by passing off staged scenes as front-line footage.
There is little doubt that most of the "400 Stupendous Scenes taken on
The Actual Battlefields of France" were filmed on this side of the Atlantic.[2] In his letter to Carl Laemmle, the president of Universal, John
D. Tippett put it bluntly: "Anything you see in America of any consequence is fake."[3]

The incentives for faking were strong because audiences had an
image of war--shaped largely by fiction films and illustrated magazines--
and the producers and exhibitors were loath to disappoint them. The war

---

[1]Motion Picture News, 17 October 1914, p. 50.

[2]Advertisement, Motion Picture News, 15 August 1914, pp. 10-11.

[3]"All War Pictures Fakes," Moving Picture World, 3 October 1914,
p. 50.

correspondent, Edward Alexander Powell, who worked with Donald Thompson in Belgium,[1] thought the average person drew ideas of warfare from the newspapers and the New York Hippodrome. The popular conception of a battle would feature

> . . . two lines of soldiers facing each other across an open field and blazing away as fast as they can work their rifles; with batteries in their immediate rear crashing out death and destruction at five-second intervals; the sky filled with the fleecy patches of cotton-wool which are bursting shrapnel; waves of infantry rolling forward in an attempt to carry the trenches with the bayonet; men falling everywhere; the fields carpeted with dead and dying men; orderlies and aides-de-camp dashing here and there on foam-flecked horses; aeroplanes circling overhead and dropping occasional bombs; the crash of the field-guns, the rattle of musketry, the cheers of the soldiers, the orders of officers, and the blare of bugles combining to make a racket which splits the ear-drums.[2]

The war Powell had seen in Flanders was remote from the popular notion. The noise was rarely deafening, there was little shouting and confusion, the troops emerged from the trenches but rarely, and most shells were not on target. "But there is no glory, mind you, no flag-waving, no hip-hurrah-and-here-we-go business, nothing even remotely approaching the spectacular," wrote Powell.[3]

"The front simply can't compete with the studio," wrote Homer Croy. "The best war pictures are made in Los Angeles."[4] And Hollywood perpetuated the myths of warfare, even after the United States entered the conflict in April 1917. Four months later, a military instructor criticized the industry for its melodramatic portrayal of war:

---

[1]See supra, pp. 101-02, 105-10.

[2]Powell, Fighting in Flanders, pp. 143-44.   [3]Ibid., p. 145.

[4]Croy, "Handing It Down To Posterity," p. 132.

> When will Moving Picture directors learn that battles are
> not mere matters of rifle and artillery fire, smoke-balls, and
> haphazard charges and countercharges? . . . If it's a good pic-
> ture from a photographic standpoint, that's all they seem to
> care, and the result is a confused jumble of which neither the
> soldier nor the civilian can make head or tail.
>
> . . . The director's way of meeting a charge is to climb out of
> a trench, or over a breastwork, and meet it with a counter-
> charge in the open. The soldiers' way of trying to stop the
> same form of attack is to stick tight to whatever defenses are
> available and shoot fast and straight. It is fortunate for us
> that Motion Picture directors were not in command of our forces
> at Bunker Hill and Gettysburg.[1]

Audiences expected the real war to be as colorful and exciting
as the fictional one--not the gray, tedious affair recalled by soldiers,
cameramen and correspondents such as Powell. While most war footage was
not faked, it is also true that it generally lacked the thrill of the
staged battle. Many of the larger film and newsreel companies refrained
from faking, but some of the smaller concerns were less scrupulous. In
November 1915, the Literary Digest published an illustrated account of
the techniques employed in faking war films in Britain:

> Agricultural laborers, farmers' sons, and village youths
> drest [sic] in the uniforms of the British and German armies,
> are drilled in their new duties and initiated into the mys-
> teries of disappearing bayonets, exploding fake shells, trench-
> warfare, and make-believe "gassing." Stroll along a quiet,
> country footpath bordering some rolling grassland sloping to
> the sea and you may come upon a horde of yelling men whose
> spiked helmets and wicked-looking bayonets glint in the sun-
> shine as they charge toward you. If you take cover nimbly and
> watch, you will see they are rushing a trench filled with khaki-
> clad British soldiers. You shudder involuntarily as you see
> those glinting bayonets sinking into human flesh three or four
> inches, but you find later that the points are protected with
> little felt buttons and that they are attached to the barrel
> end of the rifle by a spring that allows them to retract several
> inches upon striking a solid substance.

---

[1]Fred Gilbert Blakeslee, "Movie Battles That Make Mars Blush,"
Motion Picture Classic, August 1917, p. 16.

As the soldiers ford a stream in their mad charge, columns
of water splash high into the air. After awhile you realize
that these columns are caused by dropping shells from concealed
artillery. You wonder how it is that all these country "supers"
are not maimed or even killed until you find out that the water-
columns are caused by electrically exploded bladders filled with
gunpowder and hidden beneath the surface of the stream. As the
charging "Germans" reach the opposite bank and make straight for
the "British" machine guns, terrible explosions occur. They
are the shells still "dropping" from the British artillery.
The explosions are electrically controlled by a stage-director
or producer, and are caused by burying small cans of gunpowder
here and there under the ground to be rushed. At the proper
moment the fake mines are exploded by throwing a switch or
pressing a button, thus sending clods of earth, a cloud of
smoke, and a dummy figure or two into the air. All the vivid
effects of a big shell bursting on the ground are thus obtained.[1]

Another simple but effective device was used to convey the im-

pression of thousands of troops leaving for the front--without having to

hire an army of extras:

. . . the producers used an ingenious leather-band machine,
which, in conjunction with a broad window built into the scenery-
wall, is all that is necessary. The spectators in the theater
see women at the window waving out to the departing troops.
The tops of rifles with bayonets fixt [sic] move past the window, concealed from the spectators, an operator turns a leather
band passing over two fly-wheels about twelve feet apart. Attached to the top of the band are rows of bayonets. As the
handle is turned the bayonets move along with the realism of a
marching regiment, rifles on shoulders, fastened, as they are,
to the leather band, which can be moved at any speed.[2]

While choreographed battles were easier to film than the real

thing--and looked much more spectacular--the work was not without dan-

ger. Ernest Dench recalls what happened when fake mines connected by

wires were detonated at the director's cue:

. . . one of these not only produced a miniature earthquake,

---

[1]"Fake War Movies," Literary Digest, 13 November 1915, p. 1079.

[2]Ibid.

but sent debris in the direction of the camera man and broke many windows in the studio close by, besides necessitating many repairs to the roof. The noise produced harmed the hearing of members of the producing forces, many having to wear artificial ear drums in consequence.[1]

Dench believed that footage from the war zone would make audiences more critical of films that purported to show action. They would have seen genuine pictures, and former soldiers would be quick to detect errors. "The producers, to begin with," Dench said, "will have to discontinue using powder which produces clouds of smoke and employ the genuine article--smokeless powder--in its place."[2] Britain's famous animal and bird photographer, Cherry Kearton, tried to film exploding shells at the Battle of Alost in Belgium, but he found that they were barely noticeable on the screen--there was a flash and that was all:

There are no dense volumes of smoke and the soldiers do not fling their rifles up in the air, and die in a pose; such films, Mr. Kearton declares, are fakes. In warfare to-day smokeless powder is the only kind used, for it is the only kind which does not give the position away to the enemy.[3]

Cameramen who worked at the front were often critical of the war movies made in the United States, saying that they misrepresented the nature of warfare. Captain F.E. Kleinschmidt, who was travelling with the Austrian Army, wrote to Moving Picture World, describing his impressions of the front:

. . . A modern battlefield really shows little or nothing, and the real scenes are diametrically opposed to the usual "posed" battle scenes with which our public has been regaled so much. In real life a man who has been hit by a bullet does not throw up his hands and rifle and then fall in a theatrical fashion and roll a few times over. When he lies in the trenches and

---

[1]Dench, Making the Movies, p. 170.

[2]Ibid., p. 170.   [3]Ibid., pp. 164-65.

is hit he barely lurches a few inches forward or quietly turns
over on his side. The real picture is not as dramatic as the
fake picture, . . .[1]

In the same letter, Kleinschmidt says that he wishes he could
film at night; ". . . as I am writing these lines the heavens are illu-
minated by burning houses, searchlights and rockets."[2] Some companies
did claim to have shot "night scenes;" according to the film historian
Earl Thiesen, writing in the 1930s, such scenes were faked by the simple
device of intercutting negative and positive film in the finished
prints.[3]

Another form of manipulation was the re-creation of a newsworthy
event after the fact, using the same individuals who had taken part.[4]
Louis de Rochemont, a young newsreel cameraman,[5] used this technique in
1915 to cover the arrest of a German saboteur, Werner Horn, who was
charged with demolishing a bridge at Vanceboro, Maine. When De Rochemont
and the other newsreel cameramen arrived in Portland, where the arrest
had taken place, they discovered that Horn was already in prison. After
his competitors had left, De Rochemnot persuaded the sheriff to re-enact
the arrest. Both the officer and the saboteur obliged, and the footage

---

[1]W. Stephen Bush, "Genuine War Films," Moving Picture World, 14
August 1915, pp. 1134-35.

[2]Ibid., p. 1135.

[3]Earl Thiesen, "Story of the Newsreel," International Photographer, September 1933, p. 25.

[4]The storming of the Post Office at Vera Cruz in Mexico, re-
enacted for the benefit of Victor Milner is another example of this
practice. See supra, pp. 26-27.

[5]Later to become famous as the founder and producer of The March
of Time.

was widely exhibited by both Mutual and Universal. Other companies charged De Rochemont with fraud, but he argued that the newsreel camera-man should enjoy the same privilege as the newspaper reporter in re-creating an event.[1]

A similar technique was used in an edition of the short-lived American War News Weekly[2] in July 1917, although in this case there is no way of knowing if the event ever happend in the first place. The newsreel's eighth edition purported to show New York Harbor Police searching for three interned Germans who had escaped from Ellis Island.[3] The operation begins with the police running out of their quarters to-wards the camera; the operator is again ready on the patrol boat when the police come on board. The next shot shows the launch under way; this must have been taken from another craft. A suspicious vessel is stopped and searched, but allowed to proceed; the police then arrest three characters found hiding on a lighter. The police launch casts off, again moving towards the camera; when the prisoners are brought ashore, the camera is waiting on the dockside. The camera operator then sets up outside the police station for the final shot in the sequence, the arri-val of the prisoners. Unfortunately, the framing is not quite correct; for a moment, the leading policemen stands still at the edge of the pic-ture, and then, apparently at the cameraman's cue, marches into the

---

[1]Raymond Fielding, American Newsreel, pp. 149-50.

[2]Launched soon after America entered the war, it claimed to specialize in American war news. See infra, pp. 246-8.

[3]A copy is in the collection of John E. Allen at Park Ridge, N.J. (See Appendix).

building followed by his colleagues and the prisoners.

Although the retake was an acknowledged--if not always accepted--
practice in the industry, the veracity of the medium was seldom questioned by audiences, who were generally unversed in the grammar of film.
Even some film historians seemed blind to the possibilities of fraud.
As late as 1919, Austin Lescaboura, describing the work of the newsreel
cameraman, wrote: "Above all, be it remembered that he must 'get it'
the first time. There is no such thing as a 'retake' in screen report-
ing. It's either a case of getting it the first time or losing it; and
to lose it means one more cameraman without a job."[1]

Because a considerable but unknown amount of World War I footage
has been lost, it is impossible to calculate how much faking went on.
In surviving films, it is possible to make an educated guess by putting
oneself in the position of the camera operator and asking: could this
shot have been obtained from this angle? Although some cameramen had
more nerve than sense, shots taken from positions that appear to be directly in the firing line should be regarded with scepticism. The Battle of Przemysl by Albert K. Dawson has been lost, but a frame enlargement survives which purports to show the Austrian troops storming the
fortress. Kevin Brownlow is not convinced of its authenticity. "It
looks suspiciously like a staged scene," he says, "for the camera is in
a position commanding an excellent view of the assault, and the explosion appears to be simulated."[2] In the Chicago Tribune feature With the

---

[1]Lescaboura, Behind the Motion-Picture Screen, p. 228.

[2]Brownlow, The War, p. 16.

Russians at the Front, the front line at Lomza is apparently safe enough to allow the cameraman to take up a position in which the troops rush out of their quarters towards him; soldiers are seen firing from the breastwork, and some fall back, apparently wounded.[1]

The British Official cinematographer Lieutenant Geoffrey Malins recalls a conversation with an officer after an engagement. The officer had asked Malins what he was doing at the front, and looked amazed when the cameraman said he was filming. Malins continues:

> "Well, I'm damned," were his exact words. "I never thought you fellows existed. I've always thought war pictures were fakes, but--well--now I know different," and giving me a hearty shake of the hand he went on his way.[2]

Although there is no reason to doubt the authenticity of most of Malins' film, Brownlow has identified a sequence in The Battle of the Somme (1916)[3] that may have been faked. It shows soldiers going over the top: for the first shot, the camera, which should have been low in the trench, is almost as high as the soldiers themselves; the troops are shown walking towards the enemy trenches, crossing barbed wire at ankle height; two men fall somewhat unconvincingly near the camera. To film the sequence, Malins must have exposed himself to enemy fire. But, according to Brownlow, it may have been filmed at a trench-mortar battery school in France; another British cameraman, Bertram Brookes-Carrington, said he met a soldier who claimed Malins shot scenes at the school.

---

[1]See supra, p. 90.

[2]Malins, How I Filmed The War, p. 104.

[3]The first of the four "battle" films shot by Malins and Mc-Dowell. For its exploitation in the United States by Charles Urban, see infra, pp. 172-3.

"Little else in the _Somme_ is faked," says Brownlow, "and for such a scene to be reconstructed suggests that censorship demanded it."[1]

Faking was not confined to scenes from the front. In 1917, the _American War News Weekly_ featured an item purporting to show a "Procession in Cambridge, Massachusetts, in honor of Mrs. Fowler, official flagmaker of the U.S. Government." The Division of Films of the Committee on Public Information discovered that the government had no official flagmaker, and denounced the film as a fake; it ordered all prints to be withdrawn from circulation.[2]

Whether films were genuine or faked, they often failed to live up to the claims of their makers. Producers hoped to attract exhibitors with extravagant publicity in the trade press; exhibitors drew audiences by advertising and lobby displays. Although criticism was sometimes expressed in the trade magazines, there were few effective restraints on the hyping of films, and action was rarely if ever taken against false and misleading advertising. The practice was more common in the single feature-length releases, whose success depended on attracting bookings, than in the newsreels which generally had a guaranteed distribution.

The war was not the stuff of which movies are made. Filming was difficult and dangerous, censorship rigorous, and often the footage obtained hardly seemed to justify the effort expended. "War is about the

---

[1]Brownlow, _The War_, p. 65.

[2]Memo from J.S. Johnson to Charles Hart, head of the CPI's Division of Films, in "Correspondence of the Division of Films" (Judicial and Fiscal Branch, National Archives, Washington, D.C.).

most undramatic thing ever staged," wrote Homer Croy in 1919. "It needs a William C. De Mille. Dramatically the war was a failure--it couldn't stand the California competition."[1] To spice up the war, producers resorted to faking footage and re-staging scenes. From manipulating the medium to fit the story, it was only a short step to manipulating the story itself. World War I was the first major conflict in which film became an instrument of propaganda.

* * * * *

---

[1]Croy, "Handing It Down To Posterity," p. 132.

CHAPTER 8

WAR FILM AS PROPAGANDA

. . . The war has demonstrated the superiority of the photograph and film as a means of information and persuasion. Unfortunately, our enemies have used their great advantage over
us in this field so thoroughly that they have inflicted a great
deal of damage. Nor will films lose their significance during
the rest of this war as a means of political and military persuasion. For this reason it is of the utmost importance for a
successful conclusion to the war that films should be made to
work with the greatest possible effect wherever any German persuasion might still have any effect.
                                    General Ludendorff,
                                    German Chief of Staff, 1917.[1]

Although film grew in importance as a medium of communication--

and therefore as a vehicle for propaganda--as the war progressed, it was

but one of several channels into which the Allies and the Central Powers

directed their efforts at opinion management. Newspapers undoubtedly

had more influence; as literacy rose, so did readership, and the propa-

gandists of all nations attempted to manipulate the American press.

Books, magazines and pamphlets enjoyed a wide circulation, and wall

posters carried information and opinion--all were conduits for propa-

ganda. Much of American society was still rural and relatively isolated

from outside issues and pressures; in small communities, the spoken word

was an effective form of communication. People travelled for miles to

---

[1]Letter from Ludendorff to the Imperial Ministry of War in Berlin,
quoted in Lief Furhammer and Folke Isaksson, Politics and Film (New York:
Prager, 1971), pp. 11-12.

hear a famous speaker, to attend a political rally, to go to church, or to gossip in the cafe and post office. Radio was still being developed; not until the 1930s did it become a truly mass medium, and a target for the propagandists. The telegraph was the principal means of long-distance communication, although the telephone was more widely used every year. There were about 12,000 motion picture theaters in the United States,[1] but most moviegoers were city and town dwellers; the business was expanding, but its heyday had not arrived.

The British demonstrated a keen interest in the role of American opinion early in the war. Indeed, Britain's first propaganda move occurred the day after it entered the war; on 5 August 1914, the British navy cut the cables between the United States and Germany.[2] No other means of rapid communication existed between the two countries, and so the most effective form of propaganda, the news, was suppressed at a crucial time--when first impressions were being made and opinions established.

Much of America's foreign news came from Britain, in any case. Before the war, few American newspapers maintained a large European staff. Their London bureaus supervised correspondents on the Continent, and filled out their stories with background material from British newspapers and magazines; the head of the New York Times London bureau, Ernest Marshall, was British, and so were most of his staff.[3] With most

---

[1] George Creel, How We Advertised America (New York: Harper and Brothers, 1920), p. 125. Today, there are about 16,000 theaters in the United States.

[2] Peterson, Propaganda for War, p. 12.   [3] Ibid., p. 6.

of their German sources of information removed, American newspapers
secured their war news where it was available--and that was from Britain.
It was inevitable that the day-to-day picture of the war which the American public received had a distinctly British perspective.

Britain's control over the flow of news gave the government a
powerful lever for directing American opinion. In the first two decades
of the century, newspapers were the dominant medium; according to historian Horace Peterson, they comprised "the sole reading material for
ninety per cent of the American people."[1] German propagandists informed
their home office that "everything must be communicated to the American
public in the form of 'news' as they have been accustomed to this, and
only understand this kind of propaganda."[2] The British understood this
too, and manipulated American opinion in a quiet but effective manner.

In September 1914, the British Foreign Office set up a War
Propaganda Bureau under Charles Masterman, a member of the cabinet. The
offices were in Wellington House, the home of the Insurance Commission
in Buckingham Gate, London, and the bureau soon became the principal out-
let for books, pamphlets and other propaganda. While a separate Press
Bureau put out news stories, Wellington House concentrated on the production, translation and distribution of books, pamphlets and speeches, and
the placing of extracts and articles in foreign newspapers and magazines.[3]

The Canadian-born Sir Gilbert Parker was responsible for propa-

[1]Ibid., p. 7.

[2]British Foreign Office, American Press Resumé, 10 September
1915, quoted in ibid., p. 7.

[3]Peterson, Propaganda for War, pp. 16-17.

ganda in the United States; starting with a staff of nine, by early 1917, he had 54.[1] That staff compiled a mailing list, gleaning names from the American Who's Who; eventually, it contained over 260,000 names.[2] Prominent Americans were persuaded to speak for Britain's cause, reports on opinion in the United States were secured, and the staff prepared a weekly American Press Resumé, which analyzed friendly and hostile stories, and suggested ways of persuasion.[3]

The first test for British propaganda came in the Belgian campaign, where the Germans were ruthless in dealing with suspected partisans. Every civilian shot or hanged provided the rationale for a story detailing alleged German atrocities. The accounts were embellished by horrifying pictures from Wellington House artists.[4] Irresponsible freelancers on the Continent soon learned that atrocity tales had a news value considerably higher than routine war stuff, and the British and French censors did nothing to prevent them from filing stories based on gossip in bars and hotel lobbies.[5] Germany protested strongly against the publication of such stories, claiming that Britain's control of the Transatlantic cable weighed the scale heavily in the Allies' favor. Edward Alexander Powell of the New York World was among the correspon-

[1]Ibid., p. 16.

[2]Mary Esther Sprott, "A Survey of British War-Time Propaganda in America Issued from Wellington House," (Master's Thesis, Stanford University, 1921), quoted in ibid., p. 16. The Times History of the War, vol. 21, p. 101, says the Wellington House mailing list contained "over 200,000 names of influential persons throughout the Union."

[3]Peterson, Propaganda For War, p. 23.   [4]Brownlow, The War, p. 6.

[5]Crozier, American Reporters, pp. 40-41.

dents who criticized the Germans' treatment of Belgian civilians. In *Fighting in Flanders*, he recounts his meeting with the staff officers of the German Ninth Army, and General von Boehn's claim that the atrocity stories were false.[1] But other American correspondents who travelled with the German Army dismissed the allegations of German outrages as baseless.[2]

While contemporaries accepted that a newspaper might support or deny the atrocity claims according to the side it favored, some believed that films could settle the whole dispute. Writing in *Moving Picture World*, W. Stephen Bush noted that a prominent committee of Belgians was on its way to the United States to give President Wilson evidence of the atrocities:

> . . . Supposing these men had motion pictures of such outrages. Whether the president would receive them or not the members of the committee would be in a position to lay their evidence before the American public by putting it on the screen of the motion picture theaters of the country. If, on the other hand, these reports of outrages are false or greatly exaggerated, it would be easy enough to disprove them by showing the actual conditions in the cities and villages where the wanton destruction is claimed to have occurred.[3]

Bush did not countenance the notion that the film can be as colored or distorted as the printed word--that the evidence of film is not absolute, and it can be used for propaganda. The content of such a film would have been shaped by the people who made it in deciding to show one scene and not another, in the use of close-ups, in the language

---

[1]Powell, *Fighting in Flanders*, pp. 124-28.

[2]See supra, pp. 110-11.

[3]W. Stephen Bush, "War Films," *Moving Picture World*, 19 September 1914, p. 1617.

of the titles. Bush claimed that, "in the forum of public opinion, . . .
the film is accepted as conclusive evidence."[1] It was a dangerously
naive view, and it was not shared by everyone in the industry--and certainly not by the propagandists. But the novelty of the motion picture
medium may have fostered such faith in the audience; it was this trust
that the propagandist set out to exploit.

With the United States still neutral, Wellington House could not
take the risk of operating a propaganda bureau within the United States,
although agents were sent on special assignments. Indeed, the propaganda
activity was conducted in an atmosphere of secrecy, and was deliberately
low-key. Books and pamphlets sent to the United States bore only Sir
Gilbert's name and address, never any mention of Wellington House.[2] As
the historian, James Duane Squires, remarks: "The whole appearance was
that of a kindly, friendly Englishman, who more or less was doing only
his simple duty by his many American friends in sending them this literature, and inviting their observations on it or on the war in general."[3]
Sir Gilbert realized that the most effective propagandists in America
were not the British--but the Americans themselves. He and his staff
tried to enlist influential Americans who would enlighten their fellows.
"The real propagandists," wrote Peterson, "were Americans--our preachers,

---

[1] Ibid.

[2] James Duane Squires, British Propaganda at Home and in the
United States, 1914-1917 (Cambridge: Harvard University Press, 1935),
p. 52. See also Peterson, Propaganda For War, p. 20.

[3] Squires, British Propaganda, p. 52.

teachers, politicians and journalists."[1]

J. Stuart Blackton of Vitagraph needed little convincing; in his view, America's economic and political interests were closely identified with those of the Allies, and the intervention of the United States was a foregone conclusion. Blackton, who was born in Britain, thought his new country should begin preparing for the conflict, and he condemned Wilson's neutrality policy. He was profoundly impressed by the views of Hudson Maxim who, in his book Defenceless America, had revealed the pitiful state of the country's armed forces.[2] Maxim, who was famous for inventing a smokeless powder,[3] declared unequivocally in the frontispiece: "The quick-firing gun is the greatest life-saving instrument ever invented."[4] Blackton determined to turn the book into an epic film to convince Congress and the country of the peril at hand. It had the ironic title of The Battle Cry of Peace.[5]

In the opening scene, Hudson Maxim delivers a lecture on preparedness, which impresses a young banker. His fiancée, however, is the daughter of a millionaire who believes America must have peace at any price—a character that many contemporary viewers would have identified

[1]Peterson, Propaganda For War, p. 32.

[2]Brownlow, The War, p. 32.

[3]His brother, Sir Hiram Stevens Maxim, invented the machine gun that bears his name.

[4]Quoted in Creighton Peet, "Hollywood at War 1915-1918," Esquire, September 1936, p. 60.

[5]Kevin Brownlow examines the influence of Theodore Roosevelt on Blackton, the production of the film, and its impact on audiences in "The Battle Cry of Peace" in The War, pp. 30-38.

with Henry Ford. This millionaire has a friend who is a spy for a foreign power; with other conspirators, he supports the peace movement and lobbies against army and navy appropriations. The millionaire is delivering a speech at a peace rally when a shell crashes through the wall of the building; enemy battleships shell New York, and planes drop bombs. The film then shows "an unprepared America overrun by the brutal and licentious soldiery of a foreign power which, though unnamed, uniformed its troops in a strangely close imitation of the Germans."[1] The Battle Cry of Peace implied that peace could be maintained by force alone. As a later commentator remarked:

> . . . The picture was straight military propaganda and was immensely popular. Pacifists were all yellow-bellied cowards, anyway, and every American was made to realize it after seeing Vitagraph's lurid chromo which ended up with a mother shooting her two daughters to save them from attack by drunken soldiers (enemy).[2]

The film, starring Charles Richman and Norma Talmadge, was released in the summer of 1915, and was enthusiastically received by the trade press. Motion Picture News devoted a whole page to Blackton's account of his reasons for making the film--an account in which the producer exhibited a smug kind of patriotism:

> . . . I have talked with men who are holding public offices, . . . and, with one or two exceptions, they are all in favor of protecting American freedom and American homes.
>
> I call it protecting American homes because it is just that. The freedom that we have built up, and the homes that we have fought for, are for us to protect, and we must do that

---

[1] Walter Millis, Road to War: America, 1914-1917 (Boston: Houghton-Mifflin, 1935), p. 217.

[2] Peet, "Hollywood at War," p. 60.

by being prepared to repel any devastator who invades America.[1]

The implication was that men like President Wilson and Henry Ford were not in favor of protecting American freedom and homes--a simplistic, but often effective form of propaganda. The reviewer for Motion Picture News was almost ecstatic, saying that the commercial motive for the film was secondary to Blackton's lofty aim. "The picture," he wrote, is destined to perform an inestimable service for the country by arousing the people to a proper realization of the true condition of the nation's defenses--or, rather, lack of defenses. . . . The subject is a warning, a prophecy of unmitigated calamity for a generation refusing to note the handwriting on the wall."[2]

The generation could not fail to note the writing of Blackton's publicity agents. It was all sensations and superlatives:

A Gripping Human Story of America's Unpreparedness for War, Pronounced by the Nation's foremost military, scientific and clerical minds as the Camera's Masterpiece of the Age. See the bombardment of New York City, the invading horde, Wall Street in flames, the vivid battle scenes, submarine torpedo attacks, the thrilling cavalry charges, the aeroplane raid, the great naval battle, 30,000 soldiers, 5,000 horses, 17 aeroplanes, battleships, submarines, giant artillery, machine guns--each contributing toward making this the Greatest of all Photo Spectacles.[3]

America's foremost peace advocate, Henry Ford, was also a target for Blackton's publicity machine; on 1 December 1915, a plane flew over

---

[1]"Prepare Against Invasion, Is Vitagraph Film Lesson," Motion Picture News, 31 July 1915, p. 49.

[2]W.R. Andrew, "The Battle Cry of Peace Is Epic of Patriotism," Motion Picture News, 21 August 1915, p. 82.

[3]Advertisement, Chicago Sunday Tribune, 31 October 1915, pt. 2, p. 3.

Detroit, scattering advertising matter for the film.[1] Ford bought space

in major newspapers to charge that The Battle Cry of Peace was propa-

ganda for the warmongers and the munitions makers; he pointed out that

stock for Maxim's munitions corporation was on the market. The predict-

able row ensued, and Vitagraph filed a $1 million suit for damages

against Ford.[2] A few legal motions were made before the matter was for-

gotten.

The Battle Cry of Peace was warmly endorsed by advocates of pre-

paredness; Theodore Roosevelt had seen Blackton's screenplay, and had

brought together a number of influential people who pledged their sup-

port. The historian Walter Millis says that the film ". . . was soon

inculcating an enthusiasm for big armament appropriations and fears and

hatred for the Germans in theaters throughout the length and breadth of

the United States."[3] Blackton echoed the themes of Battle Cry in later

films--Wake Up America! and Womanhood, The Glory of the Nation.[4] Accord-

ing to Kevin Brownlow, "Vitagraph became an unsolicited output for Well-

ington House;"[5] when Sir Gilbert Parker visited the United States, he

stayed with Blackton and issued highly complimentary comments on his

work.[6] He had always said the best propagandists were the Americans

[1]Ramsaye, A Million And One Nights, pp. 726-27.

[2]Ibid., p. 727.   [3]Millis, Road to War, p. 218.

[4]While Battle Cry was effective propaganda for preparedness in
1915 and 1916, America's entry to the war made it suspect. The authorities feared that its depiction of the horrors of war would discourage
recruiting. All prints were recalled, re-edited and retitled, and it was
released again under a new title: The Battle Cry of Peace became The
Battle Cry of War.

[5]Brownlow, The War, p. 24.   [6]Ibid.

themselves.

Blackton's film proved to be the catalyst for a surge of motion pictures advocating preparedness; other producers, eager to mix patriotism and profit, were jumping on the bandwagon. Not untypical was Guarding Old Glory, released soon after Battle Cry. Its producer was F.O. Nielsen of Chicago, who, according to his blurb in the trade press, had realized "the deadly peril which menaced our peace loving country on account of its unpreparedness."[1] It carried endorsements from the Secretary of War, Lindley M. Garrison, and from Major General Leonard Wood. "No red blooded American will want to miss seeing it!" said Nielsen, "No red blooded American can sit still while seeing it!"[2]

The film industry was far from united in its support for the Allies. For every Blackton or Nielsen, there was a Hearst, a Selig, a Laemmle or a Lubin who, at least in the eyes of the Allied propagandists, might favor the Central Powers.[3] Many prominent figures in the industry were of German, Polish or Jewish descent; the producers might try to flood the neutral market with pro-German films, while the theater owners might refuse to show anything that favored the Allies. But economic factors were more important. By 1915, the American economy was riding on a boom caused by orders from the Allies; simultaneously, the British

[1]Advertisement, Motion Picture News, 21 August 1915, p. 69.

[2]Ibid.

[3]Some film companies actively supported German and Austrian war charities. For example, in June 1916, over 12,000 people attended a picnic at the Selig Polyscope Company zoo in Los Angeles, the proceeds of which went to the German-Austrian Relief Fund. See Motion Picture News, 15 July 1916, p. 78.

naval blockade reduced trade with the Central Powers to a trickle.
Britain was the international entrepôt for the motion picture industry.
During 1916, American producers exported more film than ever before--
$10 million worth[1]--and most of it went to, or through, Britain.

Although America exported many more feature films than it bought
from abroad, most of the newsreel traffic went the other way. Pathé was
a French-based firm; its cameramen were accredited to all the Allied
armies, and the footage received and exhibited in the United States
naturally reflected the Allied war effort. Mutual also took most of its
film on the Allied side of the lines, and Universal organized its European coverage from London. Of the major newsreels, only Hearst had
strong German connections, and the British blockade effectively prevented the export of large quantities of film from the Central Powers to
the United States. Those which arrived were usually carried by passengers on liners--an uncertain and irregular method of shipping. While
motion pictures showing the war effort of the Central Powers were
screened in the United States, most were single features of from four to
nine reels; they appeared frequently enough to arouse interest, but not
so often as to form part of the regular diet of war news for the moviegoer. That was supplied by the regular newsreels, whose footage featured
principally the Allied armies.

Feature-length films of the Allied war effort were not, at least
in the first years of the war, an unqualified success in America. Early
in 1915, Charles Urban could not find a New York theater available for a

---

[1]Brownlow, The War, p. 78.

press screening of <u>Britain Prepared</u>; he had to settle for a hall owned by Wurlitzer, the organ manufacturer.[1] Although the reviews were favorable, no bookings were forthcoming, and only the efforts of British sympathizers rescued the film. They set up the Patriot Film Corporation of New York, and arranged special screenings for influential people. But it was not until May 1916--more than a year after the original press screening--that the film, now titled <u>How Britain Prepared</u>, opened at the Lyceum Theater in New York. The pro-German press denounced it as propaganda, and many exhibitors refused to book it; the Patriot Film Corporation folded with a loss of 20,000 pounds.[2]

The propaganda in <u>Britain Prepared</u> was mild stuff compared with the hate-the-Hun tirades of later American-made films. As its title implies, it shows a nation preparing for war; it was shot in Britain, and contains no scenes from the war zone. Cameramen were sent to film the Grand Fleet, the Royal Flying Corps, and troops in training; Urban combined this material with footage supplied by the munitions firms of Vickers and Maxim. Kevin Brownlow describes the film as,

> . . . unusual, if not unique, in the history of propaganda films. It is absolutely honest. . . . Nowhere is there an attempt to falsify a situation, or to suggest that the British are somehow superior to any other form of life. Each branch of the service, together with munitions factories and ship-building yards, is illustrated with a sober simplicity to which no one, not even a German sympathizer, could object. . . . The cheapest product from American studios portrayed war as more devastating and terrifying than this picture, but then <u>Britain Prepared</u>, true to its title, devotes itself purely to the build-up, and not a shot is fired in anger.[3]

---

[1]Brownlow, <u>The War</u>, p. 52.   [2]Ibid., p. 53.

[3]Ibid., pp. 47-48.

Some industry observers believed that the protests from German-American interests were only part of the reason for the film's failure in the United States. They thought its painstaking documentation of Britain's war preparations was dull and lacked punch. American audiences, nurtured on war dramas, expected events in Europe to be more exciting.

Despite this setback, Urban remained in the United States to promote official British films. Wellington House had chosen him for the job because of his prominence in the film trade and his American connections; born in Ohio, he had gone to London to manage the Edison agency, and had become a naturalized British subject. And the disappointment of Britain Prepared was eclipsed by the success of his next major promotion for The Battle of the Somme.

This was the first of four feature-length films by the British Official Kinematographers, Geoffrey Malins and J.B. McDowell. Most of the material was shot early in July 1916, and the five-reel film was shown in Britain the next month.[1] Urban told Motion Picture News that the original plan was to release it as a series of single-reel films, ". . . but after I had seen the first print I persuaded the War Office to combine it all and let it go out as a five-reel feature."[2] Urban said that he supervised the editing and titling, and arranged a private screening for Prime Minister Herbert Asquith and members of the Cabinet. He recalls that the impact of the film was such that they ". . . were

[1]Low, British Film, p. 156.

[2]"Urban Tells How 'Battle of the Somme' Was Obtained," Motion Picture News, 14 October 1916, p. 2393.

made to realize even more keenly than they had before the awful horribleness of modern warfare."[1]

Kevin Brownlow says the film ". . . had a traumatic effect on people in Britain, not because it contained horrific scenes, but simply because the majority of civilians had only the vaguest conception of modern war."[2] They had received a fragmentary picture of conditions at the front in the newsreels, but here, for the first time, all the elements of war were brought together. Some exhibitors thought it was altogether too shocking. The manager of a theater in Hammersmith, London, placed a sign outside which read: "We are not showing The Battle of the Somme. This is a place of amusement, not a chamber of horrors."[3] But many audiences were anxious to learn of conditions at the front; the film helped them to understand that the war was not the glorious adventure of the Hollywood dramas but a grim and muddy stalemate.

The structure of the film depends almost entirely on its titles, each of which describes several scenes. The editing is elementary, and the order of the shots seems arbitrary; there is no sense of continuity. The shots are lengthy; there is no attempt to compress real time into film time. And most of the war scenes are portrayed in wide shot; there are none of the telling close-ups which have become a hallmark of modern war coverage. As in other contemporary war films, much of the activity takes place behind the lines--the artillery in action, supply trains, troops waiting for the order to attack. As Brownlow notes, the famous

[1]Ibid.   [2]Brownlow, The War, p. 61.

[3]Kinematograph Weekly, 7 September 1916, p. 869, quoted in Low, British Film, p. 29.

"over the top" scene was probably filmed at a trench-mortar battery school.[1]

Despite its shortcomings to modern eyes, the film gave many audiences their first realistic view of a war which they had read about, but seen only in the brief scenes of newsreels. The British government took some risk in releasing it; if it shocked audiences too much, it might lower morale. In fact, it was reported to have had the opposite effect, hardening the war spirit of those who saw it.[2] And, while most of the scenes were authentic, they were only part of the story of one of the bloodiest battles ever fought. Malins and McDowell were commissioned officers, and were ordered where to go and what to shoot; the film was made under the supervision of the War Office Topical Committee, a group of film producers working for the British government.[3] Nowhere in the film is there any hint of the appalling casualty figures; on the first day of the battle, more than 57,000 British officers and men were killed --the worst day in the history of any army.

The film did outstanding business in Britain; in the first two months, it had more than 2,000 bookings and made about 30,000 pounds.[4] And, according to Malins, it achieved its propaganda objective:

> The Somme Film has proved a mighty instrument in the service of recruiting; the newspapers still talk of its astounding realism, and it is generally admitted that the great kinematograph picture has done much to help the people of the British Empire to realize the wonderful spirit of our men in the face of almost insuperable difficulties; the splendid way in which

[1]Brownlow, The War, pp. 64-65.

[2]Ibid., pp. 62, 64, and Low, British Film, pp. 157-58.

[3]Low, British Film, pp. 35, 152.   [4]Ibid., p. 29.

our great citizen army has been organized; the vastness of the
military machine we have created during the last two and a
half years; and the immensity of the task which still faces
us.[1]

Urban thought that the film in its original form was not suitable for release in America. He re-edited it, inserting footage from
Britain Prepared and scenes showing American ambulances at the front;
the overly patriotic titles were toned down.[2] The film was made into a
14-reel serial in four main parts--Jellicoe's Grand Fleet, Kitchener's
Great Army, The Munitions Makers and The Battle of the Somme. Theaters
could run two reels a week, making it a seven-week attraction.[3] When
the film opened at the American Theater in Denver, the reviewer for the
Denver Post was impressed by the organization of the war effort which it
depicted:

> One of the first impressions you gain . . . is that you are
> seeing a vast number of men engaged in some great industry. War
> has become a business. Each man seems to know his place and
> goes about his duty as though it were a trade at which he had
> been working for years methodically and effectively.[4]

Distribution was at first handled by the General Film Corporation, but Pathé took over in April 1917, and vigorously promoted the
film. The Battle of the Somme was shown in 16,000 theaters, and Urban
claimed that by the end of 1917, 65 million people had seen it.[5] The

---

[1]Malins, How I Filmed The War, p. 177.

[2]London Evening News, 17 January 1918, p. 4, quoted in Brownlow,
The War, p. 53.

[3]Ibid., p. 54, and Motion Picture News, 14 October 1916, p. 2393.

[4]Quoted in Motion Picture News, 19 May 1917, p. 3132.

[5]Brownlow, The War, p. 54.

profits were shared with war charities and 47,000 pounds was made for the American Ambulance Corps alone.

Urban also believed it had met the propaganda aim of turning American opinion towards the Allies. In Britain, the film was intended to harden the war spirit; the government wanted munitions workers ". . . to appreciate as keenly as possible the absolute dependence of the boys in the trenches upon a constant and ever increasing supply of guns and ammunition."[1] In America, it was designed to have almost the opposite effect; Urban said that it would ". . . drive home as no other agency could the realization of just what this war means to England and the civilized world."[2] The implication was that only America's intervention could bring peace.

The British propaganda effort was reorganized in December 1916, when Lloyd George became Prime Minister. A Department of Information was set up under the novelist, Lieutenant Colonel John Buchan, who had spent the summer of 1916 observing the war on the Western Front. He consolidated the work of all the propaganda groups in the department, which had four bureaus--Wellington House, which continued to produce and distribute books and pamphlets, a new bureau for motion pictures and the entertainment of foreign visitors, a political intelligence section to gather evidence on the state of public opinion abroad, and a press bureau which dressed up the news for presentation to the public.[3]

---

[1]Urban, quoted in Motion Picture News, 14 October 1916, p. 2393.

[2]Ibid.

[3]See Peterson, Propaganda For War, pp. 229-30, and Squires, British Propaganda, pp. 34-35.

America's entry into the war in April 1917 allowed the British propagandists to cease their covert activities and work openly in the United States. In June 1917, Lord Northcliffe of the Department of Information's advisory committee headed a mission to America, and spent almost six months telling the country about the war it had just entered. Northcliffe's most important propaganda move was to establish the British Bureau of Information in New York City at the corner of Fifth Avenue and 43rd Street.[1] The Bureau was subsequently absorbed by the British War Mission, which needed an agency to handle its press and public relations.[2] Even by November 1917, the British had a vast organization in the United States: the War Mission had headquarters in New York and Washington and employed 500 officials and 10,000 assistants.[3] The Bureau of Information grew quickly; by the end of 1918, it was divided into 12 departments, employed almost 100 people, and had branches in Washington, Chicago and San Francisco.[4]

The Bureau's most important propaganda work was its ambitious lecture program, which brought a host of distinguished speakers from Britain and arranged for American editors and publishers to visit Europe. The Times History of the War noted that ". . . the American public is, or was, insatiable in its appetite for addresses on war questions. Few days passed without a dozen applications for speakers reaching the British Bureau."[5] A press department circulated stories to American news-

---

[1]Squires, British Propaganda, p. 62, and The Times History of the War, p. 103.

[2]Times History, p. 103.   [3]Peterson, Propaganda for War, p. 231.

[4]Times History, p. 103.   [5]Ibid., p. 106.

papers; it was claimed that one release on the British war effort, issued on 4 August 1918, occupied 26,000 columns in American newspapers.[1]
Travelling exhibitions of war relics were also arranged.

The Bureau was the channel through which Government war photographs and motion pictures were distributed. The cinema section of the
Department of Information in London, headed by Sir William Jury, sent
feature-length films and topical material, some of which was used in
the Official War Review, a weekly newsreel compiled from footage released
by the Allies and issued by the Committee on Public Information.[2] When
the Department of Information was abolished in February 1918, Sir
William continued the work in the newly-formed Ministry of Information,
which was headed by Lord Beaverbrook.[3] The poet John Masefield reported
that these "cinemas" had been effective in shaping American opinion. He
suggested that ". . . films of Stratford and of other places dear to
Americans, such as the old Washington home with troops passing etc.,
might be shown."[4]

Charles Urban remained in the United States to supervise the
promotion and distribution of the British offical war films; he re-edited
some of them, or combined reels from several films to make special
features. Many of the films were handled by Pathé, which had a large
and efficient network of exchanges. Indeed, the success of The Battle
of the Somme was matched by the next feature-length battle film released

[1]Ibid., p. 107.   [2]Ibid., pp. 106-07.

[3]Ibid., p. 329, and Brownlow, The War, pp. 54-55.

[4]Quoted in Peterson, Propaganda For War, p. 238.

in the United States--<u>The Tanks at the Battle of Ancre</u>. Malins was at
Martinpuich in September 1916 when the first tanks went over the top,[1]
and audiences on both sides of the Atlantic were eager to see film of
these new machines of war. The premiere of the five-reel film at Carne-
gie Hall in New York in May 1917 was attended by Arthur James Balfour
and the other members of the British Mission to the United States; the
audience consisted largely of prominent New York citizens and representatives of Allied governments, and the proceeds went to the British Red
Cross.[2] Members of the New York Metropolitan Opera sang national anthems, and Laurette Taylor delivered the recruiting speech from the
Broadway play, <u>Out There</u>. Major Charles Gordon of the 43rd Cameron
Highlanders of Canada, who appeared in some of the scenes, spoke of conditions at the front. He discounted claims that realistic scenes would
discourage recruiting, holding that "he didn't believe the citizens of
the United States were cowards."[3] According to <u>Motion Picture News</u>, the
pictures were well received:

> . . . They brought forth cheer after cheer from the packed
> house, one of three largest in the city, and served to put the
> audience into just the right mood to extend a most enthusias-
> tic welcome to Mr. Balfour when, later in the evening, he
> entered his box.[4]

After the premiere, <u>The Tanks at the Battle of Ancre</u> was booked
by another New York theater, the Strand. The promoters were so confident
of success that they guaranteed the Strand management that receipts for

---

[1]Low, <u>British Film</u>, p. 157.

[2]"British Commission at Benefit War Film Showing," <u>Motion Picture News</u>, 26 May 1917, p. 3267.

[3]Ibid.   [4]Ibid.

the week would be at least $16,000. The fild did even better than they expected, and receipts for the week were estimated at $30,000; proceeds were donated to American and British war charities.[1] The novelty of the tanks drew audiences everywhere, and in mid-summer--not ordinarily the best time for moviegoing--Pathé boasted in Motion Picture News:

> A line four blocks long on each side of the theatre--The Grand Opera House of Cincinnati had it, you too can have it if you play The Tanks at the Battle of Ancre. In Omaha the crowds blocked traffic while standing in line at the Brandeis: In Indianapolis the Circle Theatre broke its record and turned thousands away: In Chicago at Orchestra hall over 41,000 persons in one week paid to see the picture: In New York The Strand broke its house record with the largest receipts in its history. In New York at Carnegie Hall the picture played to $50,000 in one performance! Why go on--it's the biggest attraction the business ever saw--Ask your nearest Pathé Exchange about it--quick![2]

In September, the B.F. Keith Circuit announced that it was booking the official British war pictures which would be shown in addition to its normal vaudeville program; the proceeds would go to war charities.[3]

In August 1917, Pathé announced the arrival of another British film, The Retreat of the Germans at the Battle of Arras. According to the company, the film had "run the gauntlet of Teuton submarines" to reach the United States.[4] The camerawork, again by Malins and McDowell, was better than in the previous battle films, and the continuity was more developed. The advance of the British force is shown in a rough

---

[1]"War Film's Big Draw," Variety, 2 June 1917, p. 20.

[2]Advertisement, Motion Picture News, 30 June 1917, p. 4025.

[3]Motion Picture News, 15 September 1917, p. 1800.

[4]"Pathé's New War Film Escapes Submarine," Motion Picture News, 25 August 1917, p. 1264.

sequence: the work of engineers, the artillery bombardment, the troops
moving forward from the trenches, the treatment of the wounded, the occupation of a German trench, the arrival of an Allied train in Arras,
troops celebrating and resting after the battle. Motion Picture News
selected scenes depicting a flame-thrower, a gas attack, and a smoke-
screen for particular mention, and there was even an element of suspense . . .

> Suddenly there is a great surprise for a young tree in
> full foliage on the left of the field on the high bank, topples
> forward slowly and then falls with a crash into the under-
> growth. Something is moving, something monstrous. It comes
> heaving and tearing its way through the bushes, snapping off
> low branches and smashing young sapplings [sic] like an ele-
> phant on stampede. Then it comes into sight on top of the
> bank, a big grey beast with a blunt nose pushing its way for-
> ward all tangled in green leaves and twigs like a brutal
> Bacchus with vine leaves in his hair. It is Old Brother Tank,
> bent on death and destruction.[1]

Much of the official British film was compiled in a series of 12
films, released by Pathé in May 1918 under the title of Britain's Bulwarks.[2] They covered many aspects of Britain's war effort: from the
home front, munitions production and German prisoners of war; at sea,
the work of minelayers and minesweepers and the bombardment of the
German U-boat base at Zeebrugge in Belgium. The first film showed
British cavalry at the front; the second, the counter-offensive of the
Germans at Messines Ridge and the British campaign in Mesopotamia. The
seventh and eighth films covered the fighting at St. Quentin; this footage, shot by Malins and McDowell, had previously been released on its

---

[1]Ibid.

[2]"Pathé Releases Big War Series May 12," Motion Picture News, 4
May 1918, p. 2686.

own in Britain as <u>The Battle of St. Quentin</u>.[1] The ninth film used

material from two other films--<u>The King's Visit to the Fleet</u> and <u>The</u>

<u>Royal Visit to the Battlefields of France</u>.[2] The last two films showed

Canadian troops on the Western Front, and the action at Vimy Ridge where

they withstood a German artillery and infantry attack.

The first official Allied war films to be exhibited in the

United States were not from Britain, but from France. In May 1915,

France became the first of the Allies to allow cameramen to accompany

its armies; the French War Office granted permission to operators from

Pathé, Eclair, Gaumont and Eclipse to work at the front.[3] The British

did not appoint official cinematographers until the end of that year.

In June 1915, the first footage reached the United States, and

Pathé took a full page in the trade press to annouce that it was present-

ing Official War Pictures.[4] The emphasis on the official nature of the

film is significant; the industry and audiences had become sceptical of

the claims of some producers to have authentic footage from the front.[5]

---

[1]Low, <u>British Film</u>, p. 157.

[2]Ibid., p. 156, and <u>Motion Picture News</u>, 4 May 1918, p. 2686.

[3]Low, <u>British Film</u>, p. 152.

[4]Advertisement, <u>Motion Picture News</u>, 19 June 1915, p. 9.

[5]An example of the fanciful stuff which producers tried to pass off as war film is <u>At The Front With The Allies</u> (1916) from the Hippodrome Film Company of New York City. A full-age advertisement in <u>Motion Picture News</u> depicted a frantic cavalry charge--the like of which Europe had not seen since the Crimean War. The blurb was equally far-fetched: "The Picture That Shows the European War AS IT IS [sic]. The Last Word in Graphic Realism--One Sensation After Another, With Sentiment. Blended in Right Proportion to Control the Military Ardor the Action Will Arouse. As Good As a Trip to the Front--And Much More Secure!" Advertisement, <u>Motion Picture News</u>, 25 March 1916, p. 1705.

Although some had, most did not; exhibitors knew how difficult and dangerous it was to work in the war zone. Therefore, the fact that Pathé's film had been approved and censored by the French military authorities was regarded as a strong point in its favor; to American theater managers, official approval meant that the film was not faked or re-staged, and consequently superior to some of the other films they were being offered. Contemporaries seemed unconcerned that official supervision of the shooting and editing might mean that they would see what the French authorities wanted them to see--a partial or distorted view of the war that stressed French achievements or reviled the enemy. To the industry, official censorship seemed a guarantee of authenticity; government-approved films were better than fakes.

Official French film was sent to the United States for all the major newsreels, although Pathé and Mutual generally used more than their competitors. It was not until late 1915 that the French government set up an agency in the United States to promote and distribute feature-length films--an organization similar to the Patriot Film Corporation established by the British. French Official War Films opened offices at 110 West 40th Street in New York City, and by the end of the year was ready to release its first five-reel feature--Fighting For France.[1] Belying its reputed pro-German bias, the Hearst organization arranged advance screenings in New York, Boston, Chicago, San Francisco and Los Angeles.[2] Distribution was handled by the Mutual Film Corpora-

---

[1]Advertisement, Motion Picture News, 1 January 1916, p. 117.

[2]"Fighting for France a Special Feature for Mutual," Motion Picture News, 8 January 1916, p. 80.

tion, which concluded an agreement with the French authorities.[1]

The film was said to ". . . represent the cream of selection from the hundreds of reels of film taken by the war photographers of France,"[2] and, from summaries in the trade press, it appears to have been superior to most of what passed for war film at that time. On the Western Front, there were shots of trenches, artillery batteries and scout planes; at sea, the bombardment of the Dardanelles and the firing of a torpedo from a submarine. There was also the usual procession of the crowned heads of Europe--King George V of Britain, King Albert of Belgium and Czar Nicholas of Russia.[3] Scenes from the fighting in the Vosges Mountains had been seen six months earlier in Pathé and Mutual newsreels.[4]

The publicity was unusually lurid. The Battle of the Vosges would show ". . . heroic French soldiers falling before your eyes. Thousands shedding their blood on battlefields of ice and snow to save France."[5] "Wonderful scenes of the terrible European slaughter" were promised.[6] But Motion Picture News did not think the film was propaganda: "Fighting for France, while frankly a picture of the activities of the Allies, is devoid of the bias and spirit of propaganda which has pervaded so many war picture releases."[7]

Despite such disclaimers, film was a particularly effective form of propaganda for the French. Although many well-known French writers

---

[1]Ibid.   [2]Ibid.   [3]Ibid.

[4]See Motion Picture News, 15 May 1915, p. 57, and 12 June 1915, p. 28, and Reel Life, 8 May 1915, p. 6.

[5]Advertisement, Motion Picture News, 1 January 1916, p. 117.

[6]Ibid.   [7]Motion Picture News, 8 January 1916, p. 80.

sent books and pamphlets to the United States, the language barrier prevented an output as great as that of Wellington House. The language of pictures, however, was international; Horace Peterson notes that the French were particularly adept at doctoring still photographs and giving false titles to them.[1] There is no evidence that such techniques were employed with film; indeed, there was no need to do so. While the French could not control the stories and pictures that American newspapers used, they exercised more influence over film traffic. Cameramen worked under military supervision; film was processed and edited under the eye of the censor. The newsreel companies received only what the French authorities thought they should; they were under no obligation to use it, but most, aware of public demand, eagerly advertised their official war pictures. The newsreel companies, particularly Pathé and Mutual, and the theaters which showed the feature-length official films, were the willing accomplices of the French propagandists--not for ideological reasons, but out of economic necessity.

The French propaganda campaign intensified after the United States joined the Allies; like the British, the French maintained a well-staffed War Mission. The language of publicity for the official war films intensified too. While America was a neutral, Motion Picture News could not have accepted this advertisement for the two-reel French film, In the Wake of the Huns:

> These pictures . . . will stir the blood of every beholder and raise it to fighting pitch. Through miles of wanton destruction, villages pillaged, orchards fiendishly cut down, nothing untouched--everything burned, dynamited or defiled--

[1]Peterson, Propaganda For War, p. 240.

you see the conquering armies of France, our allies, hot on the
trail of the perpetrators of unmentionable deeds! This is
History indeed.[1]

In the Wake of the Huns, released by Pathé, showed French troops
occupying land won from the Germans at the Battle of Arras. The image
of the Germans as a cruel and barbarous race was a constant theme in the
choice of scenes and the wording of titles. The audience is told that
villages which were not under bombardment were blown up by the Germans;
that orchards were levelled out of spite.[2] With the United States in
the war, any pretension which the official films had to objectivity
quickly disappeared.

The magnitude of France's war effort was portrayed in France in
Arms (1917)--a five-reel feature which, in content, had much in common
with Britain Prepared and Britain's Bulwarks.[3] On the home front, the
topics included the training of troops, munitions production and aeroplane construction. At the front, guns of all sizes--from trench mortars
and machine guns to field guns mounted on railroad cars--are shown in
action, with titles describing the weapon, the size of the shell and
its range.[4] The climax is an "over the top" charge, described here by
Motion Picture News:

. . . The poilus, standing in the trenches with set faces, waiting the signal for "over the top" are shown. The order is given.

[1]Advertisement, Motion Picture News, 22 September 1917, p. 1925.

[2]"Shell-Wrecked Villages in Pathé Pictures," Motion Picture News,
15 September 1917, p. 1844.

[3]See supra, pp. 168-69, 179-79.

[4]"Pathé Booms Forth with New French War Film," Motion Picture
News, 3 November 1917, p. 3090.

They scramble from the relative security of the trench out into the open, where they are at once exposed to the withering fire of the Germans, whose trenches are in plain view not far away. Men begin to fall at once, but there is no faltering. With bayonets set the poilus go forward. They reach the German trench and plunge their bayonets at the foe beneath. They jump in and soon the strings of German prisoners come forth, . . .[1]

No print of the film is available, so it is impossible to tell whether the scene is authentic, or whether, like Malins' "over the top" charge in The Battle of the Somme, it was filmed in safer surroundings.[2]

Although scenes from the Italian front had been included in newsreels, the first official Italian war films were not released until August 1917--four months after the United States entered the war. The Italian Battlefront opened at the 44th Street Theater in New York City in mid-August;[3] at the same time, a London company, Anglo Film Agencies, was offering two more Italian films, The Battle of the Isonzo and The Battle of the Alps, the proceeds of which went to the Italian Red Cross.[4]

As the least known of America's new allies, Italy felt that its contribution to the war had been underestimated. It was hoped The Italian Battlefront would boost Italy's image as a fighting nation; even though America was now in the war, the Italians wanted their part to be recognized:

It is understood that the Italian Government feels that the part which it has played in the great struggle is little understood by American army and navy men, and, anxious to have the approval and recognition of the United States mili-

---

[1]Ibid.   [2]See supra, pp. 170-71.

[3]"Italian Pictures Showing to Packed Houses," Motion Picture News, 8 September 1917, p. 1656.

[4]Motion Picture News, 25 August 1917, p. 1290.

tary forces, they have decided to present these pictures as convincing records of their achievements. Military officials who have seen the pictures declare that they had no conception of the seemingly impossible feats which the Italian army has accomplished, and make the prediction that when the history of the war is written, the Italian army will be given credit for some of the most marvelous exploits of the world war.[1]

The histories of the war were written, and few (except those of the Italians) gave the Italian army much credit. But in the short term, the official Italian films were a useful instrument of propaganda in the United States. To attract servicemen, the Italian General War Staff in Rome ordered that men in uniform should be admitted at half price.[2] The film played to packed houses at the 44th Street Theater for more than a month; some patrons paid $2 a seat.[3] Business was so good that the distributors--the Fort Pitt Theatre Company of Pittsburgh--tried to find another Broadway theater to extend the New York run.[4] Audiences were enthusiastic; as the New York Evening Telegram reported, "Mighty waves of applause thundered through the house, . . . Absorbing incidents made the Italian war pictures unforgettable."[5]

For the run at the Auditorium in Chicago, William Moore Patch of the Fort Pitt Theatre Company had an elaborate set constructed to enhance the drama of the spectacle:

. . . With the immense stage of the Auditorium at his disposal, Mr. Patch constructed a massive setting showing a section of the snow-clad Alps, over which the Italian armies are fighting. The curtain rises on a blinding snow storm, through which a lonely Italian sentinel, standing on a rocky peak, is seen. This scene dissolves into the picture proper and strikes an

[1]Motion Picture News, 8 September 1917, p. 1656.   [2]Ibid.

[3]Ibid.   [4]Ibid.

[5]Quoted in Motion Picture News, 25 August 1917, p. 1253.

atmospheric keynote for that which follows.[1]

Such showmanship was common in large theaters, and the program at the Auditorium was impeccably planned. The screening was accompanied by a 50-piece orchestra, which played appropriately patriotic music. The opening performance was attended by a high-ranking Italian officer, Lieutenant-General Guglielmotti, and his staff, and by the Italian, French, British, Belgian, Russian and Japanese consuls.[2] As theater managers knew, even the least exciting war films could be lifted by an impressive set, stirring music and the patronage of leading figures.

The Chicago press was as ecstatic as the New York Evening Telegram. Louella Parsons of the Chicago Herald wrote: "Not even 'The Birth of a Nation' produced more genuine thrills. The dramatic effects of the incidents on the battlefield are better than any other war films I have ever seen."[3] The Chicago Journal: "All through the evening the pictures --and very remarkable pictures they were--kept the audience in a fever of interest, and the applause was well nigh continuous."[4] Oma Moody Lawrence in the Chicago Evening Post: "Mary Garden never brought to this theatre so much concentrated appreciation of a performance. A longer line never formed outside the box office, not even when Caruso was most in favor."[5] Bob Reel in the Chicago American: "It has been long since Chicago has had such a pretentious cinema premiere . . . The

---

[1]"Italian War Pictures Pack Chicago House," Motion Picture News, 15 September 1917, p. 1802.

[2]Ibid.

[3]Quoted in ibid.   [4]Quoted in ibid.

[5]Quoted in ibid.

picture has a picturesque and unusual quality about it, totally different from those that have gone before."[1] The film was also well received
in Pittsburgh, Buffalo and Boston.[2]

The Italian government had similar motives for releasing Italy's
Flaming Front in August 1918. Although the United States had been in
the war for more than a year, the Italians felt they still needed to
convince their ally of their loyalty and determination. Lieutenant M.M.
Prochet, of the Sixth Italian Fortress Artillery, who was representing
his country's film interests in the United States, openly admitted the
propaganda motive. He told Motion Picture News that the film played up
the glory of war, while scenes that might offend American audiences had
been omitted:

> . . . we want to place our cause before the greatest number of
> people possible, feeling that once Italy's aims and efforts are
> fully understood in America, there will be no force strong
> enough to break the handclasp of good-will and brotherhood
> now uniting the two countries. With this idea in mind, we
> have so arranged this picture that emphasis is given the dash
> and excitement of combat, and the thrill that is brought
> forth by the contemplation of notable engineering feats, with-
> out adding scenes of carnage and destruction likely to depress
> audiences unfamiliar with the stark actualities of the war
> against the Hun.[3]

The film was first shown as a weekly serial at Samuel L. Rothapfel's Rivoli Theater in New York City. It was then re-edited, and
released as a six-reel feature on the First National Exhibitors'

[1]Quoted in ibid.

[2]Motion Picture News, 8 September 1917, p. 1656.

[3]"Italian Pictures in Six Reels," Motion Picture News, 31 August
1918, p. 1399.

Circuit.[1]

German propaganda in the United States lacked the organization and finesse of Britain's Wellington House. In the view of one historian,

> The Germans, in their propaganda activities, made almost every kind of blunder which it was possible to make. They were far too open about their activity; far too obvious in their appeals; . . . By their methods they antagonized more than they converted.[2]

While the British decided that it was more politic to conduct their American propaganda campaign from London, the Germans felt they needed an organization in the United States. There were two principal reasons: the propaganda office in Berlin dealt almost exclusively with Europe; and communications with the United States were hampered by distance, the British blockade and the cutting of the Transatlantic cable. However, the agency they set up, the German Information Service, was a makeshift and unprofessional outfit; its head, Dr. Bernard Dernburg, never had more than a dozen men on his staff, and they included consular agents, attaches and businessmen stranded in New York at the outbreak of the war.[3] Horace Peterson characterized them as ". . . a chance-medley of individuals who happened to be available at that particular time. They were inexperienced, unacquainted with the American situation, and did not demonstrate abilities of any high order."[4]

Isolation from Germany was the principal problem. When wireless communication was permitted late in 1914, it was for diplomatic and com-

[1]Ibid.   [2]Squires, British Propaganda, p. 45.

[3]Peterson, Propaganda For War, p. 136.   [4]Ibid.

mercial messages only. Later in 1915 it was possible to obtain more
information, but the material sent was unsuited for publication and had
to be rewritten.[1] The British usually had their account of an event in
the American newspapers before the Germans. This meant that German propaganda
generally received less space and prominence; first versions were
often believed, and German propagandists were forced onto the defensive
to answer British charges. While Sir Gilbert Parker and his staff had
excellent sources of information, the Germans in the United States had
no intelligence department. Dernburg did not know what the American
government was doing, what the British planned to do, or even what his
own government was considering; he had only the vaguest idea of the activities
of other Germans in America. If an intelligence department is the
eyes and ears of an army, "Dernburg's force was blind, deaf and dumb."[2]

Like the British, the Germans obtained some volunteer propagandists.
A number of professional writers prepared articles and books
for the German Information Service; but most were of German blood, or
Irish sympathizers, and were motivated by bitterness towards Britain.[3]
The bellicose tone of their work may have injured the German propaganda
effort; by contrast, the material from Wellington House seemed calm and
reasoned. While both sides based their propaganda on questionable interpretations
of events, the German arguments tended to be defensive--they
were responding to charges of violating Belgian neutrality, to charges

[1]Ibid., p. 135.   [2]Ibid., p. 137.
[3]Ibid., pp. 139-40.

of atrocities. Only when the Germans raised the issue of British interference with American trade through its naval blockade did the propaganda have some impact; the phrase "Britain rules the waves and waives
the rules" enjoyed a brief vogue.[1] But the sinking of the _Lusitania_
shocked Americans more than British searches on the high seas; the
German Ambassador, Count Johann von Bernstorff, notified his government
that "Our propaganda in this country, has, as a result of the Lusitania
incident, completely collapsed."[2] Dernburg ill-advisedly defended the
sinking of the _Lusitania_ and was forced to give up his work. In the
winter of 1915, British agents exposed the activities of the German
propagandists, and the German Information Service was disbanded--only a
little over a year after it had been established.

Several pro-German groups that had worked independently of the
German Information Service continued to operate. Early in the war, the
American Correspondent Film Company of Bridgeport, Connecticut, sent
cameramen to follow the German armies.[3] Albert K. Dawson left for
Europe in November 1914, and travelled to the Eastern Front. On his
return, the company released _The Battle of Przemysl_, which documented
the siege and capture of the fortress from the Russians.[4] "To a degree,
of course, the picture tends to glorify the prowess of the Teutonic
allies," wrote Lynde Denig in _Moving Picture World_, ". . . But an audience that is totally out of sympathy with the motives behind the armies
of the Kaiser and the Archduke Frederick may overlook the political sig-

---

[1]Ibid., p. 77.   [2]Quoted in ibid., p. 138.

[3]Ramsaye, _A Million And One Nights_, p. 690.   [4]See supra,
pp. 77-79.

nificance of the operations and marvel at scenes that so graphically suggest human tragedy and military resourcefulness."[1] Dawson later returned to Europe and rejoined the German army on the Eastern Front. In May 1916, the company released his new footage in The Fighting Germans, a five-reel film distributed by Mutual. The scenes included a close-up of the Kaiser at the front, the Crown Prince leading his regiment, and the storming of the fortified village of Ivangorod.[2] Among the other cameramen who worked for the company were John Allen Everets, who was also at the siege of Przemysl,[3] and Fritz Arno Wagner, who obtained his first experience of war coverage in the Mexican Revolution.[4] According to Terry Ramsaye, the company admitted a propaganda arrangement with Germany and Austria in August 1915.[5] Allied agents in New York kept it under surveillance and in May 1918 the company president, Felix Malitz, and its secretary, Gustave Engler, were imprisoned for their allegedly pro-German activities.[6]

Before 1917, films showing Germany's part in the war did well in the United States. Germany in Wartime (1915), shot by Edwin F. Weigle of the Chicago Tribune while staying with relatives in Germany, was successful.[7] In July 1915, a German-language newspaper in New York, the

---

[1]Review, Moving Picture World, 14 August 1915, p. 1175.

[2]Motion Picture News, 20 May 1916, p. 3042.

[3]See supra, pp. 75-77.

[4]Brownlow, The War, pp. 98-99.

[5]Ramsaye, A Million And One Nights, p. 690.   [6]Ibid.

[7]Brownlow, The War, p. 82.

Staats Zeitung, reported that it had received a number of films from the German government showing activities in the war zone; however, several prints were lost in transit. Claiming that the films "were not in any sense German propaganda," the newspaper advertised them in the trade press.[1] In October 1915, the Victory Film Company of New York bought space to promote the "Latest Big Real Battle Pictures Red Hot from the Firing Lines!" The three-reel feature, The Battle and Fall of Warsaw promised:

> Moving Pictures of German War exactly as it is--war just as the camera caught it--war as it is being waged today by the greatest fighting machine of all the ages--the culmination of 40 years of German training. These pictures are not imaginary, they are REAL [sic]. They were not staged. Plenty swell posters, photos and slides. Also a 24-ft. oil cloth hand-painted banner. Flashiest thing you ever saw.[2]

The Battle and Fall of Warsaw opened at the 44th Street Theater in New York City, and played to packed houses. The first reel showed scenes inside Germany: crowds in Berlin cheer as soldiers leave for the front, commercial life in the city, the Kaiser with the Austrian General Staff. The remainder of the film was devoted to the campaign in Poland, and the battle for Warsaw.[3] The 44th Street Theater had another profitable run with the Chicago Tribune feature, The German Side of the War, which was shot by Weigle, Donald Thompson and others.[4] The attendance for one day was 8,555, a record, and receipts for the week totalled

---

[1]Motion Picture News, 3 July 1915, p. 42.

[2]Advertisement, Motion Picture News, 16 October 1915, p. 95.

[3]Ibid.

[4]See supra, pp. 80-82.

almost $15,000.[1] Applications for bookings poured in from other parts of the country, and the 44th Street Theater booked the film for a return engagement.

Exhibitors and audiences may have confused two films which appeared at the end of 1915--one was called On the German Firing Line and the other, Germany on the Firing Line. The first was shot by Wilbur H. Durborough,[2] who spent seven months with the German army on the Eastern Front. The film, distributed by the Industrial Moving Picture Company, opened at the Stoddard Theater in Milwaukee on November 28, and played to packed houses for several weeks. Durborough attended some of the shows to talk about his war experiences.[3] Germany on the Firing Line opened at the Park Theater in New York City under the auspices of the New York Globe. It was billed as the "only moving picture taken by the German government itself;" 106 cameramen, enlisted in the German forces, were said to have risked their lives to obtain the footage.[4] Just as official approval of British and French films impressed exhibitors who had seen too many fakes, so the participation of the German authorities in this film carried weight:

> Every foot of "Germany on the Firing Line" is authenticated by the German government, who have given with these pictures the visé of their official character by cards signed, sealed

[1]"German Side of the War Makes Record Run," Motion Picture News, 13 November 1915, p. 75.

[2]See supra, p. 84.

[3]"On the German Firing Line Packs Western Houses," Motion Picture News, 18 December 1915, p. 48.

[4]"Germany on Firing Line Officially Approved," Motion Picture News, 22 January 1916, p. 413.

and stamped by the German general staff. This mark of identi-
fication cannot be shown by any other war picture dealing with
the German side of the war.[1]

Exhibitors who wanted to distinguish between real and phony
German war films were advised to ask for the Kreigsausgabe or war cards,
without which a film was not official.[2]

Germany and Its Armies of Today showed a different side of the
war--the home front. The ten-reel feature, released early in 1917 by a
company called Germanic Official War Films Inc., concentrated on conditions inside the country.[3] American newspapers had carried stories of
hunger and unrest inside Germany, and the film set out to dispel such
rumors. Berlin is shown in the third year of war, with public works in
progress. Patriotic citizens are seen hammering gold and silver nails
into a colossal wooden statue of General Paul von Hindenburg. There are
signs that the German economy was relying on women workers; women with
picks and shovels are shown repairing a railroad. There are more women
than men at the race track, although in other respects life appears
normal with concerts in the parks and other everyday activities. No one
is going hungry, according to the film: goose is still being sold at 90
cents a pound and "Even a pro-ally audience will enjoy the beautiful
sarcasm of the title, "Pitiful Victim of English Food Blockade," which
accompanies a picture of a "cop" fatter than Broadway's finest in the
old days of Tammany."[4]

---

[1]Ibid.   [2]Ibid.

[3]"Germany and Its Armies of Today," Motion Picture News, 3
February 1917, p. 758.

[4]Ibid.

From the war zone come the usual series of parades and medal ceremonies. Other scenes include the occupation of the city of Lille; the Germans tried to discount claims of atrocities by showing the feeding of the poor from the state commissary. The provisioning of the armies is the subject of another sequence, and soldiers are shown resting and fishing in lakes. The first prisoners from the Russian campaign are seen worshipping in a mosque built for them by the Germans.[1]

The remarkable feature of the film is the total absence of battle scenes, either real or faked. The omission appears to have been intentional. George N. Shorey, who reviewed the film for <u>Motion Picture News</u>, said audiences were tired of seeing the carnage of war, and ". . . there has been no great demand for such pictures."[2] <u>Germany and Its Armies of Today</u> showed the background for war but, as in <u>Britain Prepared</u>, not a shot was fired in anger--a point for which Shorey commended the producers. From the reviews, this appears to have been the most artful of the German propaganda films. Instead of trying to bolster Germany's military prestige by showing its armies in action, the image is of a peaceful, hardworking nation going about its business as if there is not a war on. It was an image designed to appeal to another peaceful, hard-working nation --the United States.

Unfortunately for German propaganda, events soon made this image look inappropriate--three months after <u>Germany and Its Armies of Today</u> was released, the United States was in the war. <u>War on Three Fronts</u> was another celluloid casualty. Shot by Captain F.E. Kleinschmidt, who had

---

[1]Ibid.   [2]Ibid.

been with the Austrian army,[1] the six-reel feature was shown several
times in New York in early 1917.[2] In April, it was announced that it
would be released through the Selznick exchanges; Kleinschmidt had said
the profits would go to the German-Austrian-Hungarian Relief Fund, which
was not one of America's favorite charities in early 1917. Although the
United States was not yet officially at war with Austria, Moving Picture
World thought the release of Kleinschmidt's film was an ill-advised
venture. Reviewer George Blaisdell said that many audiences would regard its screening as being in extremely bad taste; it was his convic-
tion "that if it is shown now many exhibitors who display the subject
will be buying a riot."[3]

Even if it is accepted that propaganda and public opinion are
viable concepts for the historian, they are constantly changing, making
it difficult to draw any but the most tentative conclusions. Propaganda
takes many forms--newspapers, books, pamphlets, posters, films, radio
(and today television), speeches and word of mouth--any one of which may
be of paramount importance at a particular time. And it would be dangerous to assume that an entity called public opinion can be manipulated.
People hold opinions, not the public; although some may agree with
others on certain issues, at no time does everyone--the public--subscribe
to a particular view. So if propaganda is to work, it must take different forms and adopt different methods of persuasion; some people will be

[1]See supra, pp. 85-88.

[2]"War on Three Fronts," Moving Picture World, 21 April 1917,
p. 447.

[3]Ibid.

influenced by one medium rather than another. And views resolutely held at one time can be discarded quickly in the light of new events.

With these qualifications, film propaganda appears to have had some effect on opinion in America, although newspapers remained the most influential medium throughout the war. British control of communications and command of the sea gave the Allies a tremendous propaganda advantage. Wellington House and film promoters such as Charles Urban were careful not to alienate Americans by being too obvious in their propaganda; the Germans, by contrast, were tactless and clumsy in their efforts at opinion management. Although the Germans had been the first to allow American cameramen to accompany their armies, the largest proportion of news-film came from the Allied side. Pathé had the most successful newsreel in the United States, and it constantly reflected the activities of the Allies; Mutual and Universal also appeared to use more material from the Allies, leaving Hearst as the main channel for German and Austrian film. Although a newsreel editor may have personally favored one side or the other, his company took what film was available--and throughout the war, cameramen in Allied countries were supplying much more than their counterparts with the Germans and Austrians.

When feature-length films on the war effort of the Central Powers were shown, they were usually well attended, and sometimes, as with The German Side of the War, an outstanding success. But again the Allies had the upper hand; for every German film, there were two or three British or French films. So it was film of the Allies which constituted the major portion of what moviegoers saw of the war; when they saw a newsreel or feature-length war film, more likely than not it would show the Allied war effort.

As Sir Gilbert Parker remarked, the most effective propagandists were the Americans themselves. The Allied cause was unquestionably bolstered by a series of films, beginning with Blackton's The Battle Cry of Peace, which called for preparedness in America; the producers were not anticipating an Allied invasion. In this area, film became part of a more diverse propaganda campaign which included newspaper editorials, books, pamphlets and speeches. The most famous and vociferous advocate of preparedness was the former President, Theodore Roosevelt, whose activities were widely reported in the newsreels.

The faking and staging of war films by cameramen and producers may have helped the propagandists of all nations. Weary of films that did not live up to their extravagant publicity, exhibitors and audiences were eager to accept any footage that carried an official label. The approval and censorship of film by Britain, France, Italy and Germany seemed a guarantee of authenticity--that the action had taken place in Flanders, not in Flushing. They were apparently untroubled by the implication that military and government control of the film-making gave the warring powers an ideal propaganda opportunity. The cameramen were either enlisted men, or strictly supervised; the authorities decided where they went, and what they filmed. Official films were edited and titled under the eye of the censor; shocking or misleading scenes were omitted. When the official films appeared on American screens, they offered audiences a fragmentary and often colored view of the war. But at least it was a view--more comprehensive than the newsreels, and more honest than the fakes and war dramas. And it set the pattern for a more ambitious program of film propaganda after America entered the war--a program conducted by an agency of the United States government.

* * * * *

CHAPTER 9

THE SIGNAL CORPS

FILMS THE WAR

For American motion picture audiences, the news value of events
in Europe increased dramatically on 6 April 1917; after two and a half
years of official, if not always practised, neutrality, the United
States was at war. Despite the dire warnings of J. Stuart Blackton and
the other advocates of preparedness, the enemy was not steaming up the
Hudson River or storming the White House. Indeed, the declaration of
war had little immediate effect on the lives of Americans. Even the
government was not sure what being at war would mean to the country.
President Wilson "apparently first thought that the American participation would be confined primarily to economic and financial contributions,
with the navy to help cope with the U-boat menace."[1] Some Congressmen
assumed that America's declaration of war by itself would be enough to
assure an Allied victory. Sen. Thomas Martin of Virginia incredulously
asked a War Department official: "Good Lord! You're not going to send
soldiers there, are you?"[2]

_____

[1]D.M. Smith, The Great Departure: The United States in World
War I, 1914-1920 (New York: John Wiley, 1965), p. 84.

[2]Quoted in Frederick Palmer, Newton D. Baker: .America at War
(New York: Dodd, Mead and Company, 1931), 1:120.

If the government did not know what the war would mean to the country, the film industry could hardly be blamed for lack of foresight. Three weeks after the declaration, F. Collins of McClure Pictures boldly predicted that "The war will in no way harm the motion picture, and indications are that business actually will be benefitted by present conditions."[1] Within a few weeks, Mr. Collins must have regretted his words. A sudden increase in the cost of living and preparations for military service depressed theater attendances, although those near the training camps boomed. With young men in the service and women in munitions factories, there was less time and money for outings. To some, moviegoing seemed unpatriotic; Americans should be spending their money on Liberty Bonds and savings stamps.

The movie industry was ready to show it was as patriotic as any other: committees were formed to cooperate with the government war effort; stars appeared at fund-raisers for the Red Cross and war charities; Charlie Chaplin, Mary Pickford, Douglas Fairbanks, William S. Hart and others travelled the country persuading thousands to buy Liberty Bonds;[2] William Desmond thrust, parried and jabbed a broomstick across a double-page spread in Motion Picture Classic to show movie fans how to use a bayonet to repel the invading hordes.[3]

---

[1]Quoted in Moving Picture World, 28 April 1917, p. 646.

[2]Douglas Fairbanks chartered a special train for a whirlwind tour and sold $1 million worth of bonds; Mary Pickford was credited with bringing in $2 million on a brief tour of California. James R. Mock and Cedric Larson, Words That Won The War (Princeton: Princeton University Press, 1939), p. 135.

[3]William Desmond, "Home Bayonet Practice," Motion Picture Classic, September 1917, pp. 44-45.

But the attitude of the government to the film industry remained decidedly ambiguous. While stars raised money and the government's Committee on Public Information exploited film for propaganda purposes, the administration refused to classify motion pictures as an essential industry. Distributors and exhibitors who had fought a war tax before the war now faced a war tax surcharge.

The declaration of war did nothing to help the film companies engaged in war coverage. If anything their problems increased: audiences wanted to see how the country was preparing for war, but government censorship was imposed almost immediately. Within a few days of the declaration of war, the Navy Secretary, Josephus M. Daniels, wrote to the newsreel companies to explain that censorship was essential to national security:

> It is requested that your company show no pictures in motion picture weeklies of American naval vessels, preparations and naval activities, and pictures of American merchant ships, unless the same have been properly passed upon by the authorities at the Navy Department.
>
> It is only by the co-operation of "all hands" that information can be prevented from reaching possible enemies of the United States or their agents in this country.[1]

Anticipating a flood of war films in the coming months, an editorial writer in Exhibitors Trade Review warned producers not to release anything that might prejudice the war effort as "there is every indication that the Federal authorities will suppress such pictures without hesitation."[2] As an example, the writer considered the effect of films

---

[1]"Government will Censor Films Showing Ships of War," Motion Picture News, 14 April 1917, p. 2343.

[2]Exhibitors Trade Review, 28 April 1917, p. 1433.

on recruiting:

> . . . A film which dealt minutely and at length with the horrors of war, depicting them on the screen in all their gruesomeness and hellishness, might very easily be supposed to have a retarding effect upon recruiting. As a matter of fact, army officers in charge of recruiting stations in various parts of the country have complained that they are having that effect. And they have threatened to take steps to have such films suppressed.[1]

The government's attitude to war films was not yet known, but the writer urged producers to do nothing that would antagonize the authorities. The film industry could not expect absolute freedom while the country was at war:

> . . . There is no time now to discuss a producer's abstract right to make and market any kind of picture he pleases. Possibly he possesses that right. But public welfare takes precedence over any private right, especially in time of war, and it is upon that principle that the Federal Government will proceed against any influence intentionally or unintentionally hostile to the public welfare.[2]

The War Department's notion of the public welfare did not apparently include a provision for civilian cameramen at the front. Following the example of the other Allies, the authorities ordered that only enlisted men should be allowed to film in the war zone, or at the training camps, airfields and munitions factories in the United States. The branch of the armed forces chosen to record America's war in still and motion pictures was the U.S. Army Signal Corps.

Formed in 1861 to provide army communication, the Corps was singularly unprepared for the demands of war. At the time of the 1916 National Defense Act, the Corps was actually smaller than when it had taken part in the Spanish-American War; it had 42 officers and 1,212

---

[1]Ibid.   [2]Ibid.

men scattered over half the world.[1] In the Mexican campaign, the army
became convinced that aviation would be used mainly for artillery spotting and reconnaissance; therefore, the Signal Corps became America's
air force (until May 1918). Photography was just another burden for the
undermanned and underequipped Corps; in April 1917, the photographic
section was just 25 strong.[2] According to its official historian,
Dulany Terrett, the Corps was 35 times larger at the Armistice than it
had been when America entered the war; in France alone, there were 1,462
officers and 33,038 men.[3] The expansion was not a painless one.

Photographic duties were assigned to the Signal Corps on 21 July
1917.[4] The priority was military intelligence; still and motion pictures
were to be used for reconnaissance and artillery spotting. Next in importance came training films; the subjects ranged from trench-digging and
first-aid to the use of gas and bayonets. Finally, still and motion pictures would provide a historical record for the War College.[5] The publicity value of the material was not even considered until the newly-
established Committee on Public Information asked the Secretary of War,
Newton D. Baker, for permission to select still and motion pictures for
public exhibition.[6] Until March 1918, film was released by the American

[1]Dulany Terrett, The Signal Corps: The Emergency (Washington,
D.C.: Government Printing Office, 1956), p. 20.

[2]K. Jack Bauer, comp., List of World War One Signal Corps Films,
(Washington, D.C.: National Archives, 1957), p. 1.

[3]Terrett, The Signal Corps, p. 21.

[4]Ibid.   [5]Ibid., p. 79.

[6]George Creel, How We Advertised America (New York: Harper and
Brothers, 1920), p. 118.

Red Cross; after that time, the Committee became the sole distributor for Signal Corps footage.

The war placed almost impossible demands on the manpower and resources of the Signal Corps Photographic Section. When the Committee on Public Information made inquiries, it emerged that the section "was a hope rather than a fact."[1] It was under-staffed, under-equipped and had no clear notion of its duties in the war. A photographic officer accompanied General John Pershing, the commander of the American Expeditionary Force, to France, to study the methods and equipment of French and British military cameramen.[2] In July 1917, a laboratory for developing still and motion pictures was secured in the St. Ouen district of Paris.[3] But it was several months before photographic units were sent and the laboratory staffed.

Most of the experienced members of the Photographic Section were needed to train new photographers and technicians at the U.S. Military School of Photography at New York's Columbia University. At first, the army did not try to recruit experienced photographers; the policy was to assign men to jobs for which they had no training, so they had nothing to unlearn before doing it the army way. It may have been appropriate for clerks and quartermasters, but motion picture and still photographers could not be created overnight. Under pressure from the Committee, the army changed its mind and professionals were drafted. The director of the Committee's Division of Pictures, Kendall Banning, and his assistant, Lawrence E. Rubel, made a survey of photographers in the country and

---

[1]Ibid.   [2]Bauer, Signal Corps Films, p. 1.   [3]Ibid.

submitted names to the Signal Corps.[1] Civilians with the right experience were given commissions, while others were sent for training. The
work of the war photographer required special qualities--quick reactions,
news judgement and initiative--as this 1917 Signal Corps circular noted:

> . . . As to the kind of men who can qualify for one of these
> appointments, it may be said that the successful newspaper
> photographer represents most nearly the type of man needed.
> That is to say, he must have a "nose for news" in addition to
> being able to properly set and expose his camera. The man
> who could take excellent pictures where the work is brought
> to him or where he is ordered to photograph a certain object,
> and when he has all the time wanted to get the conditions just
> right, might not be at all suited to this special military
> problem. For this work, the photographer must not only be
> qualified to make good pictures under these favorable condi-
> tions but he must be able to quickly judge the conditions of
> light and atmosphere under which he is working in order to
> get the best results, for every exposure will represent a new
> problem and there usually will be no time for experimentation.
> In general, while quality of work will be greatly sought after,
> it will usually give way in importance to subject. For this
> work, the photographer must possess a generous amount of ini-
> tiative and originality for he will have to act as his own
> boss, his own director, and dig up the type of picture that
> really tells the story with a comprehensiveness comparable
> with the magnitude of the great game.[2]

Photographers who had been chosen for aerial reconnaissance work
were sent to Madison Barracks at Sackett's Harbor, New York, where they
were given military training. According to Earl Thiesen, a writer on
film, they readily accepted the hardships of military life: "They
marched. They hiked. They swept floors. And they kitchen policed.

---

[1]Creel, How We Advertised America, p. 118.

[2]"Signal Corps needs photographers to produce pictorial history
of the war," circular in "Correspondence of the Office of the Chief
Signal Officer, 1917-1940," Box no. 18 (General Archives Division,
National Archives, Washington, D.C.).

It was a process of hardening."[1] One hot day, the photographers hiked
22 miles, carrying 40 lb. packs. No cameraman would dream of doing it
in peacetime, said Thiesen, but "they did it during the war and liked
it."[2] Not all the professionals found military discipline to their
liking, however, and some found ways to goldbrick--to avoid work. Some
went off to sell Liberty Bonds or visit hospitals; others had their
relatives wire "Come home at once." According to Thiesen, "there were
as many ways of softening army life as there were photographers."[3]
Kevin Brownlow has interviewed several cameramen who served in the Signal Corps, and remarks that "As more young men were drafted from the
studios of New York and California, the outfit acquired its own, distinctly anarchic atmosphere."[4]

Many cameramen who were later to become well-known in Hollywood
served in the war. The list is long and impressive: Ernest B. Schoedsack, George Hill, Victor Fleming, Larry Darmour, Faxon Dean, Fred
Archer, Farciot Edouart, Harris (Harry) Thorpe, Reginald Lyons, Lynn
Smith, C.R. Wallace, Johnny Waters, Alan Crosland, George Siegmann,
Wesley Ruggles, Ira Morgan, Al Kaufman, Eddie Snyder and George Marshall
are among the names. Not all of them went to France. Lewis Milestone
was attached to a unit in Washington, D.C., which made films about
health and medicine.[5] Josef von Sternberg was based at Columbia University, where he helped to make training films.[6] Others, through bureau-

[1]Earl Thiesen, "The Photographer in the World War," The International Photographer, November 1933, p. 5.

[2]Ibid.   [3]Ibid.   [4]Brownlow, The War, p. 118.

[5]Ibid., p. 126.   [6]Moving Picture World, 3 August 1918, p. 694.

cratic confusion, were sent to units where no photographic skills were needed: Karl Brown, who had been assistant to Billy Bitzer, was drafted into the Machine-gun Corps to look after mules.[1]

Larry Darmour almost did not make it to France at all. The assistant editor of the Mutual Weekly, he was commissioned as a first Lieutenant in October 1917, and assigned to General Pershing's staff. Darmour wanted to gain some experience of aerial photography before leaving for France, and went up for several flights over Long Island. One one trip, he secured his camera to the plane by wires but forgot to strap himself in. He was filming another aircraft, using one hand to crank the camera and the other to hold onto an upright strut, when air currents sent the machine into a dive. The pilot looped the loop with Darmour hanging on for dear life. He told Motion Picture News "that only centripetal force, the luck of the Irish, or some other scientific thing . . . saved him."[2]

In France, a photographic unit was attached to each army division, with others assigned to special duties. Each unit had a motion picture cameraman, a stills photographer, a helper and a driver. At first, most of the photographers were non-commissioned officers, and several units would take orders from a single lieutenant. General Pershing found the arrangement impractical, because of the territory to be covered, the size of the divisions and the amount of work. In March 1918, he asked the War Department to increase the establishment of the

[1]Brownlow, The War, p. 122.

[2]"Lawrence J. Darmour Is Appointed Lieutenant," Motion Picture News, 20 October 1917, p. 2746.

Photographic Section by 44 Second Lieutenants; at the same time, he said
that the developers were not needed in the war zone because most of
their work was done in Paris.[1] In April, President Wilson authorized
the increase and, from that time on, the motion picture cameraman in the
unit was usually a First or Second Lieutenant; there was a Sergeant First
Class to take stills, a Private First Class as a helper, and a driver.[2]

However, Pershing was not satisfied with the caliber of the men
that Washington was sending. Nine days after his request for the Lieutenants was granted, he complained to the Chief Signal Officer about the
latest men to arrive; he had asked for news photographers, but only one
had such experience--the rest were studio operators. "Difficult to
carry out successful photographic service without competent officer
operators such as Lieutenants Darmour, Jackson, Silio, Kingsmore or
Cugnet," he cabled. "The best news photographers needed for war photography. Two first-class motion picture director officers needed to
supervise preparation of educational war films, also 15 first-class
still laboratory and 10 motion picture laboratory men. . . ."[3]

The need for more trained personnel had been emphasized several
months earlier--not by the military, but by a well-known figure

[1]Cable from Pershing to the Adjutant General, 22 March 1918, in
"Records of the Adjutant General's Office," (Navy and Old Army Branch,
National Archives, Washington, D.C.).

[2]Memo from Adjutant-General to the Chief Signal Officer, 5 April
1918, in "Correspondence of the Office of the Chief Signal Officer, 1917-
1940," Box no. 18 (General Archives Division, National Archives, Washington, D.C.).

[3]Cable from Pershing to Chief Signal Officer, 14 April 1918, in
American Expeditionary Force records, "Correspondence of the Chief Signal
Officer, 1917-1919," Box no. 7 (Navy and Old Army Branch, National
Archives, Washington, D.C.).

in the film industry. Francis Brown, the manager of the Burton Holmes
Travelogues, submitted a plan for training cameramen to the War Department. He urged that recruits should be instructed in both motion picture and still photography, so that they would be ready to take over
from colleagues who were injured or killed. The job of a war cameraman
was dangerous, said Brown. "Military photographers must work in the
most dangerous positions, hence the casualty list is great; one battle
of any magnitude could easily eliminate the entire personnel of many
units . . . A company of fighting men can recruit from reserve regiments
of many thousands but military photographers have no such enormous re-
serves to draw upon."[1] The recruit, he said, "must be taught true military and photographic values."[2] He must learn what subjects to film,
when to film them, and how much film to use on a particular scene.
"Without such standardization and special knowledge," warned Brown,
"millions of feet of film in the aggregate will be absolutely wasted, at
enormous expense to the Government."[3] The War Department and the Committee on Public Information studied Brown's recommendations, but took no
action. At a conference at the War College, Brown was told that his
best ideas were already part of the Signal Corps program.[4]

Nevertheless, the work of the Photographic Section was hampered
by manpower shortages, official red tape and indecision in Washington
and Paris. In August 1918, the officer in charge of the AEF's Photo-

---

[1]Memo to War Department from Louis Francis Brown, November 1917,
in "Records of the Adjutant-General's Office (Navy and Old Army Branch,
National Archives, Washington, D.C.).

[2]Ibid.   [3]Ibid.   [4]Note attached to Brown's memo.

graphic Section, Captain William E. Moore, complained that up to that
time the units had been left ". . . too much to their own devices, with
the result that there either was too little activity on their part or
that all of them were working along the same lines, thus resulting in
much useless duplication."[1] Travel permits for photographers had to be
obtained from the commanding officer at Tours, and that often took
several days. Moore said he could not do his job properly under the
existing conditions: "I have no clerks, no means of transportation in
the field, and am occupying office room in a room already overcrowded."[2]

Shortage of trained personnel prevented the Photographic Section
from fulfilling its duty to provide a pictorial record of the war, said
Moore. He wrote with admiration of the work of photographers during the
American counter-offensive at Chateau-Thierry in July 1918. Many had
bravely exposed themselves to fire, and two men from the 26th Photographic Unit had been seriously wounded. But despite their efforts, the photographic record of the battle would at best be fragmentary:

> . . . The results produced by these photographic operators show
> the need, however, of additional units when divisions are going
> into action. It is impossible for four men, which is the usual
> complement of a divisional photographic unit, to cover properly
> the field of action. It is especially desirable that the back
> areas over which an advancing division moves should be thorough-
> ly covered by photographers. For example, I would cite the in-
> stances of German vandalism in the residences of Chateau-Thierry,
> the concrete and steel emplacement for the German long-distance
> gun at Fere-en-Tardenois, and the large park of captured German
> artillery near Villers-Cotteret. All these were passed over un-

---

[1]Memo from Captain William E. Moore to Major A.L. James, Chief
Press Officer, Paris, in "Correspondence of the Office of the Chief
Signal Officer," Box no. 18 (General Archives Division, National Archives,
Washington, D.C.).

[2]Ibid.

noticed by the photographers operating with the advancing divisions, because of the rapidity of their advance, and were obtained only through special efforts and by the assignment made from Paris of special photographers for this work.[1]

Although Louis Brown's fears were not, in this event, justified --casualties in the Signal Corps Photographic Section were remarkably light--there were never enough photographers for the work. Covering every aspect of a military engagement was difficult enough by itself; satisfying the demands from Washington was well-nigh impossible. Although priorities had been established, the Photographic Section found itself serving several masters. The commanders at the front wanted reconnaissance photos, particularly aerial views; the War College in Washington wanted training films and a pictorial record of America's part in the war; the Committee on Public Information needed motion pictures and stills for public exhibition. As early as November 1917, Pershing's press officer, Major Frederick Palmer, remarked that ". . . the Signal Corps photographers have been hard pressed by the very great demands upon them from home for technical photos, and their corps has had difficulty in meeting the demand for other forms of publicity."[2]

If anything, the demands increased. In the spring of 1918, Charles Hart, the head of the CPI's Division of Films, sent a former Hearst employee, Edgar B. Hatrick, to France to study the work of the Photographic Section. Hart did not think his organization was getting

---

[1]Memo from Captain William E. Moore to Major A.L. James, Chief Press Officer, Paris, 2 August 1918, in "Correspondence of Signal Corps Laboratory," Box no. 6188, Records of AEF General H.Q. (Navy and Old Army Branch, National Archives, Washington, D.C.).

[2]Memo from Palmer to the Chief of Intelligence, 7 November 1917, in ibid., Box no. 6188.

enough film and stills for use as propaganda, and he asked Hatrick for suggestions on how to revamp the Signal Corps operation.

In a memo dated May 1918, Hatrick recommended a fundamental reorganization of the Photographic Section. The propaganda work should be separated completely from military and technical photography, and an experienced newsreel editor should be put in charge. Hatrick wrote:

> This man should have his headquarters in the Intelligence Department in Paris and should have sufficient rank to get things accomplished. He should arrange for a tip system from the various points in France where our army is carrying on its work, and should also get the news report of the Havas [French national press] agency.[1]

Hatrick thought that eight motion picture and eight still photographers would be enough to do the work. They should be stationed at determined points in the war zone, but could be moved on the orders of their editor in Paris if a newsworthy event took place somewhere else. At least one man should remain in Paris to cover the arrival of military and political leaders and other events in the capital. Hatrick said that only experienced newsreel cameramen and newspaper photographers were suitable for the work,

> . . . as these men have the knowledge of making pictures in a way to interest the public. On the motion picture end, they are much better qualified than studio men, as they are accustomed to working in the field and making pictures on their own initiative and not waiting for a director to tell them when to crank.[2]

At least 2,000 feet of film, containing from 15 to 20 subjects,

---

[1] Edgar B. Hatrick, "Memoranda on the gathering of Motion Pictures and Still Photographs with the AEF for Propaganda Purposes," May 1918, in "Correspondence of Signal Corps Laboratory," Box no. 6188, Records of AEF General H.Q.

[2] Ibid.

should be shipped to the United States each week, said Hatrick; although the titles need not be edited into the film, they should accompany it. The original negative and two positive prints should be sent to Washington, while a dupe negative and one positive should be retained in Paris. Weekly shipments would ensure regular supplies of footage to the newsreels which Hatrick described as "the great mediums for propaganda distribution of this kind."[1] While the footage could also be used in feature-length films for the CPI, it was very important that ". . . a sufficient supply of film go forward each week to take care of the news weeklies as the Government gets more value from a propaganda standpoint through this medium than through any other and the Red Cross gets the revenue."[2]

Although the CPI reorganized government film distribution,[3] Hatrick's plan for a special newsreel unit within the Photographic Section was not pursued. The army could be expected to oppose any reorganization that would reduce its authority; it was not prepared to put its men under the control of a civilian agency. For that was in effect what Hatrick was proposing--the creation of a CPI newsreel organization in France. It was an idea that his superiors, Charles Hart and George Creel, knew would find little favor in the War Department or at the AEF Headquarters in Paris.

While the CPI's Division of Films wanted more footage from the war zone, the Signal Corps in Washington felt that photographers in France were spending too much time on motion picture work, and were

[1]Ibid.   [2]Ibid.   [3]See infra, pp. 250-55.

neglecting still photographs. Major Bert E. Underwood in Washington
complained that after motion picture coverage, still photography came a
poor second:

> It is known that many of the Signal Corps photographers are
> men of ability and experience, especially as news men, but it
> seems to have been considered by many of them that motion pic-
> ture work was the more important, and that after these had been
> made, the hard work was over. They seem to think that a little
> strolling around with a snapshot camera will obtain all the
> results which are expected in still work. The fact is, that to
> make still photos of good composition requires much more hard
> work and is much more difficult than to make successful motion
> pictures. Many of the results obtained with these hand cameras
> --so far as they are in focus--are intimate and interesting bits
> which will make good trimmings, but there are few strongly com-
> posed pictures; these are hard to make; one such picture, suc-
> cessfully made, however, is worth a hundred of the other type.
> The War College files are at present clogged with thousands of
> hand camera snapshot pictures.[1]

In his reply, Brigadier-General Edgar Russel of the Photographic
Section politely pointed out that Washington knew little of the conditions under which the photographers had to work. Units were arriving
from the United States without equipment or proper training; they were
hampered by poor light and bad weather; it was difficult to obtain general views of battle areas because camouflage was used to control prominent features; and the photographers were not always welcome at the
front. "Commanders of the fighting units," wrote Russel, "object to
having photographers in evidence during actions, on account of drawing
fire. Anything so conspicuous as a camera can be easily spotted by the

---

[1]Memo from Major Bert E. Underwood, office of the Chief Signal
Officer, to Brigadier-General Edgar Russel, AEF Photographic Section, 7
August 1918, in "Correspondence of the Office of the Chief Signal Officer," Box no. 18 (General Archives Division, National Archives, Washington, D.C.).

aerial observers and a liberal shelling results."[1]

Although they bore military rank and were under army orders, members of the Photographic Section were often frustrated in their attempts to work at the front. Edgar Hatrick recalled such an experience on his first visit to the American sector. With authorization from army headquarters, he and a cameraman set off to film the fighting at Chateau-Thierry. They soon ran into trouble:

> We struck a village and were stopped. A colonel came out and demanded to know what the bang bang blazes we were doing there. I told him that we were photographers from headquarters. Say, he was one mad colonel. He let loose a volley of heavy-artillery talk and said he didn't want any photographers or correspondents or any one but fighting men around there. Of course, when he found out who sent us he let us stay, rather reluctantly. But he wouldn't let us go around and work as we wanted to. Not much. He didn't want to take the slightest chance of our drawing the attention of a Boche observer, and then--shell fire. I didn't blame him. He was dead right. Pictures were important, but human lives were more so.[2]

Working at the front, the cameraman had no more protection than any other soldier and, if his apparatus was spotted, could be in serious danger. The cameramen, said Hatrick, ". . . have to take practically the same risks as any of the others, they bear the same hardships--the same long marches, the waiting for hours in the cold or even in the mud."[3] Some took their lives in their hands to obtain the shots they wanted. Under cover of darkness, one ventured into No-Man's Land, crawled into

---

[1]Memo from Brigadier-General Edgar Russel, AEF Photographic Section, to the Chief Signal Officer, 16 September 1918, in "Correspondence of the Office of the Chief Signal Officer," Box no. 18.

[2]Quoted in Charles Gatchell, "Filming the Fighting Front," Picture-Play Magazine, January 1919, pp. 22-23.

[3]Ibid., p. 23.

a shell hole, and made a pile of stones behind which he concealed his camera. When American troops went over the top at daybreak, he filmed the advance.[1] And Hatrick recounted an incident when a cameraman named Lieutenant Cooper was taking aerial views:

> . . . All at once the machine began to rock and tip. The pilot got her steadied, and, looking around, saw that his observer had crawled out and was lying flat on the back end of the machine, where he could get a better shot.[2]

A month after leaving Hollywood, Vitagraph cameraman Reginald Lyons was on the St. Mihiel Salient, where he served with the 79th Division. Film historian Earl Thiesen later recalled the terrible conditions under which cameramen such as Lyons had to work:

> . . . During the day, he shot such film as he could from holes in buildings, and from such other camouflaged vantage points where he dared to go. Late at night, he and his crew skulked forth in search of a new location. Through barbed wire entanglements, stumbling over clammy things, through stinking mud holes, they searched for a position for their camera for the coming day.
>
> Each sigh of the wind, each slight noise sent them scampering or made them hug the earth. There they would lie, hardly daring to breathe, while they hoped the enemy had not heard them. There they would poignantly await the tearing thud of an exploding shell. After a faltering reassurance that would come like a dawning day and with it an awareness of their surroundings, they found themselves, perhaps, face to face with what had once been a man, or perhaps, they had dropped into slimy mud.[3]

Harris Thorpe, who had been with Douglas Fairbanks' company in Hollywood, returned from the front with no illusions about the danger of the work. "I used to think it was a pretty lively job taking Doug's stuff when he got going good," he said, "but since I tackled this stuff

---

[1]Ibid., p. 24.   [2]Ibid.

[3]Thiesen, "The Photographer In The World War," p. 4.

--Oh boy!"[1] His replacement was Ernest Schoedsack. To his dismay, he
was not given a light camera but "this damn great Bell and Howell and
this great trunk," which he reckoned weighed a hundred pounds. Then he
was left to his own devices:

> I had no directive, no passes, no nothing. They didn't even
> give me a gas mask or a helmet, although I did get a .45 and
> some ammunition. I got a truck down to the combat zone, but
> an MP stopped me because I had no gas mask or helmet. There
> were some fresh graves by the side of the road, and one of
> them had a gas mask and helmet. The helmet was kind of bashed
> in on one side, and I remember the name inside was Kelly.
> Anyway, that got me into the combat area.
>
> There was hardly any activity in the daytime. All the
> barraging and banging around was at night. Photographically,
> there was very little you could do.[2]

Signal Corps cameramen such as Schoedsack were learning what
other Allied cameramen had realized in 1915 and 1916--that the war made
exciting reading but generally dull viewing. What action there was took
place on a featureless landscape, from which trees and buildings had
long since disappeared; all that remained was mud, shell holes and
barbed wire. The battles began with an artillery barrage, and the troops
moved forward under cover of poor light or a smoke screen. As Hatrick
noted, sweeping battle scenes were out of the question:

> In the first place, if you take a wide range of a battle
> going on all you get is a lot of shells bursting. There's no
> way of showing hundreds of men making a charge, because they
> don't go forward in close formation. You're lucky if you can
> get half a dozen figures in the range of your camera.[3]

[1]Quoted by Hatrick in Gatchell, "Filming the Fighting Front," p.
23.

[2]Ernest B. Schoedsack to Kevin Brownlow, quoted in Brownlow, The
War, p. 125.

[3]Quoted in Gatchell, "Filming the Fighting Front," p. 22.

Homer Croy, a regular contributor to the motion picture magazines, agreed; none but the ignorant or the foolhardy would attempt to
film an infantry action:

> . . . That is the Eldorado of every war photographer--to show
> the two sides coming together in No Man's Land. But it isn't
> done. The boys go over at dawn, when you couldn't get a
> clothes-line on a wide open diaphragm. You've got to have
> light for a motion picture. Even if the boys postponed it
> till noon the chances are you wouldn't come back with much. . .
>
> It simply can't be done: photographing the biggest thrill
> in modern war--close-ups of bayonet fighting. You'd better
> depend on getting some German prisoners coming back--you're
> more apt to get to to Nice on your leave. If you try to get
> hand-to-hand fighting you are apt to get a leave that will be
> too indefinite.[1]

Poor light and bad weather were constant headaches for the
photographers. Lieutenant Paul D. Miller of the Photographic Section
gloomily reported that in the month of October 1917, the work ". . .
was greatly hindered by the weather, there being but four days during
the entire month entirely free from rain, and the constant ground haze
and fog made the taking of large movements where distance was a factor
almost an impossibility."[2] In January 1918, the official cameraman for
the U.S. Marine Corps, Quartermaster Sergeant Leon H. Caverly, wrote to
his old boss Jack Cohn, the editor of the Universal Animated Weekly:

> . . . Light conditions are very bad as it is pitch dark by
> three-thirty, and besides it rains and rains and rains with
> the result that we are knee deep in mud spelled with a capital
> letter. If "war is Hell," as Sherman said, it should be
> fought in the tropics to carry out the proper idea of heat.

---

[1]Croy, "Handing It Down to Posterity," p. 71.

[2]Report from Lieutenant Paul D. Miller, AEF Photographer Section, to Chief Signal Officer, 1 November 1917, in "Correspondence of
Signal Corps Laboratory," Box no. 6191, Records of AEF General H.Q.

Incidentally light conditions would be greatly improved.[1]

Of course, none of the armies were fighting the war for the benefit of their cameramen. While General Pershing was concerned about photographic coverage, he was not about to follow Pancho Villa's example, and orchestrate his battles for the camera. And the strategy of war on the Western Front dictated the use of poor weather to cover advances. "No difference how much influence you may have with the general," said Croy, "he won't put it off till a clear day."[2] As Brigadier-General Russel told Washington: "In raids and advances, every advantage is taken of poor light conditions and although the photographers have taken many chances, and several have been wounded by exposing themselves to fire, little success has been attained in action pictures. When conditions are good for fighting they are, of necessity, poor for photography, and vice versa."[3]

If infantry engagements were difficult to film, what was left for the cameraman? Not tanks, according to Croy. "Tanks are picturesque; they fill the screen and look like something, but good tank pictures are few and far between," he wrote.[4] Filming them on maneuvers was easy, but a shot of a tank going over the top was a different matter. As noted earlier, some cameramen, notably Malins, were successful in filming

---

[1]Quoted in Motion Picture News, 12 January 1918, p. 264.

[2]Croy, "Handing It Down to Posterity," p. 71.

[3]Memo from Brigadier-General Edgar Russel, AEF Photographic Section, to the Chief Signal Officer, 16 September 1918, in "Correspondence of the Office of the Chief Signal Officer," Box no. 18.

[4]Croy, "Handing It Down to Posterity," p. 71.

tanks in action,[1] but the enthusiasm which greeted such scenes suggests

that they were comparatively rare. Battles in the air were also filmed,

but, as Croy remarks, it was often a matter of luck:

> . . . They never tell you when they're going to pull off something. You may stick around for a week with your "long tom"[2] and never get anything more than an observation balloon on fire. You get an airfight only by chance. And then when you do see two men come together and crank her up . . . and one of them drops and your heart climbs up in your blouse pocket . . . you find out after a couple of minutes that he was just doing a feint. Heavens--the miles of motion picture film that has been wasted on tail-spins![3]

Even when a cameraman courted danger by working in the forward

trenches, his efforts were not always reflected by the film he shot.

Film could make the front line look deceptively peaceful, as Croy

remarked:

> . . . It may be hotter there than the pit of Kiluweah,[4] but it doesn't look it. The air may be as full of bullets as a hayloft full of motes, but you can't see them. They don't show on the film. The scene may look as peaceful as Sunday morning in Watertown, Mass., but as a matter of fact a man's life isn't worth two whoops in Wheeling if he shows his head over a parapet. Hell is tethered outside, but on film it looks like children's day in Dayton.[5]

War, said Croy, was about the most undramatic thing ever staged.

Audiences, accustomed to war dramas and orchestrated battle scenes,

---

[1]See supra, p. 176.

[2]Long focus lens.

[3]Croy, "Handing It Down to Posterity," pp. 71-72.

[4]Probably a reference to Kilawea, the world's largest volcanic mass on Hawaii Island. It contains the vast Halemaumau ("house of everlasting fire") pit of molten lava--the legendary home of Pele, the Hawaiian fire goddess.

[5]Croy, "Handing It Down to Posterity," p. 132.

expected hystrionics that the front line could not provide:

> You scheme and carry your life on a platter to get a good
> picture and when you do get a scene it looks as if it had been
> taken back at Fort Lee. The front simply can't compare with
> the studio. The best war pictures are made in Los Angeles.
> There they look like something. You can see men dying in
> winrows [sic]. But in the real thing, you never see anybody
> throw up his hands, stagger and die on the ten yard line.
> They don't do it. Out on the real Champ de Mars men are
> loath to oblige.[1]

Despite the dangers of working in the war zone, casualties among
Signal Corps photographers were remarkably light. Records list just one
fatality--First Lieutenant Ralph Estep, who was killed by a shell near
Sedan four days before the Armistice. The plates from his camera
recorded the last moments of his life.[2] Reginald Lyons was gassed three
times, lost the sight of one eye, and spent 11 months in hospital.[3]
Faxon Dean, whose father had covered the Mexican Revolution for Mutual,
spent five months in hospital recovering from injuries suffered in a
plane wreck.[4] Corporal Daniel J. Sheehan was struck by a gas bomb and
taken prisoner by the Germans.[5] Two men in the 26th Photographic Unit
were seriously wounded at Chateau-Thierry.[6] Others had more narrow
escapes than they cared to recall; Larry Darmour returned from the front
holding a camera pitted by machine-gun bullets.[7] But the dire prophecies

---

[1]Ibid.   [2]Ibid., p. 70, and Brownlow, The War, p. 128.

[3]Thiesen, "The Photographer In The World War," p. 6.   [4]Ibid.

[5]Croy, "Handing It Down to Posterity," p. 70.

[6]Memo from Captain William E. Moore, AEF Photographic Section,
to Major A.L. James, Chief Press Officer, Paris, 2 August 1918, in
"Correspondence of Signal Corps Laboratory," Box no. 6188, Records of
AEF General H.Q.

[7]Thiesen, "The Photographer In The World War," p. 4.

of Louis Brown[1] were not fulfilled, and most of the cameramen came
through the war unscathed--in body if not in mind. The psychological
effect was more difficult to erase; even in the 1930s, war experiences
seemed vivid:

> Though fifteen years have passed, recalling the episodes
> of the war brings a sombre expression to their eyes. Memories
> of the sizzling gas shell and its yellowish-white smoke, of the
> screaming flight and thump of large shells, the menacing whine
> of the lighter shell, of jumping from one "fox hole" to another
> with a large camera have left a stamp on the war cameramen.[2]

The allusion to "a large camera" was a pointed one; many photographers found that the size of their equipment limited their movements.
"When you're packing a motion picture camera across a chewed-up terrain
you're just about as busy as a one-armed man carrying a trunk up a back
stairs," wrote Croy.[3] Ernest Schoedsack _was_ given a trunk, and wished
he could exchange his Bell and Howell for a lighter camera.

The Debrie was generally regarded as the best for field work; it
was robust and light enough to move around, although the operator generally needed a tripod to obtain steady shots.[4] However, the Debries
were in short supply; the Signal Corps sent other cameras, but many were
unsuitable. In April 1918, Pershing complained about the latest deliv-
ery: the five Pathé cameras with outside magazines were "useless for
field work" and the single Debrie arrived without a tripod. "Equip all

[1]See supra, pp. 209-10.

[2]Thiesen, "The Photographer In the World War," p. 4.

[3]Croy, "Handing It Down to Posterity," p. 71.

[4]For a comparison of the hand-cranked cameras, such as the
Debrie, which required a tripod, and the Aeroscope, powered by compressed
air and held stable by a gyroscope, see supra, pp. 132-7.

photographic field units in future with 400 foot inside magazine field type motion picture cameras such as DeBrie [sic], Gillon, Pathé or Moy-Schustich," he cabled.[1] He also wanted every operator to have two cameras in case one was damaged.

In his proposal for the reorganization of the Photographic Section, Edgar Hatrick said each operator should be equipped with two light field cameras, such as the Debrie, and two tripods.[2] Since the Debries were in short supply, he recommended the manufacture of a camera similar to that used by operators for the Hearst-Pathé News; they could be made quickly and cheaply by a Chicago manufacturer named Schustek.[3] Hatrick reported that only two Signal Corps cameramen in France had serviceable Debries; the new cameras sent from the United States were unsuitable because they had outside magazines:

> . . . A few days ago, eighteen men arrived from the States, six of this contingent being motion picture operators. All of these operators were equipped with Pathé professional cameras which are very poor for field work. They could be used for covering a review of some other set event, but it would be almost impossible to use them at the front as they are too heavy and very unwieldy on account of the magazines being on the outside. The tripods that these men had were also impractical on account of their weight. The Debrie tripod is about the best tripod for this work, and I understand that some of these are being made.[4]

---

[1]Cable from Pershing to Chief Signal Officer, 14 April 1918, in AEF records, "Correspondence of the Chief Signal Officer, 1917-1919," Box no. 7.

[2]Hatrick, "Memoranda on the gathering of Motion Pictures," May 1918, in "Correspondence of Signal Corps Laboratory," Box no. 6188.

[3]Ibid. Schustek may have been another spelling for the Schustich of the Moy-Schustich camera.

[4]Ibid. Here, Hatrick may be referring to the same incident mentioned by Pershing in his cable to the Chief Signal Officer on 14 April 1918. See supra, p. 209.

In July 1918, the Signal Corps was considering how to modify the
Universal camera for use in France. The wet weather was taking its toll
of wooden cameras: the wood warped and split, the doors jammed, and the
magazines swelled. The idea was to use aluminum for the camera body and
magazines; the weight would be reduced and the camera could survive rough
use.[1] But there is no evidence in Signal Corps records that the idea was
pursued.

To handle the volume of film from the front, the Signal Corps
expanded its laboratory facilities. At first, it had been expected that
most of the processing would be done near the front line in mobile units.
A typical unit was a truck, with developing equipment, a darkroom and,
on the roof, a water tank which was refilled from village wells and
roadside pools with a hand pump. These mobile units were valuable when
pictures were needed quickly. A dispatch rider would deliver the plates
to the truck, and then rush the finished prints back to the front line;
Croy estimated that a print could be ready 15 minutes after the picture
was taken.[2] This method was important for intelligence and reconnaissance work. Photos taken from the air or by cameras with long-focus
lenses helped artillery officers to direct their fire; during an advance,
aerial photos were laid out on the ground to form a mosaic map.

Although motion pictures had a military value, they were not
normally needed as quickly, so most of the processing was done in Paris.
In February 1918, the Signal Corps laboratory was transferred from St.

---

[1]Intra-office memo from Lieutenant S.G. Boernstein to Lieutenant
J.M. Dawson, 4 June 1918, in "Correspondence of the Office of the Chief
Signal Officer," Box no. 1378.

[2]Croy, "Handing It Down to Posterity," p. 70.

Ouen to the Pathé chateau at Vincennes, where its equipment and cutting rooms occupied the fourth floor.[1] It was here that the first of several stages of censorship took place. Army censors scrutinized footage to ensure that it contained nothing that could be of value to the enemy. The film was dispatched from Paris to the War College in Washington, where other censors decided what could be released for public exhibition. When the Committee on Public Information took over the distribution of Signal Corps film from the Red Cross in March 1918, it too served as a censor. The film therefore had to pass three censors before it could be seen by the American people.

Sometimes, there was a fourth censor. The American army had an agreement with the French under which each could censor motion and still pictures shot in its sector of the front; the American censor could scrutinize film of American troops shot by a French cameraman, and the French censor had to approve Signal Corps film of French soldiers. The American and French censors met every Wednesday and Saturday at the Maison de la Presse in Paris to view the material.[2] There was a similar agreement with the British censor in Paris, Captain B.W. Kenney.[3]

These arrangements were designed to remedy a chaotic system of film release among the Allies. Pershing and his staff realized that it was impractical, and impolitic, to try to prevent the cameramen of the

[1]Bauer, Signal Corps Films, p. 1.

[2]Memo from Lieutenant (later Captain) Joe T. Marshall, Assistant Press Officer in charge of photographic censorship, 1 September 1917, in "Correspondence of Signal Corps Laboratory," Box no. 6187.

[3]Memo from Francis C. Wickes, Assistant Press Officer, Paris, 13 September 1917, in ibid., Box no. 6188.

other Allied armies from filming the American Expeditionary Force. As Pershing's press officer, Major Frederick Palmer, told the Chief of Censorship Division in Washington:

> . . . As long as our Army is scattered all over France, and French photographers have the freedom to move about France, they will continue to take photographs of American soldiers and American subjects. Once our censorship stops these photographs, we shall of course find ourselves in conflict with the French authorities and with the French official war photographers who will maintain their rights to photograph in the regions of France which are not in the zone of advance.[1]

Palmer recommended that the American and French postal services collaborate to prevent unauthorized material from reaching the United States.[2] But he admitted that his staff were powerless to prevent films and stills from leaving the country. "We have no control," he wrote, "over the censorship of French mails, which may carry photographs to America; and we have likewise no control over passengers going to America on French steamers and even, as far as I know, over those going on American steamers."[3]

In September 1917, the War Department cabled Pershing that unofficial photographs of the American forces were reaching the United States; he was asked to ensure that only Signal Corps cameramen took still and motion pictures, and that they should not be released in France, but sent to Washington.[4] Pershing replied that he had authority to

---

[1]Letter from Palmer to the Chief of the Censorship Division, Washington, D.C., 1 December 1917, in ibid., Box no. 6187.

[2]Ibid.

[3]Memo from Palmer to the Chief of Intelligence, Washington, 7 November 1917, in ibid., Box no. 6188.

[4]Cable from War Department to Pershing, 13 September 1917, in ibid., Box no. 6187.

release material to the other Allies for propaganda purposes; it would be a mistake, he said, to send the material to Washington because by the time it reached the Allies it would be so outdated that its publicity value would have been lost.[1] The War Department agreed,[2] and the American censors in Paris distributed some film to French and British newsreel companies. But Palmer refused to allow cameramen from these companies to film American units at the front. In July 1917, the director of the French Eclair Journal had requested a general permit for his operators, telling Palmer that, "Tout ce qui touche à votre pays et à vos soldats intéressant au plus haut degré l'opinion publique française."[3] Palmer refused the request, telling the company that only official American and French photographers would be allowed to work in the AEF's sector.[4] In December 1917, the rule was relaxed and Pershing was allowed to accredit civilian cameramen, but it appears that few permits were issued.[5]

The general censorship rules were similar to those adopted by

---

[1]Cable from Pershing to War Department, 11 October 1917, in ibid., Box no. 6187.

[2]Cable from War Department to Pershing, 19 October 1917, in ibid., Box no. 6187.

[3]"Everything concerning your country and your soldiers of the greatest interest to French public opinion." Letter from director of Eclair Journal to Palmer, 19 July 1917, in ibid., Box no. 6187.

[4]Letter from Palmer to director of Eclair Journal, 24 July 1917, in ibid., Box no. 6187.

[5]Report by Secretary of War to House of Representatives, 6 July 1918, in "Correspondence of the Office of the Chief Signal Officer, Box no. 18.

the other Allies:[1] no place names should be used, no units identified,
no new weapons shown, and American casualties should not be revealed.
But the censorship had a political as well as a military purpose. The
United States wanted to field an independent army, and rejected requests
from the other Allies to amalgamate American units with their forces.
While the strength of the American Expeditionary Force was being built
up, the War Department and Pershing believed that speculation about the
deployment of the troops would be dangerously premature. Palmer sent
word to his staff that ". . . no mention is to be made of the artillery
and infantry going into battle, and no article is to pass which urges
American troops be sent into battle soon."[2]

The regular reports of the American photographic censors in
Paris[3] indicate that only a small proportion of the film shot was not
passed and sent on to Washington; from January to May 1918, 712 scenes
were passed and only nine held--three marching scenes in Neufchateau, a
street scene in a French village, camouflaged guns, three scenes showing
the 1st Division and a shot of the 26th Division Headquarters.[4] The 712
scenes--a total of 21,360 feet--were shipped to the War College; some
material was also released to the British, French and Italian authorities

[1]For the British rules on photographic censorship, see supra,
p. 96-7.

[2]Quoted by Assistant Press Officer Francis Wickes in memo to
American censors, 13 September 1917, in "Correspondence of Signal Corps
Laboratory," Box no. 6188.

[3]These were compiled by Lieutenant (later promoted to Captain)
Joe T. Marshall, the Assistant Press Officer in charge of photographic
censorship in Paris. Copies are in the correspondence files of the Signal Corps Laboratory.

[4]Report by Marshall in "Correspondence of Signal Corps Laboratory," Box no. 6187.

for use in newsreels and other films. By this time, many of the Signal
Corps cameramen knew what they had to do to satisfy the censor; they were
working for the army, not for a commercial company, so there was little
point in causing trouble by filming a prohibited subject. Only part of
the material received by the War College was released to the CPI; most
was kept to provide a historical record of the war. One of the few
groups privileged to view this footage were members of the United States
Congress, for whose exclusive use two motion picture projectors were in-
stalled--one in a committee room of the House of Representatives and the
other in a room adjoining the Senate Chamber.[1]

To many Americans, the Bolshevik Revolution in October 1917 was
merely a sideshow to the main event in Europe. Russia was a long way
away, news travelled slowly, and few Americans knew much about the issues
and personalities involved. Donald Thompson was one of the few American
cameramen to return with usable footage; it was released in December
1917 under the title The German Curse in Russia.[2] Another was Lieutenant Norton C. Travis, who travelled to Russia as a member of an American
Red Cross mission. In Petrograd, he filmed the customs house under fire
and the seizure of a factory by its workers. He told the New York Tribune
". . . that he could have ground away all day at scenes of the populace
looting stores, factories and residences."[3] From Petrograd, he went to
Minsk where he toured the hospitals. The front line was only 42 miles

---

[1]Croy, How Motion Pictures Are Made, pp. 265-66.

[2]See supra, pp. 128-30.

[3]Quoted in "Tragedy and Comedy in Making Pictures of the Russian
Chaos," Current Opinion, February 1918, p. 106.

from the city, and Travis spent 18 days in the trenches, shooting some
75,000 feet of film. He told the magazine Current Opinion of his per-
ilous journey to the front line:

> As we approached our objective the roar of artillery became
> louder; shells burst about us, constant rifle fire sounded like
> the popping of fire-crackers amid the greater din, and from our
> shelter on the hill we looked down upon trench-gashed and wire-
> enmeshed fields, swept by searching lights, and that stretched
> away for a thousand miles, the honey-combed, battle-scarred
> ground presenting the appearance of the bed of a glacier.
>
> In the dark of four o'clock in the morning we crawled on
> our hands and knees down the zigzag of the parallel to the
> trenches, two hundred feet from the first-line enemy trench.
> We were very quiet. The least clash of metal, the least unus-
> ual sound would, we knew, be heard by the enemy's sensitive
> listening instruments in the ground, and would bring on us,
> from artillery stationed a mile and a half in the rear, an
> immediate rain of shells.[1]

Overhead, said Travis, aircraft were dropping bombs while gunners
on the ground tried to shoot them down. Gradually, he became accustomed
to the sights and sounds of warfare and, in his words, ". . . stood
around in the rear of the trench amid hurtling shells and whistling
bullets as unconcernedly as did the rest."[2] Travis said that about half
the German shells did not explode on impact, and the unexploded shells
in the ground were a constant danger. He thought that filming in the
rear was more dangerous than working in a forward trench, because most
of the shell fire was directed towards the area immediately behind the
lines. "I never could inure myself to that awful sound--the shriek of a
shell travelling through the air," he said. "It always made my blood
curdle and turn cold. Then, bang! Oh, the relief of that explosion
after the horror of suspense!"[3]

---

[1] Ibid., p. 107.   [2] Ibid.   [3] Ibid.

Travis, like Thompson, filmed the Women's Death Regiment on the front line near Minsk. He reported that there were 2,500 women aged between 15 and 30; the corporals and sergeants were women, but they were commanded by men. Travis described them as "of sturdy Slav physique and . . . accustomed to the work of men in the fields."[1] The most horrifying incident he filmed followed a Russian attack. Red Cross workers from both sides went out to pick up the dead and tend the wounded. Said Travis: "The Germans snatched sheets from the stretchers they bore, disclosing machine-guns, and opened fire on doctors, nurses and orderlies at their work of mercy, mowing down women and men alike."[2] Travis gloomily concluded that after this episode, both sides fired on the Red Cross.

Travis returned to New York with 120,000 feet of negative; Motion Picture News said the film would be edited and released by the Red Cross.[3] Travis had been allowed to move fairly freely in Russia, and made a 6,000-mile trip on the trans-Siberian railroad. He was one of the last foreign cameramen to enjoy such privileges. After the October Revolution, American photographers and correspondents were not welcome in Bolshevik Russia. The new government withdrew from the war in December, and under the terms of the Treaty of Brest-Litovsk, the Germans occupied the Ukraine. Representatives of the Committee on Public Information found that their propaganda material got no further than the Russian border; facing Bolshevik hostility, they packed up and left

[1]Ibid., pp. 106-07.   [2]Ibid., p. 107.

[3]"Travis Returns with Red Cross Films," Motion Picture News, 2 February 1918, p. 716.

Petrograd and Moscow for Archangel and Vladivostok.[1] It was a time of

famine and disorder throughout Russia; in Omsk, Admiral Alexander Kol-

chak, supported by Japanese forces and former Czech prisoners of war,

had established a White government and was attacking the Red armies. An

Allied Expeditionary Force was sent to help Kolchak, and American troops

landed at Vladivostok in the fall of 1918. With them were five Signal

Corps photographers.

According to one of the two motion-picture cameramen in the

party, Phil Tannura, the work was pretty routine. "In Vladivostok we

shot nothing but parades--diplomats meeting with the Chinese generals

and admirals," he told Kevin Brownlow.[2] With the head of the photo-

graphic unit, Captain Howard Price Kingsmore,[3] he travelled west on a

Red Cross train to the Ural Mountains where the Czechs were fighting the

Red Army. He filmed political prisoners in Omsk, and came away convinced

that the revolution had been necessary. Tannura was in Russia for a lit-

tle over a year, managing to obtain his release by training another man

to do his work.[4]

---

[1]Brownlow, The War, p. 164.

[2]Quoted in ibid., p. 167. Tannura's comment is confirmed by the
footage of the Allied operations in Vladivostok released by the Committee
on Public Information. Official War Review no. 27 (in National Archives
--see Appendix) showed street scenes, the harbor where American troops
are guarding war materials, wrecks of Russian warships, municipal officials, the staff of the U.S. Consulate and American, Russian, Czech,
Japanese and Italian military officers.

[3]Who apparently had served with the Signal Corps Photographic
Section in France. His name is mentioned in a cable from Pershing to
the Chief Signal Officer, 14 April 1918. See supra, p. 209.

[4]Brownlow, The War, p. 164.

The other motion-picture man, Lieutenant L. William O'Connell,
was detailed to film Kolchak's activities at Khabarovsk, north of Vladivostok. He travelled on the trans-Siberian railroad, and for a time
rode on the engine with the driver and fireman. In Khabarovsk, he saw
a train packed with refugees, all of them hungry and many suffering from
typhus. No village would accept them, so the train went on to Vladivostok, with many dying on the journey.[1] Another Signal Corps camera-
man--the Russian-born Carl von Hoffman[2]--filmed Kolchak's unsuccessful
attack on the Bolshevik Army; all but 2,500 feet of his film was destroyed during Red attacks.[3]

While the film record of America's part in World War I was
largely the work of Signal Corps cameramen, other branches of the military also had motion picture and stills photographers. The United States
Navy appointed official photographers, and, soon after the country went
to war, the Marine Corps publicity bureau enlisted Leon H. Caverly, and
made him a Quartermaster Sergeant in the Reserve Corps.[4] In civilian
life, Caverly had worked for the Mutual Weekly as a South American correspondent, and for Jack Cohn at the Universal Animated Weekly. He was
with the first regiment of Marines to leave for France, and filmed their

---

[1]Quoted in ibid., p. 167.

[2]In November 1917, a malicious rumor claimed that Hoffman had
been interned at Fort Leavenworth, Kansas, because he was suspected of
enemy sympathies. However, Variety reported on 7 December 1917 that he
had been commissioned as a first lieutenant in the Signal Corps (p. 49).

[3]Moving Picture World, 31 July 1920, p. 899.

[4]Lieutenant Charles P. Cushing, "What Movies Mean to the Marines,"
Picture-Play Magazine, September 1917, p. 56.

embarkation and arrival.[1] With an assistant, stills photographer Private Lester Woodward, he shot scenes at training camps and in the war zone, but found that bad light and rain made photography difficult.[2] The Marine Corps also made recruiting and training films in the United States.

The work of the Signal Corps photographers did not end with Armistice Day. The War Department wanted a record of the work of the American forces in the liberated and occupied areas; divisions sent into Germany were accompanied by photographers, who filmed conditions in the country, welfare and medical work and the usual quota of military parades. Wherever they went, wrote Earl Thiesen, they were known as the "Mary Pickfords,"[3] and, with the German economy in ruins, they would barter with chocolate, cigarettes and soap. Harris Thorpe carried about two dozen bars of soap; according to Thiesen,

> . . . He would walk into a store and grin, then nonchalantly flop a cake of soap on the counter. The German tradesman's eyes would bulge and he would yell something to the living quarters in the rear. A rapid shuffle of feet announced his chattering frau and a number of his offspring. They would carefully pick up the soap and rub it, smell it, pass it around, and when thoroughly convinced it was soap, the bargaining began. Harry [sic] Thorpe lived on the best of the land.[4]

Although America was in the war for less than two years, the amount of footage shot by Signal Corps cameramen was phenomenal--more

---

[1]Charles Carter, "Making American History," _Picture-Play Magazine_, November 1917, p. 31.

[2]See Caverly's letter to Jack Cohn, quoted supra, p. 219-20.

[3]Thiesen, "The Photographer In The World War," p. 6. Jack Painter--one of the Signal Corps veterans interviewed by Kevin Brownlow --says another reason for the nickname was the 'P' (for photographer) armband which the cameraman often wore.

[4]Ibid.

than either the French or the British shot throughout the whole war.
In the month of the Armistice, when the Photographic Section reached its
maximum output, over 117,000 feet--22 miles--of negative was made.[1] American cameramen shot almost 600,000 feet in Europe, while 277,000 was shot
in the United States.[2] Croy estimates that only about 15 per cent was
released for public exhibition; the rest was used for intelligence, reconnaissance and as a historical record.[3] Most of the films are now in
the National Archives in Washington, D.C.; they cover all aspects of the
draft and the mobilization of the American forces, their arrival and
training in France, and the engagements in which they took part such as
the battles at Chateau-Thierry, the Argonne at St. Mihiel; the divisional
histories alone occupy 121 reels.[4]

* * * * *

---

[1]Croy, "Handing It Down to Posterity," p. 132.

[2]Bauer, Signal Corps Films, p. 1.

[3]Croy, "Handing It Down to Posterity," p. 132.

[4]Bauer, Signal Corps Films, p. 8.

CHAPTER 10

AMERICA'S FIRST PROPAGANDA MINISTRY

I have found most success in using patriotic propaganda in
the news weekly, ... The way I generally do is to open up
with some big thrill. This gathers your audience into your
lap as it were. Carry them along (making sure you don't give
the thrill too soon or else you will slip the climax) and then
follow up by some weaker stuff. Arrange your magazine so that
it ends with a wallop.

Samuel L. Rothapfel, writing in <u>Motion Picture News</u>.[1]

If anyone could spice up a piece of dull war footage (without

overplaying it), it was Rothapfel. The manager of New York's Rialto

and Rivoli theaters, Rothapfel--Roxy to his many friends and admirers--

had established a deserved reputation as a businessman and exhibitor.

He was also a natural showman--and he needed that talent for some of

the material he was receiving in 1918.[2]

Rothapfel was writing about the <u>Official War Review</u>, a weekly

newsreel distributed by Pathé for the Committee on Public Information.

---

[1]Samuel L. Rothapfel, "Rothapfel Gives Some Hints on Weeklies,"
<u>Motion Picture News</u>, 24 August 1918, p. 1220.

[2]For an examination of the life and work of Rothapfel, see
Ben Hall, <u>The Best Remaining Seats: The Story of the Golden Age of
the Movie Palace</u> (New York: Clarkson N. Potter, 1961), pp. 26-30,
54-5, 80-88, 256-8. Rothapfel was a frequent contributor to the
motion picture magazines, and his articles on the use of music, scenery and special effects provide useful insights to the art of exhibition. See the <u>Motion Picture News</u> article in footnote 1; also,
"Dramatizing Music for the Pictures," <u>Reel Life</u>, 5 September 1914,
p. 23, and Rothapfel Tells of Advance of Weeklies," <u>Motion Picture
News</u>, 31 August 1918, p. 1374.

The Committee, which has been dubbed "America's first propaganda min-istry,"[1] was set up by President Wilson on 13 April 1917, one week after the United States entered the war. For the Official War Review, the Allies--the United States, France, Britain and Italy--contributed material shot by their military cameramen; the Committee's Division of Films censored and edited the footage into a weekly release.

The Official War Review did good business, yielding a gross income of $334,622 for its 31 issues.[2] Rothapfel urged every exhibitor to subscribe to it, not merely for patriotic reasons, but because it "will create many patrons."[3] A full-page advertisement by the Committee and Pathé in September 1918 portrayed a soldier in a foxhole, read letter from home, and asked somewhat rhetorically:

> What is he doing over there? That's the question that is being asked today in a million American homes. "He" is helping to make history. "He" is one of the many on whom the hope of Democracy rests. How does he live? What are his amusements? What sort of country is he in? What sort of men are those with whom the Americans are making a solid front against the foe? Every member of those million families may find those questions answered in OFFICIAL WAR REVIEW which contains the official, exclusive pictures of Great Britain, France, Italy and United States.[4]

Official, yes; exclusive, perhaps. But the moviegoer seeking an accurate account of the progress of the war, and the problems

---

[1]James R. Mock and Cedric Larson, Words That Won The War (Princeton: Princeton University Press, 1939), p. vii.

[2]The gross income from the sale and rental of films was given in the Report of the Chairman of the Committee on Public Information (Washington, D.C.: Government Printing Office, 1920). Also in ibid., p. 141, and in Creel, How We Advertised America, p. 125.

[3]"Rothapfel Tells of Advance of Weeklies," Motion Picture News, 31 August 1918, p. 1377.

[4]Advertisement, Motion Picture News, 7 September 1918, p. 1461.

confronting the American Expeditionary Force, would not find it in the Official War Review. Instead, it offered a fragmentary, and sometimes distorted, picture of the war--a collage of marching soldiers, supply trains, artillery batteries, hospitals, field kitchens, prisoners, troop reviews and visiting generals and politicians. Military setbacks were not shown; the supply problems of the AEF ignored. The official films, Terry Ramsaye wrote later, "resembled a story of the war about as a scrapbook resembles a historical novel."[1]

The CPI was charged with the dual role of propaganda and censorship--with spreading the American gospel to people at home and abroad, and with seeing that they didn't know too much (or enough to damage their morale). The Committee developed according to no set plan; it had the virtues, and the problems, of improvisation, as its historians, James R. Mock and Cedric Larson, have remarked:

> Main objectives were fixed, but two hours never passed
> without a new idea for achieving them. Bureaus were thrown
> together in an evening on the flash of someone's four o'clock
> inspiration, and on some other day might be as speedily closed
> down, merged with another office, or directed to assume
> entirely new duties.[2]

Its chairman was the Missouri-born George Creel;[3] his career in journalism had taken him from Kansas City to Denver, where he became that city's police commissioner. He was a staunch supporter of Wilson, and in 1916 defended the President's policy in a book entitled

---

[1] Ramsaye, A Million And One Nights, p. 784.

[2] Mock and Larson, Words That Won The War, p. 48.

[3] President Wilson appointed him on 13 April 1917--the same day he created the Committee.

<u>Wilson and the Issues</u>. He was called in primarily to rectify a chaotic system of government news releases, which had angered journalists and administration officials alike. But the work of the Committee soon grew, and began to move into the less restricted field of opinion management.

The Committee's <u>Official Bulletin</u>, containing government announcements and censored news items, was distributed to public buildings. Posters in the general store and on telephone poles were designed by the Committee's artists. Clergymen read Committee sermons, and school teachers explained the war from Committee pamphlets. Movie programs began with a Committee film encouraging the audience to conserve coal or buy savings stamps; in the interval, they would hear a pitch from one of the Committee's Four Minute Men, a national group of volunteer speakers who talked for exactly that length of time in support of the Red Cross, Liberty Loan or another patriotic venture.

Creel said he did not believe in formal censorship; it should, he said, be voluntary and self-imposed. Every newspaper in the United States received a card headed "What the Government Asks of the Press." It requested that no information be printed about troop movements, ship sailings, convoys, the location of bases and minefields, the number of soldiers sent to France, shipbuilding and munitions production, and the testing of new weapons.[1]

The film industry was asked to observe similar restrictions, and the Navy Secretary, Josephus M. Daniels, wrote to the newsreel

[1]Harvey A. DeWeerd, <u>President Wilson Fights His War: World War One and the American Intervention</u> (New York: Macmillan, 1968), p. 244.

companies to seek their cooperation.[1] "Voluntary" guidelines for

motion picture and stills photographers were outlined by the CPI in a

four-page pamphlet, published in August 1917.[2] It listed six categories

of pictures that should not be taken or distributed without official

sanction:

1) Army fortifications, magazines, wireless plants, navy yards,
   munitions factories, newly installed military equipment,
   ports of embarkation and land defenses in the United States.

2) The construction and testing of new military weapons and
   equipment; examples included aeroplane and submarine
   instruments, sighting mechanisms, range-finders and communications devices.

3) Troop movements that reveal the deployment of forces, special duties or new military formations.

4) The location of minefields and the warships of the American
   or an Allied navy.

5) Scenes that "tend to misrepresent or to arouse prejudice
   against friendly nations."

6) Scenes from Allied countries that have not been passed by
   the censors of those nations.

The fifth and sixth categories were broad enough to give the

Committee considerable leeway in deciding what could be exhibited.

And a rider to the list apparently gave the Committee carte-blanche to

censor anything it chose:

> Whether or not specifically prohibited by these rulings,
> when pictures are plainly of a character that require official
> consideration, representatives of motion-picture companies and
> distributing agencies, exhibitors, illustrative news bureaus,

---

[1]See supra, p. 202.

[2]The Committee on Public Information, Information Concerning
the Making and Distribution of Pictures that show the activities of
the Army and Navy (Washington, D.C.: Government Printing Office,
1917). See also "Government Rules for Film Men During the War,"
Motion Picture News, 1 September 1917, p. 1436.

editors, and others are themselves expected to withhold publication.[1]

Who was to decide what required "official consideration?" The
Committee's Division of Films. It was this gray area--the unspecified
pictures that "plainly . . . require official consideration"--that was
to be the source of several disputes with film companies, notably
Universal in the case of its film on airplane production, The Yanks
Are Coming.[2]

The pamphlet also laid out the procedure for obtaining permits
to film the work of the Army, Navy and other government departments,
and munitions production. The Committee was to be the clearing-house
for the applications, referring them to the relevant agency. Appli-
cants should state specifically what they wanted to film, and the use
they intended to make of the footage. All film, stills and drawings
should be submitted to the Committee for approval. In the case of
film, three prints were required: one would be kept as a record by
the military or government agency, and one by the Committee, while
the third would be returned to the company, bearing the imprint
"Passed by the Committee on Public Information, Washington."[3]

The CPI soon found that it was difficult to enforce these
rules. The film companies resented them, while the army and navy and
government departments were often willing to grant permits to cameramen

[1]CPI, Information Concerning the Making and Distribution of
Pictures, p. 4.

[2]See infra, pp. 272-3.

[3]CPI, Information Concerning the Making and Distribution of
Pictures, pp. 4-5.

without bothering to tell the CPI. The predictable result was bureau-cratic confusion, with permits issued and denied according to no set formula. Cameramen and their editors preferred to seek permits directly from the military authorities, rather than routing their applications through the CPI. In February 1918, the Universal _Animated Weekly_ sent a telegram to the Signal Corps headquarters in Washington, asking for permission to film the manufacture of airplanes at the Curtiss Company in Buffalo, New York. Universal stressed its patriotic motives; it believed the subject would be "of incalculable value as aid towards recruiting in present crisis."[1] Lieutenant Colonel George O. Squier wasn't impressed by Universal's public spiritedness; he turned down the request, replying that "under pres-ent conditions, it appears inadvisable to permit motion pictures being made of Government airplanes in course of manufacture."[2]

But several months earlier, the Commanding Officer of the army base at Fort Wood, New York, had apparently allowed filming by the Community Motion Picture Bureau of Boston. The CPI protested to the Signal Corps; the films, it claimed, included "matter of a technical and military nature which the Committee does not deem to be suited for publication."[3] In particular, the CPI objected to close-ups of technical apparatus and Signal Corps instruments and some troop

[1] Telegram from Universal _Animated Weekly_ to Lieutenant Colonel George O. Squier, 6 February 1918, in "Correspondence of the Office of the Chief Signal Officer," Box no. 18.

[2] Telegram from Squier to the Universal _Animated Weekly_, 6 Feb-ruary 1918, in ibid., Box no. 18.

[3] Memo from the Office of the Chief Signal Officer to the Com-manding Officer, Fort Wood, New York, 8 November 1917, in ibid., Box no.18.

244

scenes. Major Roy H. Coles of the Signal Corps passed on the complaint to Fort Wood, telling the Commanding Officer that the Committee wanted to know under what authority the film had been made, and whether any restrictions on subject-matter had been imposed.[1]

Before the American Expeditionary Force embarked for Europe, interest in the United States centered on the army camps where drafted and enlisted men were training. The film companies believed that scenes of the soldiers on parade, in training and at leisure would be a popular item for the newsreels. "Recognizing that the nation is interested heart and soul in the prosecution of this war," Motion Picture News reported, "the Gaumont Company is bending every effort to satisfy the country's legitimate demand for pictorial news of the conflict that is already upon us."[2] For its Mutual Weekly, Gaumont promised scenes of recruiting, of soldiers and sailors in camp and of submarine chasers--scenes obtained "despite the rigorous military and naval censorship now exercised over news cameramen."[3] Mutual Weekly No. 118 featured the physical examination of Navy recruits, the Navy's first woman yeoman, and an airplane carrying a motorcycle; it was a reel "that will appeal to all red-blooded Americans."[4] In June 1917, a one-reel film on the training of a Navy recruit, Manning Our Navy, was released by Mutual.[5] Most of these short features had a distinctly

[1]Ibid.

[2]"Gaumont Company Is Covering War in Its Single Reels," Motion Picture News, 28 April 1917, p. 2665.

[3]Ibid. [4]Review, Motion Picture News, 28 April 1917, p. 2670.

[5]Motion Picture News, 9 June 1917, p. 3626.

patriotic flavor. <u>Our Fighting Forces</u>, a two-reel Pathé film released
in May 1917, showed recruiting, troops in training and warships; it
was "calculated to stir any audience to the grand climax when an
inspiring vision of Liberty, in the symbolic colors of the Union, calls
upon the sons and daughters of America all to do their bit."[1]

In September 1917, the director of the CPI's Division of
Pictures, Kendall Banning, allowed cameramen from the <u>Hearst-Pathé News</u>
to film soldiers in training at military camps throughout the country.
A report in <u>Motion Picture News</u> indicated how the official censorship
would take place: "As rapidly as the pictures are taken they will be
forwarded to Washington to be passed by the official censors, after
which they will be shown each week in the releases of the <u>Hearst-Pathé
News</u>."[2] The newsreel company had learned from bitter experience that
the censorship rules were not to be flouted with ease. In June,
<u>Hearst-Pathé</u> footage of American troops embarking for France had been
held by the authorities because it was feared it contained information
useful to the Germans.[3] It was returned in July and shown in the <u>Hearst-
Pathé News</u>, but the delay deprived it of its impact; Universal was
ready with film showing General Pershing's arrival in France and his
reception in Boulogne and Paris.[4]

Confusion over the permit system persisted well into 1918. In
June of that year, the U.S. House of Representatives called for a report

---

[1] "Appropriate War 'Specialities' from Pathé--Fine Scenics,"
<u>Motion Picture News</u>, 2 June 1917, p. 3434.

[2] "Life in Cantonments in Hearst-Pathé News," <u>Motion Picture
News</u>, 8 September 1917, p. 1615.

[3] <u>Motion Picture News</u>, 14 July 1917, p. 236. [4] Ibid., p. 226.

on the photographic activities of the Signal Corps from the Secretary
of War.[1] The Representatives wanted to know if Signal Corps cameramen
were filming war preparations in the United States, such as training,
munitions and aircraft production, and if any permits had been granted
to civilian cameramen. The reply by Newton D. Baker was prepared by
the CPI chairman, George Creel, and the Chief Signal Officer, General
George O. Squier; it indicated that the rules for permits were not too
hard and fast:

> . . . With the exception of certain camps where secret tests
> are being made, cantonments [temporary barracks] have been
> free to photographers from the beginning of the war. With
> respect to ordnance and airplane production, the military
> authorities have not deemed it wise to expose secrets to
> other than those in uniform and while permits have been
> given in some cases, the general policy has been to exclude
> private photographers from factories where ordnance and
> airplanes are being made.[2]

Some film producers preferred to rely on personal contacts
rather than the official channels. Such a character was Robert R.
Reynolds, a retired cavalry captain described in the trade press as
"an amalgamation of soldier, author, journalist and outdoor sportsman
who is familiar with the producing end of the motion picture business."[3]
He was one of the founders of a new company, the Cinema War News
Syndicate of New York, that tried to cash in on public interest by
launching the American War News Weekly, a newsreel devoted entirely to

---

[1] H. Res. 402, 65th Cong., 2d sess., 29 June 1918.

[2] Report by Secretary of War to House of Representatives,
6 July 1918, in "Correspondence of the Office of the Chief Signal
Office," Box no. 18.

[3] "Independent Producer to Put Out American War News Weekly,"
Motion Picture News, 21 April 1917, p. 2498.

America's part in the war.[1] A week after the United States entered the
war, it was reported that Reynolds was in Washington, obtaining credentials from government officials. "It is believed," said the Exhibitors
Trade Review, "that Capt. Reynolds' wide acquaintanceship in both
branches of the service will add materially in his getting the
pictures the public want to see."[2]

There's no evidence that Reynolds was able to obtain privileges
that were denied to other companies. The first edition of the American
War News Weekly was released in May 1917 with the extravagant publicity
that had become the industry's hallmark. Reynolds, exhibitors were
told, had deployed his forces throughout the United States and was
ready to bring audiences film that was "hot from the barrels of the
foremost rifles."[3] American troops weren't doing any fighting at
that time, so Reynolds had to be content with more routine material;
the first edition featured the launching of a submarine at Portsmouth,
Virginia, and a women's war farm on Long Island.[4] Indeed, the American
War News Weekly never got to Europe.

Reynolds tried to interest exhibitors by giving the newsreel a
military flavor; he described himself as its chief of staff, and his
men were billed as "cameraspondents"--an ugly contraction that lasted
about as long as the newsreel itself. Reynolds liked to pose for

[1]This newsreel provides a good example of how film sequences
were staged. See supra, p. 151-2.

[2]Exhibitors Trade Review, 14 April 1917, p. 1302.

[3]Advertisement, Exhibitors Trade Review, 14 April 1917, p. 1294.

[4]Review, Motion Picture News, 12 May 1917, p. 2963.

pictures in full dress uniform;[1] theater managers were offered "life-size paintings of your special war correspondent for lobby display and autographed photographs for distribution to your patrons . . ."[2] He was also much given to rhetorical flourishes. The eighth edition[3] opens with Reynolds at his desk, talking on the telephone and tapping out a Morse Code message; "Captain Reynolds despatches his weekly newsletter from Washington, D.C.," says the title. He can't have had much to say: America's contribution to the war was represented by a reunion of Confederate veterans, the dedication of a hall at American University in Washington, a staged operation by the New York Harbor Police,[4] the donation of a California ranch for animal welfare, Mayor Curley of Boston and city officials watching the departure of Massachusetts' "Fighting Ninth" for Europe, and a five-year-old in uniform raising money for charity with the aid of "Rex, the only dog in the world that can drive an automobile." Hard-hitting stuff. Other editions showed scenes from the training camps: No. 19,[5] for example, featured artillery practice at Fort Oglethorpe, Georgia, and a tour of the camp, as well as a champion Girl Scout and some of the 10,000 dogs that were being taught, not to drive automobiles, but to help the Red Cross. The American War News Weekly, despite its pretentious publicity, offered nothing new, and folded in a few months.

_____

[1]See Exhibitors Trade Review, 14 April 1917, p. 1302.

[2]Ibid., p. 1268.

[3]In the collection of John E. Allen (see Appendix).

[4]For an analysis of this sequence, see supra, p. 151-2.

[5]In the Library of Congress collection (see Appendix).

The CPI took no action to restrain Reynolds; he had no military secrets to divulge on the screen. Indeed, the granting of permits and the censorship of footage was only part of the Committee's film work. George Creel was conscious of the propaganda value of film, and, although a newspaperman by training, had long been interested in the medium. Indeed, he even appeared in an unmemorable low-budget Western. In 1919, when he was editor of the Rocky Mountain News in Denver, he rode out to watch the shooting of the Heart of a Cowboy. The producer, "Bronco" Billy Anderson, had a problem--his chief villain had fallen ill. "Mr. Creel was seized upon as a substitute, and was soon posing before the camera as Steve Peters, cattle rustler and all-around badman."[1] It was not an auspicious debut: Creel "was very villainous and never was asked to pose again, because he 'took the play' away from the star."[2] Creel liked to show the one-reel film to friends; a screening for the White House staff was held in July 1918.

In 1913, when Creel was an editorial writer in Denver, he wrote the scenario for a serious film on the city's crime problems, Saved by the Juvenile Court. The producer who had enlisted Creel decided it was wiser to leave Colorado than to pay the debts he had accumulated there, so the project foundered. But when Creel became the city's police commissioner, he decided to use the film and it was

[1] Washington Herald, 19 July 1918, in "Papers of George Creel," Box no. 5, Manuscripts Division, Library of Congress, Washington, D.C.

[2] Washington Times, 19 July 1918, in "Papers of George Creel," Box no. 5.

released under the new title of <u>Denver's Underworld</u>.[1]

"At the very outset," Creel wrote in his account of the work of the CPI, "it was obvious that the motion picture had to be placed on the same plane of importance as the written word."[2] In July 1917, Creel met the leaders of the National Association of the Motion Picture Industry (NAMPI). "At last the government and the motion picture theaters of the United States are to be linked together in what will probably be the greatest propaganda in history," <u>Motion Picture News</u> confidently predicted.[3] But while cooperating committees were established and compliments exchanged, the CPI politely but firmly resisted the patriotic offers of the film industry.

The Committee's Division of Films was set up by Presidential order on 25 September 1917,[4] with Charles S. Hart as director. He had been advertising manager at <u>Hearst's Magazine</u> at a reported $10,000 a year and came to the CPI for $3,900, having been lured away from a possible Ordnance Department commission.[5] Starting from scratch, he built up a staff of almost 50 in eight months and opened offices in New York and Washington, D.C.

[1] Ramsaye, <u>A Million And One Nights</u>, p. 611.

[2] Creel, <u>How We Advertised America</u>, p. 117.

[3] "Creel Confers with N.A.M.P.I. for Giant Film Drive," <u>Motion Picture News</u>, 21 July 1917, p. 371.

[4] From April to September 1917, the Committee's film work was handled by its Division of Pictures. Its first director was Kendall Banning, but he left after a short time to accept a commission as a major. Two volunteers--Louis B. Mack, a Chicago lawyer, and Walter Niebuhr--supervised the motion picture work until the Division of Films was established. Creel, <u>How We Advertised America</u>, pp. 118-9.

[5] Mock and Larson, <u>Words That Won The War</u>, p. 136.

Hart had no background in the film industry, a fact noted by the trade press. "With the exception of J.E. Brulatour, Chairman of the National Cinema Commission, not an important man in the industry enjoys any authoritative connection with the vast Government motion picture work," complained Moving Picture World.[1] Hart said he was chosen because, unlike some people in the industry, he had no axe to grind;[2] those who believed he was promoting Hearst's interests disagreed.

Hart found that the government film effort was in sore need of direction. Despite offers by the industry to distribute the latest releases free to the troops, the Committee granted exhibition rights for the training camps to the YMCA and the Knights of Columbus, which could not afford new films, and relied mostly on government topicals and older releases. The Committee had also given the Red Cross the sole rights to distribute footage shot by Signal Corps cameramen--an arrangement that astounded and exasperated the trade press:

> In the name of common sense, why start the Red Cross in the film business? It would be much more reasonable to ask them to operate a chian of grocery stores. Try the better plan used by each of the Allied countries--a Government Pictorial Service to sell War Pictures directly to the distributor. That plan works out with the same result, i.e., the British Pictorial Service turns over the net proceeds of its business to the War Relief Fund. The charitable organization is saved from the undignified scramble for business and

---

[1] Henry McMahon, "Uplifters Boss War Films: Secret Events Revealed Showing How and Why the Government Failed to Accept the Film Industry's Offer of Hearty Aid," Moving Picture World, 26 January 1918, p. 482.

[2] Kinematograph Weekly, 5 December 1918, p. 56, quoted in Brownlow, The War, p. 115.

devotes all its energies to succor and help.[1]

The newsreel companies, which had to go to the Red Cross to buy footage, complained of a chaotic system, with negatives unsorted and shots uncatalogued. In March 1918, Red Cross officials, headed by George Murrane, a New York banker, met CPI staff at the Committee's headquarters in Washington and agreed to hand over the distribution rights for official war film. Hart had been dismayed at the inefficient distribution of the footage which, he claimed in a telegram to Creel, had reduced its effectiveness as propaganda:

> . . . When this film is received from the Red Cross, the four editors of Pathé, Universal, Mutual and Gaumont divide the weekly supply into four packages, one for each company. They then hold a dice-throwing contest, the winner having first choice, the second highest man second selection, etc. In other words, the news weeklies do not duplicate pictures. As an instance the Red Cross recently had the first pictures showing the operation of liquid gas. This prize of the night was won by Universal which has half the circulation of Pathé. Consequently this important picture for propaganda was distributed only in a very limited way. Our present plan eliminates entirely this system and secures 100 percent distribution of all Government pictures edited by the Government.[2]

Hart's "present plan" was more ambitious than a mere takeover of the distribution rights to American war films; he wanted his division to handle all the Allied war film shown in the United States. Up to this time, agents for the Allied governments had been selling U.S. rights to their films to the highest bidder. Hart wanted to consolidate the film into a single release, the Official War Review. It would have about 1,000 feet of film each week (at the then-standard

[1]McMahon, "Uplifters Boss War Films," pp. 483-4.

[2]Telegram from Charles S. Hart to George Creel, 11 April 1918, in "Correspondence of the Division of Films" (Judicial and Fiscal Branch, National Archives, Washington, D.C.).

silent film speed of 60 feet per minute, it would run about 15 minutes). Half would be Signal Corps material, and the rest would come
from the other Allies. In April 1918, Hart wrote to Edmond Ratisbonne
of the French Pictorial Service:

> . . . It is our opinion that the Official French War Pictures
> can be shown to much better advantage through this Official War
> Review than under your present arrangement. We realize the
> importance of the financial returns you are receiving at pres-
> ent from the news weeklies, and will arrange to pay you $400 a
> week during the life of this agreement for the exclusive rights
> to the weekly French pictures in the United States. The amount
> of footage to be devoted to the French pictures under this pro-
> posed arrangement would be determined by the interest of the
> pictures. However, we will agree that a minimum of 100 feet of
> French pictures will be used in each issue.[1]

Ratisbonne agreed, as did Captain G.M.L. Baynes, who represented
the British and Italian governments. "It was the first contention of
the representatives of the British, French and Italians that the War
Review should be offered to the highest bidder," Creel wrote later,
"but the Committee on Public Information insisted that the four film-
news weeklies of the United States should be given prior consideration."[2] So the CPI made what it thought was a fair proposal: Pathé,
Universal, Mutual and Gaumont would receive the same reel every week.

Creel and Hart should have known the industry better; asking
four rival companies to distribute the same reel may have been patri-
otically sound, but it wasn't good business. The companies wanted
films that their competitors didn't have; they asked the CPI for a
weekly supply of separate material for each of them, an arrangement

---

[1] Letter from Charles S. Hart to Edmond Ratisbonne, 12 April
1918, in "Correspondence of the Division of Films."

[2] Creel, How We Advertised America, p. 123.

not unlike the dice-throwing Hart had deplored.[1] As he had noted, the newsreels did not duplicate pictures.

Creel was unhappy about the plan, because the division of the footage into four parts would reduce its impact as propaganda. However, he agreed to give the weeklies a total of 2,000 feet a week, to be divided between them (he didn't specify how they should do it). The flat rate would be $5,000--at first the CPI wanted $9,000--and each company would pay for the proportion it used.[2] Creel said that the Allied representatives felt that the price "robbed them of fair and demonstrated profits," but the CPI persuaded them to accept it.[3]

But when the contract was drawn up, only Paul Brunet, the president of Pathé, signed. The others said they would do so only under protest; one company sent letters to President Wilson and members of the cabinet, claiming not only that the films should be free of charge, but hinting at a government subsidy.[4] As _Variety_ wryly remarked, "Charles Hart . . . isn't quite certain that four concerns at present issuing news weeklies are altogether guided by patriotism in their dealings with his department."[5]

The proposal was withdrawn, and the _Official War Review_ was

---

[1]"Explanations Clear War-Films Row," _Motion Pictures News_, 13 July 1918, p. 201.

[2]Ibid., and "War Films Bureaus Confuse Industry as to Exact Duty," _Variety_, 31 May 1918, p. 37.

[3]Creel, _How We Advertised America_, p. 123.

[4]Ibid., pp. 123-4.

[5]"War Films Bureaus," _Variety_, 31 May 1918, p. 37.

offered to the highest bidder. Pathé was awarded the contract; 80 percent of the proceeds were to go to the Committee, and the company guaranteed a "showing in 25,000 theaters as a minimum."[1]

But weekly releases and longer features did not consume all the footage, so from June 1918 material was made available to the newsreel companies at the flat rate of $1 a foot. The CPI reserved the right to supervise the editing "to conform to the policies of the American government."[2] Revenue from the Official War Review and the miscellaneous sales was ploughed back into film production and distribution.

The first edition of the Official War Review was released by Pathé on 1 July 1918, and it appeared weekly until after the Armistice-- 31 issues in all. The CPI and Pathé bought full-page advertisements in the trade press to promote the newsreel, and some of the writing bordered on cheap sensationalism. President Wilson deplored the Hate-the-Hun elements of propaganda, yet Creel and Hart lent their names to advertisements like this:

> The sort of enemy we are fighting: you may see him as he is
> in OFFICIAL WAR REVIEW No. 10. Upon a German officer captured
> during the latest drive the Allies in France was discovered
> an order commanding the Hun armies to 'destroy everything.'
> In Official War Review No. 10 is shown how thoroughly this
> damnable order was followed. Scenes of wanton destruction
> and murder are shown that would shame a tribe of head-hunters.[3]

---

[1]Creel, How We Advertised America, p. 124. The deal may have been for 25,000 weekly screenings; since (on p. 125) Creel estimates that there were 12,000 motion-picture theaters in the U.S., and that the Official War Review was shown in over half of them, this seems the most likely interpretation.

[2]"War-Films Row," Motion Picture News, 13 July 1918, p. 201.

[3]Advertisement, Motion Picture News, 14 September 1918, p. 1637.

Earlier in the war, American correspondents had been instru-
mental in discounting rumors of German atrocities in Belgium.[1] But,
with the United States in the war, almost anything went. Huns and
head-hunters were not about to claim their First Amendment rights, and
the campaign of abuse and innuendo went unanswered.

The reviews in the trade press were just as virulent. Here,
Moving Picture World describes a sequence in Official War Review No. 14:

> . . . Just what kind of people the plain soldiers are in the
> ranks of the German army is a question paramount in the minds
> of all Americans at home. In this reel are shown thousands
> of Germans who have been captured by the French and are being
> marched to the rear. These pictures vividly show the low
> order of mentality of the Germans in ranks, but at that these
> prisoners appreciate their good fortune in falling into the
> hands of their enemy, for they grin and nod, and bow and
> scrape for their warm food which to them seems to be the
> treat of a lifetime.[2]

In the same reel, hundreds of Austrians captured by the Italians
are shown being fed and receiving medical aid. As British soldiers
return from the front, "the smile of victory illuminates their dirt-
streaked faces."[3] And there is "a stirring picture of a brave American
soldier who was severely wounded in holding the post and now stands
before his admiring fellow doughboys while the cross of war is pinned
upon his blouse."[4]

Prisoners of war, troops returning from the front, a medal
ceremony--these had been standard fare for the newsreels since the

[1] In a telegram to the Associated Press. See supra, pp. 110-11.

[2] "Official War Review No. 4 Is a Stirring Release," Moving
Picture World, 3 August 1918, p. 698.

[3] Ibid.   [4] Ibid.

beginning of the war. The action in this reel is confined to scenes
of artillery batteries firing on the Western and Italian fronts, a
supply train and the ruins of a French village. If the Signal Corps
cameramen were obtaining film of the fighting, it was not being
released in the United States. These titles from Pathé News No. 63,
which describe a sequence of official war film, give a fair indication
of what was regarded as war news:

. . . 1. After a hard day's work, even the horses need a bath,
and the Yankees find convenient ways of giving it to them.
2. Proud of the trophies they captured from the Huns. 3. His
French comes slow-l-y. 4. The mascots of the company.
5. Everything is kept in tip-top shape. 6. They fought in
the war's greatest battle, and all know how they fought.
General Passage decorates 104th Infantry, 26th Division.
7. General Edwards, commander of the Division, congratu-
lating the men. 8. A new honor on an old flag.[1]

In other reels, American soldiers are shown marching, eating
meals, wearing gasmasks, playing baseball, listening to music and
dancing with French soldiers.

More serious than this superficiality was the omission of
vital facts about America's war effort and military policy in France.
Since the outbreak of the war, the administration had been sensitive
to criticism. The government, and General Pershing, wanted to field
an independent American army, and not amalgamate its forces with
Allied units; the AEF should have its own zone of operations, communications and harbors. But the Americans were using French ports and
French artillery, British ships and British steel helmets; far from
being the arsenal of democracy, the United States was receiving a

[1]"Short Subjects in Review," Motion Picture News, 31 August
1918, p. 1433.

greater tonnage of supplies and weapons from France and Britain than it shipped to Europe.[1] It was natural for the Allies to want the American soldiers to go into action as soon as possible: why not draft them into British and French units? Pershing resisted amalgamation; officially, the United States was not an Allied but an Associate power, and no country with a grain of national pride would provide men for another nation's army; he was worried about the language barrier and had a low estimation of French morale.[2]

Not a hint of these issues crept into the Official War Review or the other newsreels; differences between the Allies were not good for public confidence in the United States. While the troops trained in France and supply lines were established, adverse publicity was to be avoided.[3] A later commentator may have been rather severe when he claimed that "American setbacks were not shown and their advances were too fast for even the speediest newsers."[4] But there is no question that the authorities controlled the supply and use of newsfilm. Footage shot by Signal Corps cameramen was developed and censored in Paris; then it was sent to the War College in Washington, where it was decided what might be released to the public; this material was passed to the CPI which made the final selection.[5]

---

[1]On the equipping and supply of the AEF, see DeWeerd, President Wilson Fights His War, pp. 206-8.

[2]On the amalgamation controversy, see ibid., pp. 210-13, 300-4.

[3]See the memo from Pershing's press officer, Major Frederick Palmer, to his staff, supra, p. 229.

[4]Thiesen, "Story of the Newsreel," p. 25.

[5]For an analysis of American censorship, see supra, pp. 226-30.

One of the least documented stories of the war was the AEF's supply problems, and the mismanagement of munitions production in the United States. Reports reached the War Department of congested ports and railroads; in the winter of 1917-1918, American troops lacked warm clothing and hospital equipment. Factories in the United States produced heavy guns in sufficient quantities too late for use at the front; yet so much powder and explosives were being manufactured in the United States that the Ordnance Department ran out of storage space. The problems went unreported in the Official War Review which took its viewers to the Alps to see cable cars and dogs carrying ammunition to forward positions,[1] to Palestine where the British were laying railroad tracks,[2] and to the usual round of troop inspections and medal ceremonies.

When the Official War Review covered the supply effort, it portrayed it in optimistic terms. "You'll like this when you know that Austrian prisoners are opening these boxes," says the title for the dockside scenes. Lumberjacks from Oregon and Washington fell trees; a sawmill is working at full capacity; a refrigeration plant is under construction--it will make a million pounds of ice a day and store ten million pounds of beef; locomotives are assembled and repaired; camouflage nets sewn; and hundreds of loaves of bread baked.[3]

With action at a premium, the only sight of the enemy in most

---

[1]Official War Review, nos. 19 and 28, in National Archives (see Appendix).

[2]Official War Review, no. 19.

[3]Official War Review, no. 9, in National Archives.

260

newsreels was in the comparative security of a prisoner-of-war camp.
Official War Review No. 18 shows prisoners from the province of
Lorraine, which France claimed: "Forced into German uniforms against
their wills, their spirit still survives, and many later march back to
fight the Hun." Austrians captured by the French in Italy, ". . . seem
to be happy to be out of it, to have food--the same rations as the
Poilu--and safety."[1]

Similar themes are evident in the three feature-length documentaries released by the Committee--Pershing's Crusaders, America's
Answer and Under Four Flags. While the Official War Review had gone
to the highest bidder, the CPI decided to arrange the bookings for the
features itself; it went into the motion picture business as both producer and distributor. The theatrical manager George Bowles, who had
made a name for himself by exploiting D.W. Griffith's Birth of a Nation,
was charged with advertising, advance sales and business management;
at one time, he had eight road companies in different parts of the
country.[2] The tickets were cheap, too; the Commissioner of Internal
Revenue decided that patrons for official films should not have to pay
the theater tax because the CPI was a government agency.[3]

Each feature was launched with official screenings in a number
of large cities, backed up by a publicity campaign. There were displays in hotel lobbies and department store windows, signs on street

---

[1]Official War Review, no. 18, in National Archives.

[2]Creel, How We Advertised America, p. 121.

[3]Note in "Correspondence of the Division of Films" (Judicial
and Fiscal Branch, National Archives, Washington, D.C.).

cars and advertisements in local newspapers, with some space bought
for the CPI by patriotic citizens. Speakers were provided for churches,
clubs and schools; leading citizens were personally invited, and
employers urged to buy blocks of tickets for their workers. When
Pershing's Crusaders was premiered at the Grand Opera House in
Cincinnati on 29 April 1918, Hart sent a telegram to the editors of
the city's newspapers:

> . . . As it is most desirable that these pictures of the
> activities of our boys over there and over here be seen by
> as many people as possible, this committee will greatly
> appreciate whatever unusual publicity you may give to this
> presentation. To hit the Hun propaganda in the solar
> plexus is the aim of this picture. We hope that you will
> do your best to help us land this punch.[1]

And in case the message didn't get through, Howard Herrick,
the CPI's advance man in Cincinnati, sent telegrams to the city's
theater critics.[2] The film was a resounding success, bringing in
receipts of $600 for the first day; it had been scheduled for a week's
run, but after three days the manager of the Grand Opera House
requested another week. When it opened in St. Louis the following
month, Bowles sent telegrams to 30 prominent men in the city, asking
for their "personal cooperation and influence" in making the picture
a success.[3]

The eight reels of Pershing's Crusaders covered America's
preparations for war--from Liberty Loan rallies and munitions production

---

[1]Telegrams dated 23 April 1918 in "Correspondence of the
Division of Films."

[2]Telegrams dated 29 April 1918 in ibid.

[3]Mock and Larson, Words That Won The War, p. 140.

to the training of soldiers in the United States and their arrival in
France. "It is a revelation of a nation aroused in all its might,"
said Motion Picture News. "Here is the truth about the war. It's
Uncle Sam's answer to the lies of the Hun."[1] The film was officially
presented in 24 cities, and then handled by regular commercial
distributors who acquired the state rights; in California, Michigan
and North Dakota, the CPI films were distributed by the State Councils
of Defense.[2] Proceeds for the CPI from Pershing's Crusaders totalled
over $180,000.[3]

Even more successful was the second feature, America's Answer
(released in Europe under the title America's Answer to the Hun).
According to Creel, it broke all records for the number of bookings
and the range of distribution.[4] The Committee had devised a propor-
tionate selling plan, under which the rental charged each house was
based on its average income. Therefore, ". . . the same film might
be obtained for a few dollars a week by a crossroads theater but
$3,000 a week by a Manhattan picture palace."[5]

America's Answer covered the build-up in France and the first
engagements at the front. Creel wanted Wilson, who was somewhat wary

[1]"Official War Film at Lyric," Motion Picture News, 1 June
1918, p. 3245. Pershing's Crusaders opened at the Lyric Theater in
New York on May 21.

[2]Mock and Larson, Words That Won The War, p. 137.

[3]Ibid., p. 141, and Creel, How We Advertised America, p. 125.

[4]Creel, How We Advertised America, pp. 124-5.

[5]Mock and Larson, Words That Won The War, pp. 137-8. See also
ibid., p. 124.

of personal publicity, to appear in the film, and, on 24 July 1918,

wrote:

> My Dear Mr. President,
>
> I feel that the time has come when we should have a motion picture of you for Government use. Our second great feature, 'America's Answer,' will be released next week, and we want it for inclusion in that film.
>
> I know how you feel about it, but this one sitting will relieve you of all future importunities.
>
> Respectfully, George Creel.[1]

Wilson obliged, although a year earlier he had told a film industry gathering:

> I have sometimes been much chagrined in seeing myself in a motion picture. . . . The extraordinary rapidity with which I walk, for example; the instantaneous and apparently automatic nature of my motions; the way in which I produce uncommon grimaces, and altogether the extraordinary exhibition I make sends me to bed very unhappy.[2]

Wilson appears in the opening montage of America's Answer: a glowering sky, men of different walks of life poised for action, "Our Leader," Pershing addressing troops; wipe to convoy at sea.[3]

The titles, written by Kenneth C. Beaton, appear trite to

---

[1]Letter from Creel to Wilson, 24 July 1918, in Papers of George Creel, Box no. 2 (Manuscripts Division, Library of Congress, Washington, D.C.).

[2]Ernest A. Dench, "The President as a Movie Fan," Motion Picture Classic, July 1917, p. 64.

[3]Pershing's Crusaders is in the National Archives (see Appendix).

modern eyes, but apparently inspired contemporary audiences.[1] As
American troops debark in France, viewers are told: "The sacred,
shell-swept soil of France ne'er answered to the tread of braver men
than these," and "Old Glory knows no alien soil when there is work to
be done in Freedom's name."

Variety most accurately described America's Answer as "the sort
of government film as is shown in the weeklies, made up into a two-hour
show."[2] Indeed, the second reel--showing the supply effort in France--
had been released previously as Official War Review No. 9.[3] The film
tries to inject humor in places: "How would you like to have the hat
check privilege?" the audience is asked as soldiers sort through a
mountain of hats. The climax is the action at Cantigny, where an
artillery barrage and a not-too-spectacular infantry advance are shown.

However, some striking scenes were left out of the film.
Captain Robert R. Warwick of the Signal Corps Photographic Section
brought the footage to the United States from France, and stayed to
advise the CPI on the titling and editing.[4] In a memo to the AEF
headquarters in Paris, he reported that the film had been retitled,

---

[1]The flowery language was characteristic of feature films of
the period, and is found in the work of D.W. Griffith, Henry King,
Thomas Ince and other directors. Titles were used as much to create a
mood as to explain what was going on in the film. Kevin Brownlow says
that while fiction writers got between one and ten cents a word, motion
picture title writers received about $2.20 a word; they were paid "not
for the number of words they wrote so much as the number they avoided
writing--while still managing to tell the story." For an analysis of
film titling in this period, see Brownlow, The Parade's Gone By (New
York: Albert A. Knopf, 1968), pp. 294-99.

[2]Review, Variety, 2 August 1918, p. 38.

[3]See supra, p. 259.

[4]Warwick was one of the best known film stars of the period.

because the first titles lacked dignity. But he was also dissatisfied with the choice of scenes:

> . . . My only criticism of their arrangement of the film is their fear of presenting scenes which, in their opinion, were too morbid and might depress the public, such as a very impressive burial scene and several very striking hospital scenes. I disagreed with them in this, as I believe the seriousness of this war can only be brought home to them by the presentation of its true details.[1]

But the cuts were made, and the film opened at the George M. Cohan Theater in New York on Monday 29 July 1918.

Creel was at the screening to tell the audience about the work of the Committee, at home and abroad. The film, he said, ". . . represents one phase of America's fight for public opinion. . . . America's Answer cannot be made by any single class or by any single endeavor. There is a firing line in the United States as well as a firing line across the water. The answer must be given also by the millions who remain in civilian life, working in field and factory, shop and store, in the office and in the home."[2]

The reviewers were ecstatic. "Not a man or woman in the crowd . . . failed to feel the pull of the war, the urging of its influence, the sense of participation in it," said the New York Times.[3] Describing the climax, the New York Herald said: "Nothing finer has been shown in moving pictures in New York than that great battle

[1] Memo from Captain Robert R. Warwick to Lieutenant-Colonel W.C. Sweeney, 26 July 1918, in "Correspondence of Signal Corps Laboratory," Box no. 6191.

[2] Speech at premiere of America's Answer, 29 July 1918, in Papers of George Creel, Box no. 5.

[3] "America's Answer Stirs War Spirit," New York Times, 30 July 1918, p. 9.

scene."[1] "Besides real films of this sort," added the New York Sun,
"efforts of cinema directors, however thoughtfully conceived, pale
into comparative insignificance, as well they might."[2] Only Variety
stopped short of euphoria; the film was thrilling and interesting, but
". . . why not have woven a little heart interest story through the
genuine scenes from the front?"[3]

America's Answer was shown in about half the 12,000 theaters
in the United States and yielded over $185,000 for the Committee.[4]
While it was popular with patrons, the Division of Films made it clear
to exhibitors that it would be unpatriotic to refuse it. A full-page
advertisement in the trade press exerted subtle moral pressure:

> All Exhibitors in North America: . . . Our Government requests
> that you run these live pictures of our own sons, brothers and
> friends--filmed at the gates of Hell and brought back through
> the submarine-infested seas--in the same worthy spirit that
> put America in this world war. In this instance, Distributors
> and Exhibitors should be above commercialism. . . . The cost
> to you will be the consistent minimum and you are asked not to
> haggle and barter and hold off, but to be personally as
> anxious to exhibit them as our intrepid soldiers are to
> establish democracy with the blood of their stalwart bodies.[5]

Under Four Flags[6] was being edited when the Armistice was

---

[1]Review, New York Herald, 30 July 1918, in Papers of George
Creel, Box no. 5.

[2]Review, New York Sun, 31 July 1918, in Papers of George
Creel, Box no. 5.

[3]Review, Variety, 2 August 1918, p. 38.

[4]Creel, How We Advertised America, p. 125, and Mock and Larson,
Words That Won The War, p. 141.

[5]Advertisement, Motion Picture News, 21 September 1918, p. 1818.

[6]There are prints in the National Archives and Library of
Congress (see Appendix).

signed. It was retitled and released with some scene changes in November 1918. It reviewed the war from the time that General Foch became Commander-in-Chief of the Allied forces to the Armistice; of particular interest to American audiences was footage of two of the major actions involving the AEF--at Chateau-Thierry and on the St. Mihiel Salient. Motion Picture News devoted a whole page to the feature, giving a synopsis and suggestions for exhibition and advertising. Indeed, the writer tried hard to make the film appear to be a typical product of the Hollywood studios: "The stars are Generals Foch, Haig, Diaz and Pershing--the support is the united armies of France, the British Empire, Italy and the United States--the best cast ever assembled for a motion picture!"[1]

The official films were not an instant hit abroad. The Division of Films correspondence file, now in the National Archives, contains telegrams to Canadian theater managers, urging them to book the films--and follow-up telegrams asking why they haven't replied. The situation was even worse in neutral lands, such as the Scandinavian countries, where the Germans were using American entertainment films to carry their own propaganda. As Creel wrote later:

> . . . What the war-weary foreigners liked and demanded was American comedy and dramatic film. They had to have their Mary Pickford and Douglas Fairbanks and Charlie Chaplin and Norma Talmadge. The Germans, either by outright purchase of picture-houses or else by subsidizing exhibitors, were largely in control in every neutral country, and used American entertainment film to put across their propaganda material. As a result, we stood to be left out in the cold.[2]

---

[1]"Under Four Flags," Motion Picture News, 30 November 1918, p. 3269.

[2]Creel, How We Advertised America, p. 275.

The Trading-with-the-Enemy Act provided that no film could be exported without a license from the War Trade Board. Creel secured a ruling from its chairman, Vance McCormick, that every application for a license had to be endorsed by the CPI. And the Committee informed distributors and producers that they couldn't export entertainment films unless they included some CPI material: 20 percent of every shipment should be "educational matter," no film should be sold to any exhibitor who refused the CPI's films, and no pictures should be sold to theaters where German film was being used.[1] Creel said the restrictions had an almost immediate effect: Swedish and Norwegian theaters stopped showing German films within a few weeks, although the CPI had less success in Switzerland and Holland.[2] But the result, as Creel put it, was that "Charlie Chaplin and Mary Pickford led Pershing's Crusaders and America's Answer into the enemy's territory and smashed another Hindenburg line."[3]

Advising the Division of Films on the assembly and presentation of its feature-length films was Samuel L. Rothapfel, the enterprising New York theater manager who brought the art of the showman to film exhibition. According to Creel, his work at the official screenings was most valuable, with help "in the matter of scenic accessories, orchestra and incidental music."[4] Indeed, Rothapfel was well aware that the war film, by itself, was often dull and uninspiring; although the titles might arouse patriotic feelings, the films needed a more

[1]Ibid., p. 276.   [2]Ibid.

[3]Quoted in Mock and Larson, Words That Won The War, p. 142.

[4]Creel, How We Advertised America, p. 122.

emotional impact. Music, he believed, could carry the audience along, even if the pictures didn't. Writing in Motion Picture News, he advised exhibitors: "Music plays an all important part in presenting these pictures and a general scheme to follow is to use good common sense and to get some advice if you don't know."[1]

At the Rialto and Rivoli theaters in New York, Rothapfel and his staff edited their own weekly newsreel from footage supplied by the CPI and the news weeklies. Starting with between 6,000 and 8,000 feet, they selected between 2,500 and 3,000. The scenes chosen, said Rothapfel, should appear in the right psychological order:

> . . . For instance, we may start the Magazine with marching troops or some subject that will immediately enthuse the audience and then follow in sequence, such as the troops arriving at camp, their embarkation on transports, their arrival in France, then intimate scenes showing them in their billets or on the front line. You see this gives you a sequel and will hold the interest of the audience for about ten to fifteen minutes. . . .
>
> . . . Then we start another sequel--it might be concerning activities at home, such as conservation, war activities, etc. This, of course, has a relation to the first unit, then we continue with war work, women's activities, such as the Red Cross, war charities, etc. After that comes the foreign element which of course includes all our Allies. Then to subside a bit from so much war stuff we get topics of interest that have happened during the week . . . Last of all we generally wait for the Punch.[2]

Sound effects could be used to liven up the footage, but Rothapfel urged great care in handling them:

> . . . if you do not know how a big gun sounds and the noise it makes don't use any effects until you find out. It is

---

[1]"Rothapfel Gives Some Hints on Weeklies," Motion Picture News, 24 August 1918, p. 1220.

[2]"Rothapfel Tells of Advance of Weeklies," Motion Picture News, 31 August 1918, p. 1374.

more than simply a smash on the drums because some shells shriek through the air and some sound like the whirr of an express train. The effects we get are by a simultaneous crash of cymbals and then a rumble on the organ with the biggest pipes we have.[1]

But it was music, said Rothapfel, that really lifted the war film, and he proceeded to list the pieces most appropriate for the standard war scenes. When the troops leave on the transports, "a good old chestnut can be used such as Good Bye Broadway, Hello France;" for naval scenes, he recommended the Jack Tar March, Before the Mast and Our Jackies; when the troops land in France, start on the chorus of Over There. No lack of suggestions for scenes at home--Keep the Home Fires Burning, It's Time for Every Boy to be a Soldier, What Kind of an American are You, There's a Million Heroes and My Dough Boy.[2] For scenes of the other Allied armies, Rothapfel recommended the respective national anthems. However, there was a problem with the British: "Rule Britannia unfortunately is not so well known. We have played it in our theatres time and time again and not a soul would rise, but the moment the strain of the Marseillaise is played everybody would jump to their feet."[3] There's no telling whether Rothapfel would have had more success with the official British national anthem, God Save The King.

Keeping the audience in their seats was often as much of a problem as making them stand up at the right moment. "Understand me, it is not good policy to make the people rise out of their seats during the performance by playing the national anthems, . . . yet it would be

---

[1]"Hints on Weeklies," p. 1220.

[2]"Advance of Weeklies," p. 1374.   [3]Ibid.

undignified, bad taste and disrespectful if, for instance, the President of France was shown on the screen, or the King of Britain, and the national anthem was not being played."[1] All this standing up and sitting down, said Rothapfel, could ruin the pace and psychology of the performance.

The showman always reserved the best till last--for the climax or "Punch" as he called it. Here, he gives an example of the orchestrated finale to a newsreel presentation at the Rivoli:

> . . . . The last shot in the issue of the War Review released by the Committee on Public Information shows the Defense of Rheims and the burning of the city, and then the title which reads, 'In Spite of Kultur the Cathedral Still Stands.' What we did was to get a piece of film from 'Joan the Woman,' which shows Joan of Arc leading her mignons to battle. We faded this picture in on another machine over the burning city of Rheims (using the two projectors at the same time), then faded it out denoting of course that the spirit of France, as exemplified by Joan, could never be equalled; then we faded in again on the second machine the title, 'The Steel Wall of France,' and the huge body of French troops marching across the ruins. The music that we used for this subject was the 'Allegro Movement' from Robespierre Overture, by Littolf, and as Joan appeared we raised our trumpets high and started the chorus of the 'Marseillaise' which took the people right out of their seats. The applause lasted fully a minute and a half after the picture had closed and didn't cease for a moment but instead grew louder and louder and held up our performance.[2]

While the Committee's films did good business, the CPI itself was the butt of criticism from many quarters. Congress wanted to know who was allowed to take film, and who had contracts for exhibition.[3] The film industry resented what it saw as government interference in its affairs, and unfair competition; Moving Picture World said, ". . .

---

[1]Ibid.   [2]Ibid., pp. 1374, 1377.

[3]See supra, p. 245-6.

it is evident that the Government and its auxiliary agencies have gone
into motion picture production, distribution and exhibition with a
minimum of counsel from the wise heads of the industry and the maximum
of direction by those unacquainted with the films."[1] And there were
disputes over the Committee's attempt to suppress some films--the most
serious of which led to charges of pro-Hearst bias.

The Division of Films certainly had a number of former Hearst
employees on its staff, Charles Hart among them. And when it banned a
Universal film on aircraft production, The Yanks Are Coming, the
company's vice-president, Robert Cochrane, became convinced that the
CPI was in Hearst's pocket. Creel, he told Motion Picture News,
". . . is so completely under the Hearst control, and so surrounded
with Hearst influences, that he will take advantage of his official
position to aid Hearst in every way possible . . . In other words,
Mr. Hearst practically controls the Creel Committee, so far as films
are concerned."[2]

Although the Dayton-Wright Airplane Company had cooperated with
Universal in the making of the film, the company had failed to secure
the necessary permits from the CPI. Universal said it would defy the
Committee, and the film was advertised to open at the Broadway Theater
in New York on 23 June 1918. Carl Byoir of the CPI was in the ticket
line that night, and Justice Department agents were reported to be in
the house in case the theater tried to show the film. Instead, a sign

[1]"Uplifters Boss War Films," Moving Picture World, 26 January
1918, p. 483.

[2]"Truce in the Universal-Creel Row," Motion Picture News,
6 July 1918, p. 62.

was hung in the lobby: "The Yanks Are Coming, advertised to be tonight, stopped by the Creel-Hearst Committee."[1]

The film was banned because Creel and Hart knew that it gave a false picture of aircraft production. Congress had made a large appropriation for building planes, and the film suggested that many would soon be in France. But although more than $1 billion was spent on combat aircraft, not a single one reached the battle zone before the end of the war. Creel could not reveal the real reasons for banning the film without causing the public disillusionment he wanted to avoid, so he replied to the charges of Hearst bias. Universal, he told the press, did not have the necessary permits, and had planned to exploit the film for its own profit.[2] "The only question in issue is whether private greed shall have power to nullify the government's efforts to protect its military secrets," he said. "The charge of Hearst influence is merely an attempt to muddy the water and is as absurd as it is indecent."[3] Hearst himself made public a letter which showed that, far from wanting to influence the CPI by placing his men there, he had strongly protested to Creel ". . . at that gentleman's habit of drafting his men into Government service." The loss of Charles Hart, he added, was one "that I do not know how to repair."[4]

More charges of Hearst influence on the CPI were brought by

---

[1]Mock and Larson, Words That Won The War, p. 149.

[2]During the war, the proceeds of many films on military subjects were donated to war charities.

[3]Mock and Larson, Words That Won The War, p. 150.

[4]"Truce in the Universal-Creel Row," Motion Picture News, 6 July 1918, p. 57.

Universal when the <u>Hearst-Pathé News</u> showed a film of American tanks in action. Universal claimed that the other companies had not been allowed to film them. Actually, both Hearst-Pathé and Universal were granted permits; the Hearst-Pathé cameramen filmed the tanks, but Universal delayed until the War Department changed its mind, and refused to honor the permit. The film was shown on the <u>Hearst-Pathé News</u>, but was recalled when the new order was issued.[1]

When the Armistice was signed, Creel hoped that the CPI would be allowed a breathing space to clear up its business. But the Committee was disbanded as quickly as it was set up, by order of Congress on 30 June 1919. There was no time or money for an orderly liquidation as Creel told Wilson a year later:

> . . . No one was left with authority to receipt for funds, rent a building, employ a clerk or transfer a bank balance. The foreign representatives of the Committee, returning with records and monies, were unable to report, accumulating checks that could not be deposited, and approved bills could not be paid. To add to the confusion, the Committee was dispossessed on July 20, and the ledgers and files of two years were loaded into army trucks and dumped in vacant offices in the old Fuel Administration building.[2]

Creel told Wilson that, for the past ten months, he and other former CPI officials had been travelling to Washington at their own expense to finish the liquidation. He was angry about a Senate report that held him up to be ". . . one who had 'finished a joyride' and then deserted his post, leaving checks and valuable papers scattered

---

[1]Ibid., p. 62, and Mock and Larson, <u>Words That Won The War</u>, p. 148.

[2]Letter from George Creel to Woodrow Wilson, 24 May 1920, in Papers of George Creel, Box no. 2.

over the floor."[1]

It was an ignominious end for "America's first propaganda ministry." And while with hindsight the Committee may be criticized for its suppression of news and attempts at opinion management, propaganda was not a dirty word in those days. Creel and his staff were doing what they (and most other Americans) regarded as their patriotic duty to maintain morale at home, and spread America's message abroad. The Official War Review and the longer films gave Americans a view of the war that was fragmentary, and sometimes distorted; yet at least it was a view, and the reaction of critics and audiences suggests that the films were generally appreciated. It was a war which did not lend itself to pictorial coverage, and it was perhaps too much to expect cameramen, inexperienced in war coverage and encumbered by heavy equipment and official red tape, to produce the action footage to which later audiences have become accustomed. As one plaintively remarked:

. . . Every time I go up to the front they show me craters and tell me what unusually fine stuff I could have had if I'd been there about daybreak--when there wasn't enough light for taking pictures--or the day before, when it was raining, or some other time when I just didn't happen to be there. But whenever the sun is shining right, and the camera man's on the job, things suddenly become peaceful. I hope the folks back home know that we're doing our best to give 'em the real stuff.[2]

---

[1] Ibid.

[2] Lieutenant Charles P. Cushing, quoted in Charles Gatchell, "Filming the Fighting Front," Picture-Play Magazine, January 1919, p. 22.

CONCLUSION

Writing about the news films of World War I six decades later is a venture fraught with pitfalls. Some of the evidence is missing-- many newsreels and feature-length documentaries as well as written testimony and official records. But potentially more dangerous is the seductive mental trap of hindsight. Our perceptions of the role and influence of film have been enhanced by the development of the medium. We know how films are shot, processed, edited and screened--a knowledge that was not shared by most moviegoers in World War I. Removed from the pressures of living in a country at war, we can dispassionately examine how film was exploited for propaganda purposes.

To modern observers, their attitudes anaesthetized by film coverage of World War II and television reports from Vietnam, the news film of the Great War seems poorly shot and the subject-matter often tedious; the absence of the sounds of war lends an air of unreality; the music and sound effects that brought these films to life for contempo-rary audiences cannot be reporduced. It is difficult to understand why crowds lined up for blocks to buy tickets for The German Side of the War or why audiences cheered every scene of America's Answer. Most of the "action" takes place behind the lines, the shots are static, there are few telling close-ups, the editing is pedestrian and the titles florid. Yet to dismiss the war films of this period because they do not meet our expectations of what war films should be is rather like blaming Thomas Edison for not being born a century sooner.

We cannot beam ourselves back to Samuel L. Rothapfel's Rialto or Rivoli Theater in New York to join the audience for a war film; even if we could, our knowledge of films would bar us from sharing the experience of the person in the next seat. But we have the next best experience--the testimony of those audiences, the cameramen, the producers and the propagandists as recorded in the trade magazines, newspapers, books and official documents.

And if for a moment we can forget what we have seen of the D-Day Landings and the Tet Offensive, we get a different picture on the screen of our mind. We see cameramen overcoming the problems of distance, heavy equipment, obstructive military authorities and physical danger to obtain film. We see producers and exhibitors exploiting it for commercial gain, and propagandists exploiting it for political or psychological advantage. We see the growing pains of an industry that, 10 years earlier, had been regarded by some as a mere fad. We see the failure of some companies, but the success of more; World War I helped producers such as Pathé and Universal to consolidate their business. We see newsreels becoming an integral part of the motion picture program--and, consequently, part of the media diet of filmgoers.

Newsfilm in World War I offered audiences a picture of the war that was always fragmentary, and frequently distorted too. Faked films were still peddled to unsuspecting exhibitors; even in authentic films, scenes were sometimes restaged for the camera. Censors excised scenes that they thought would depress audiences; propagandists inserted uplifting titles; everyone indulged in extravagant and misleading

publicity. But none of this could obscure the stark realities of war
that these films brought to audiences for the first time. It was the
first major war to be covered on film, and it was not the frantic,
romantic affair served up by the studios of New York and Hollywood.
While the newsfilm of World War I may seem uncompelling to modern eyes,
we should not forget that today's coverage is not without its faults.
Donald Thompson may have been pan-happy; some modern news photographers
zoom with abandon. World War I photographers used a tripod whenever
possible; too often these days, it is left in the truck. But the sound
provides an immediacy that makes us overlook the inadequacy of the
visuals. We are accustomed to the fast-paced news report, with stand-
uppers and fonts, in which the events of several hours are compressed
into a briskly edited 90-second package. But war proceeds at a slower
tempo; perhaps the pace of the World War I newsfilms is closer to the
real time of the events. If they lack action and excitement, it was
because that was the nature of the war. It was a drab, dirty, tedious
and dangerous business. And it showed on the screen.

* * * * *

REVIEW OF SOURCES:

FILMS AND LITERATURE

1) FILMS:

In studying the factual films of World War I, the films themselves are not paradoxically, the principal research source. So many
have been lost or mutilated that the researcher who relies on film alone
can offer only an incomplete and rather subjective study. For his
history of the newsreel, The American Newsreel, 1911-1967, Raymond
Fielding worked primarily with written materials, in particular the
motion picture trade magazines. When I met him at the University of
Houston to discuss my research, he suggested I do the same. It was
good advice.

Another eminent film historian, often quoted in the text of
this thesis, put the problem succinctly. "We are sitting on a celluloid time bomb," writes Kevin Brownlow.[1] Almost all silent film was
photographed and printed on unstable nitrate stock; unless kept in
precisely the right conditions, it will deteriorate or, worse, explode.
On 7 December 1978, fire destroyed 27 million feet of 35 mm Universal
newsreel footage stored in the vaults of the National Archives at
Suitland, Maryland.[2] Universal had given the film, most of it outtakes,
to the American people in 1973, and Fielding, who spent a year

---

[1]Brownlow, The War, p. xiii.

[2]Gordon Hitchens, "Third Major U.S. Archive Fire; History Lost:
Is Govt. Reliable?" Variety, 13 December 1978, pp. 5, 48.

appraising it, described it as "historically priceless."[1] It was the
third major fire to destroy American archive films in a little over a
year; some people inside and outside the industry say that nitrate
film is simply too dangerous to keep and should be destroyed. "This is
a serious matter," writes Brownlow, "for the films being junked are
not simply ephemeral entertainment . . . They represent the history of
our century, a history that was often captured on celluloid at great
risk."[2]

The problem, inevitably, is money. Most film archives do not
have the funds to transfer large amounts of nitrate film to safety
stock. The work proceeds as and when the money is budgeted; in the
meantime, the film deteriorates further. Most film archives do not
allow researchers to view nitrate film; however, I was able to see
some nitrate footage in John Allen's collection at Park Ridge, New
Jersey.

Even if a print has been transferred to safety stock, it may
be in a form that tells the researcher little or nothing. Many newsreels have been bastardized for later compilations--a scene selected
here, a single shot there. Often, they were not restored to their
original form, and without the titles, the date and location of a
scene cannot generally be identified. So it is difficult to view
these films as contemporary audiences viewed them because most of them
do not exist in their original form.

Some film archives now catalog their World War I material by
subject, not by date or provenance. Hearst-Metrotone has reels of

---

[1]Quoted in ibid., p. 5.   [2]Brownlow, The War, p. xiii.

"World War I scenes," that are little more than a collage--scenes from different years, places and companies edited together. The Sherman Grinberg Film Libraries, now home to the Pathé newsreel collection, has an excellent card index. A film researcher seeking shots of aeroplanes and tanks can quickly find which stock shots are available. But the academic researcher is frustrated by titles such as "1918: With the Stars and Stripes Abroad--The busiest men at the training camp are the gunners as they prepare a fiery message of steel for the Kaiser."[1] Without a precise date and the number of the newsreel, the information is of little value. Often film footage is so jumbled that only persistence--and a good measure of luck--can yield results. The eighth edition of the American War News Weekly[2] in John Allen's collection is followed immediately by a single scene from Pathé News No. 67 and a pictorial history of the war, compiled in 1919. The Theodore Roosevelt collection in the Library of Congress has a feature entitled Theodore Roosevelt in the Great War that was made up by taking scenes from many newsreels. Since titles are often missing, it is deceptively easy to think that one shot is part of the preceding scene when, in fact, it may be from an entirely different film.

Persistence sometimes pays off. Leafing through the catalog in John Allen's archive, I came across a familiar name--Przemysl. The reel contains footage from the 1915 Chicago Tribune feature, The German Side of the War.[3] Most of the titles have been preserved, so I was

---

[1] Scene title from Pathé collection, Sherman Grinberg Film Libraries, New York.

[2] See supra, p. 248.   [3] See supra, pp. 80-2.

able to note the scene numbers: in the reel, they appear in the
following order--53, 55, 56, 57, 59, 62, 4, 16, 23, 25, 26, 28, 41.
And, as if to trap the unwary researcher, scenes 62 and 4 are separated
by film of the Allied offensive in Alsace in 1918!

The largest collection of World War I footage in the United
States is in the National Archives in Washington, D.C. The Signal
Corps films are interesting and well-indexed,[1] but since most of the
material was intended as a historical record of the war and was not
seen on American theater screens, a large part of the collection is
not relevant to this study. The footage that was released was used in
the Official War Review and in the CPI's feature-length documentaries.
The National Archives has six editions of the Official War Review--
nos. 9, 18, 19, 27, 28, 31--and prints of Pershing's Crusaders and
America's Answer.[2] There is also (on videotape) a copy of Donald
Thompson's War As It Really Is.[3]

The final CPI feature Under Four Flags is in the Library of
Congress; unfortunately, it is incomplete (most of the first reel is
missing) and in places the picture quality is poor--most likely due to
nitrate deterioration before it was transferred to safety stock. There
is one edition of the American War News Weekly--no. 19. In a compilation
film, there are five scenes from The German Side of the War--nos. 93,
94, 95, 96 and 104. Donald Thompson's Somewhere in France is on

---

[1]By K. Jack Bauer, in List of World War I Signal Corps Films
(Washington, D.C.: National Archives, 1957).

[2]For the films of the CPI, see supra, pp. 255-67.

[3]See supra, pp. 124-6.

nitrate stock, and cannot be viewed. There is the newsreel footage of Theodore Roosevelt and the compilation film, Theodore Roosevelt in the Great War.

John Allen's collection has a wealth of World War I material, but most of it is on nitrate, and, as indicated earlier, the footage is not generally identified by origin or title. However, careful reading of the catalog can lead the researcher to relevant footage. The eighth edition of the American War News Weekly is complete, and there are the 13 scenes from The German Side of the War. There is some footage from Pathé and other newsreels.

The Chicago Tribune's other 1915 feature, With The Russians At The Front,[1] is in the Museum of Modern Art in New York. There is also an edition of the Universal Current Events from September 1918, and some other newsreel footage.

Most of the surviving newsreel footage is in commercial archives, where it is generally catalogued by subject, not by date or original title. The Sherman Grinberg Film Libraries have the large Pathé collection; there is a card file in New York, but the film is kept in Los Angeles. Hearst-Metrotone in New York has a smaller collection.

Film archivists and historians are now examining and cataloguing the films uncovered in the most sensational film "find" in years. Hundreds of reels of silent film were found buried at Dawson City in the Yukon; stored in the ground, their deterioration was slowed by the perma-freeze. There are between 40 and 50 reels of newsfilm, about

---

[1]See supra, pp. 89-90.

two-thirds of them from the war period. It will be some time before
they can be catalogued and transferred to safety stock, but when the
work is done they may provide some new insights to the war film of
the period.

2) CONTEMPORARY MAGAZINES, NEWSPAPERS AND BOOKS:

Without a substantial amount of film from the period available
for study, the researcher must go to other primary sources, of which
the trade press is by far the most important. The two principal
industry magazines--Moving Picture World and Motion Picture News--
provided a mixture of news, reviews, opinion and advertisements.
Published weekly, they were the main channel for news about film
production, bookings and business deals. Through advertisements,
theater managers learned of the latest films to be released; they
could read reviews, and discover how much business features were doing
in other cities. With some gaps, both magazines gave a weekly synopsis
of subjects in current newsreels. There were special articles on
subjects ranging from the experiences of cameramen to the use of film
music. The line between news and opinion was sometimes not too well
defined; short news stories about the latest release from Pathé or
Mutual might conclude with phrases such as "this reel is without bias,
and should appeal to all your patrons, whatever their sympathies," or
"no patriotic exhibitor should fail to book this stirring feature."
But in as much as the magazines reflected the industry they were
serving, such comments provide an insight to contemporary attitudes.

Exhibitors Trade Review, also published weekly, was similar in
content and layout to Moving Picture World and Motion Picture News;

however, I was unable to find a complete set for the World War I period. Variety devoted most of its space to theater and vaudeville; after the United States entered the war in April 1917, there were more articles on film, including reviews of the official films and news stories on the CPI. Two British trade magazines--The Bioscope and Kinematograph Weekly--should also be mentioned because they contained stories on cameramen at the front and on British films released in the United States.

While these publications were the main source of news for the industry, other magazines concentrated on features. The movie fan magazines contained little of use to this study, although I found a couple of useful stories in Motion Picture Classic. The Mutual Film Corporation published Reel Life--a helpful guide to the company's productions. The most valuable sources were three monthly publications: Motion Picture Magazine, Photoplay Magazine, and Picture-Play Magazine. All contain detailed and interesting features on the experiences of cameramen such as Wilbur Durborough, John Allen Everets, Merl LaVoy and Donald Thompson, and on the general problems of war coverage; among the contributors were well-known contemporary film writers such as Ernest Dench and Homer Croy.

Some general-interest magazines, with a readership not limited to the film industry or movie fans, occasionally published articles about the war coverage. Among those quoted in this thesis are Current Opinion, Literary Digest, The Photographic Times, and The Scientific American.

Daily newspapers are an obvious source for material about war

films--and a source which, unfortunately, has been little exploited.
An analysis of major newspapers in the United States for this period
would take several years, but the results could be most valuable; news
stories and reviews would help the researcher to form a more accurate
impression of how certain films were received by audiences. The Chicago
Tribune would be a good choice for a case study, since it was closely
involved in the industry as a producer of newsreels and feature-length
documentaries. Some of the quotes from newspapers in this thesis are
drawn from other sources, principally the trade magazines. Others
were taken directly from the newspapers; the New York Times, for
instance, was the source for articles on Pancho Villa's deal with
Mutual,[1] and the Donald Thompson film The German Curse in Russia,[2]
and for a review of America's Answer.[3] Thompson returned to his home
town, Topeka, in December 1915 for the screening of Somewhere in
France; a study of the issues of the Topeka Daily Capital for November
and December 1915 provided ample material.[4]

As far as I can discover, no American cameraman published an
account of his war experiences comparable in scope and detail--or
hyperbole--to that of the British Official War Kinematographer,
Lieutenant Geoffrey Malins, in How I Filmed The War. However, shorter
accounts appear in several books published during the war. Ernest
Dench's Making The Movies relates the experiences of cameramen such as
J.M. Downie, the Frenchman Bizeul and Cherry Kearton; Dench also makes

---

[1]See supra, pp. 20-23.   [2]See supra, pp. 128-30.
[3]See supra, p. 265.   [4]See supra, pp. 115-123.

some good points about the difficulties of war coverage. Albert K.
Dawson's account of his work with the German army during the Galician
campaign is in The Camera Man by Francis Collins; the author also
discusses the problems of the war cameraman. Donald Thompson's experiences in Belgium are well treated by the war correspondent Edward
Alexander Powell in Fighting in Flanders.

Several books have passages on technical advances and the
design of cameras for use in the trenches;[1] Homer Croy's How Motion
Pictures Are Made and Behind the Motion-Picture Screen by Austin
Lescaboura are useful sources. For British propaganda in the United
States,[2] the best contemporary work is The Times History of the War
Vol. 21, although it has few specific references to film; it may
reflect British attitudes, because it was published in 1920, before
the propaganda effort was subjected to historical analysis. The work
of the Committee on Public Information is faithfully documented by its
chairman George Creel in How We Advertised America; although it smacks
of self-righteousness in some passages, it is an invaluable guide to
the ideas and policies that guided the Committee's use of films, and
its dealings with the newsreel companies.

3) OTHER PRIMARY SOURCES--OFFICIAL RECORDS, CORRESPONDENCE AND PAPERS:

The records and correspondence of the War Department, the
American Expeditionary Force and the Signal Corps are standard research
materials for military and political historians, but few (if any) film
historians have gone to these sources for the World War I period. The
records occupy hundreds of boxes in the National Archives, but they

[1]See supra, Chapter VI. [2]See supra, pp. 157-179.

are well indexed so records relating to military photography can be located fairly easily. Many of them are concerned with the use of stills and motion pictures for purely military purposes, such as target practice, reconnaissance and training, and are not relevant to this study. However, others have a direct bearing on questions such as the make-up of photographic units, censorship and relations with the Committee on Public Information. Three groups of records were particularly helpful:

a) <u>Records of the Office of the Adjutant General, Washington, D.C.</u>:

These include a cable from Pershing requesting that lieutenants be assigned to photographic units, Louis Brown's plan for the organization of war photography, and the resolution from the House of Representatives seeking information on Signal Corps photographic work and the issuing of permits.

b) <u>Records of the American Expeditionary Force General Headquarters, Paris</u>:

The regular reports of the photographic censors in Paris are in this group; they give details of the footage shot, the number of scenes passed and the films dispatched. There are letters, memos and cables from Pershing, Palmer and other officers on the censorship of the mails, the reciprocal censorship arrangements with the French and British, and the problems of photographic units at the front, such as casualties, weather and excessive demands from Washington. Captain Warwick's memo on the editing and titling of <u>America's Answer</u>, Edgar Hatrick's plan for a CPI newsreel unit and a copy of the British censorship rules are also in these files.

c) Records of the Office of the Chief Signal Officer, Washington, D.C.:

These contain more letters, memos and cables on the work of the Photographic Section, including the lively exchange between Major Bert E. Underwood in Washington and Brigadier-General Edgar Russel in Paris over the work and problems of the photographers.[1] A copy of the Signal Corps circular specifying the qualities it needed in war cameramen is in these files, as is the report of the Secretary of War, Newton D. Baker, to the House of Representatives on the photographic work of the Signal Corps. Applications from film companies to take pictures in military camps and munitions and airplane factories are also included.

The meticulous record-keeping of the military is a boon to the researcher; almost all the papers are signed and dated, so it is possible to identify policies and patterns, if they exist. These files also contain copies of records from other branches of the military and government agencies; sent for information only, they were kept with the army's own records. The originals, and other copies, may exist, but the fact remains that the army files contain documents that may not be readily available in other places. Hatrick's report and the British rules for photographic censorship have been mentioned; while I was unable to find the CPI's rules for photographic permits and censorship in the Committee's own records, I came across a copy in the AEF files.

The records of the Committee on Public Information are not nearly as complete as those of the military. Less efficient office

---

[1] See supra, pp. 214-216.

practices may be to blame, as well as the hurried dismantling of the agency after the Armistice.[1] But the National Archives have not helped the historian by destroying some of the CPI's records--not a deliberate act of censorship or expungment, but the routine disposal of old documents to make way for new ones. The Judicial and Fiscal Branch says that the records destroyed were of little use to the historian; since I didn't see them, I can't agree or disagree. However, the correspondence of the Division of Films and the Division of Foreign Pictures have been retained and they contain some interesting documents. These files record the efforts of the Division of Films to promote its features; there are letters and telegrams to theater managers in major American and Canadian cities. There is some revealing material on the Official War Review--Charles Hart's proposal to take over the distribution of footage from the other Allies.[2] and his telegram to Creel describing the "dice-throwing" of the newsreel editors and his plan for 100 percent distribution.[3]

George Creel's papers are in the Manuscripts Division of the Library of Congress; the relevant files contain material on the work of the CPI and his correspondence with President Wilson. Creel was highly sensitive to press coverage and opinion; he kept voluminous books of clippings of newspaper stories and reviews of the official films. Also in these files are Creel's speeches; of particular interest is his address at the premiere of America's Answer.[4] There is his official report on the work of the Committee, most of which was reproduced in

---

[1]See supra, pp. 274-5.   [2]See supra, pp. 252-3.
[3]See supra, p. 252.   [4]See supra, p. 265.

How We Advertised America. The correspondence with Wilson includes Creel's bitter letter, complaining about the hasty action of Congress in dissolving the Committee, and defending his reputation.[1]

4) SECONDARY SOURCES--BOOKS AND PERIODICALS:

World War I had received scant attention from film historians until 1979 when The War, The West and The Wilderness by Kevin Brownlow was published. The first section of the book is devoted to war films, and the people who made them. The scope is wider than that of his thesis; Brownlow studies fiction films as well as those that were, or purported to be factual; he covers British productions as well as American ones; and he has excellent personal interviews with directors and cameramen, some of which I have quoted. While he was a good chapter on the Mexican Revolution, he does not outline the previous history of war coverage by cameramen; he does not examine the newsreel business in detail, although the issues of faking, re-staging and theatrical presentation are treated in a more general context; Allied propaganda in the United States is covered briefly, but he sensibly concentrates on the impact of particular films such as The Battle of the Somme; he does not go into detail on the official films of the CPI. These are not intended as criticisms of Brownlow's book, for it is by far the best treatment of World War I films to date; however, these points indicate where his book and this thesis overlap, and where they diverge. On the work of the war cameramen, I was able to find some new material to amplify known accounts and Brownlow's interviews; the material on Donald Thompson has, to my knowledge, never been used. I attempted to

_____

[1]See supra, pp. 274-5.

put the film propaganda of the Allies into its historical context and to examine, albeit briefly, more of these films. On the work of the Signal Corps, Brownlow has some delightful anecdotes and interviews; my research of military records sheds light on the organization of the photographic work, the problems encountered by the cameramen, and the disputes between the AEF and Washington. My analysis of the work of the CPI's Division of Films, its dealings with the newsreel companies, the Official War Review and the longer official films is, to my knowledge, the first detailed study of American government film propaganda in World War I. Brownlow and I have been in correspondence: he has given me some useful tips, and I have been able to tell him about certain films in American archives that he had feared were lost.

As mentioned earlier, I also discussed my research with the film historian Raymond Fielding. It was his book, The American Newsreel, 1911-1967, that first aroused my interest in the subject. The first chapter of this thesis, on the coverage of previous wars, and the second, on the newsreel business, are based on his work. His chapter on World War I provided me with the material for my thesis proposal, and his bibliography lists several useful articles from the trade press, notably from Moving Picture World. Fielding examined that magazine page-by-page for the war period; he suggested I do the same for Motion Picture News. As I hope this thesis has shown, that line of research proved most fruitful.

Rachel Low's The History of the British Film, 1914-1918 is of more peripheral relevance to this study. Although it provides a comprehensive analysis of fiction film production and the theater industry, newsreels and longer features such as the "battle" films of Malins and McDowell are not treated in great detail. British propaganda in the United States has been covered in at least three books. The Times History of the War Vol. 21 was mentioned in 2). The 1930s saw the publication of two studies of British propaganda--British Propaganda at Home and in the United States, 1914-1917, by James Duane Squires, and Propaganda For War: The Campaign Against American Neutrality, 1914-1917, by Horace C. Peterson. The latter is the more complete, although neither deals specifically with film as an instrument of propaganda.

Brownlow's book is the best study of fiction films in the war, but several periodical articles are useful in this area. In "Hollywood at War, 1915-1918," Creighton Peet examines the "hate-the-Hun" phenomenon in films, and the impact of features such as The Battle Cry of Peace. In "Hollywood and World War I, 1914-1918," film historian Timothy J. Lyons offers a good survey of the industry's depiction of the war in fiction films, and the attitudes of contemporary audiences. Michael T. Isenberg analyses how film images of the war conditioned the thinking of moviegoers in "The Mirror of Democracy."

The role of the CPI is analyzed in two works. In the article "Wilson, Creel and the Presidency," Elmer J. Cornwell argues that the Committee helped to strengthen the prestige of the office of the presidency. James R. Mock and Cedric Larson study all aspects of the Committee's work in Words That Won The War; it traces the background, methods and aims of the CPI, and has a section on the work of the Division of Films.

Magazine articles on cameramen and newsreels in World War I were published occasionally through the 1920s and 1930s. The most useful are Stuart Mackenzie's survey of the history of the newsreel in American Magazine in 1924, and Earl Thiesen's article on war photographers in The International Photographer in 1934.

No survey of literature on film history can leave out Terry Ramsaye's A Million And One Nights. It is a fascinating collection of anecdotes and opinion, written in idiosyncratic style. Ramsaye has a keen eye for the bizarre story, the ironic twist, and many film historians must be indebted to him for material found nowhere else. Yet for the researcher, the book is infuriatingly vague; events are mentioned without dates and places, characters jump in and out of the text like figures in a comic opera. Ramsaye was writing a personal history, and it reads that way; he wouldn't let a footnote within a yard of the page.

* * * * *

APPENDIX: SOURCES OF

FILMS AND BIBLIOGRAPHY

This section is organized in the same way as the review of
films and literature. It is divided into four parts: 1) Sources of
the films; 2) Contemporary magazines, newspapers and books; 3) Other
primary sources--official records, correspondence and papers; 4) Secondary sources--books and periodical articles.

1) SOURCES OF THE FILMS:

These are arranged chronologically, and are listed by title,
date of release and producer. I have not included, for reasons of
space and clarity, the large commercial newsreels. The Pathé collection is in the Sherman Grinberg Film Libraries, and the National
Archives still has a considerable quantity of Universal footage
(despite the 1978 fire). But editions of the newsreels are scattered
in film archives throughout the United States and the world; any list
would be incomplete and too long to be helpful. The only newsreels
listed below are those to which special attention was given in the
text, namely the Official War Review and the American War News Weekly.

Britain Prepared (1915), Charles Urban (Imperial War Museum, London).

The Battle Cry of Peace (1915), J. Stuart Blackton (fragments in George
        Eastman House, Rochester, New York).

The German Side of the War (1915), Chicago Tribune (13 scenes in collec-
        tion of John E. Allen, Park Ridge, New Jersey, and five scenes
        in Motion Picture Division, Library of Congress, in reel
        entitled Newsreel Clips From Various Newsreels, No. 9).

With The Russians At The Front (1915), Chicago Tribune (Film Study
     Center, Museum of Modern Art, New York).

Somewhere in France (1915), Donald Thompson (copy on nitrate stock in
     Motion Picture Division, Library of Congress).

The Battle of the Somme (1916), Geoffrey Malins and J.B. McDowell for
     British War Office Topical Committee (Imperial War Museum).

War As It Really Is (1916), Donald Thompson (Motion Picture Branch,
     National Archives).

The Battle of St. Quentin (1916), Malins and McDowell (Imperial War
     Museum).

The Tanks at the Battle of Ancre (1917), Malins and McDowell (Imperial
     War Museum).

American War News Weekly, No. 8 (1917), Cinema War News Syndicate,
     New York (John E. Allen).

American War News Weekly, No. 19 (1917), Cinema War News Syndicate
     (Motion Picture Division, Library of Congress).

The Retreat of the Germans at the Battle of Arras (1917), Malins and
     McDowell (Imperial War Museum).

Official War Review, Nos. 9, 18, 19, 27, 28, 31 (1918), Committee on
     Public Information and Pathe´ (National Archives).

Pershing's Crusaders (1918), Committee on Public Information (National
     Archives).

America's Answer (1918), Committee on Public Information (National
     Archives).

Under Four Flags (1918), Committee on Public Information (National
     Archives and Motion Picture Division, Library of Congress).

Theodore Roosevelt in the Great War (1919), compilation of newsreel
     scenes, (Theodore Roosevelt Collection, Library of Congress).

2) CONTEMPORARY MAGAZINES, NEWSPAPERS AND BOOKS:

     Since most of the articles quoted in this thesis come from the

trade magazines--in particular Motion Picture News and Moving Picture

World--an alphabetical listing in which the name of the magazine is

mentioned every time seems unnecessary. Consequently, I have decided

to group the trade press articles under the name of the publication, and
to list them chronologically. I have omitted small news items, newsreel
synopses and advertisements, although these are referred to in footnotes.
Where no author's name is given, the article is anonymous.

a) Exhibitors Trade Review:

"Kleinschmidt War Films, Showing Actual Fighting, To Be Sent Throughout
    Country After N.Y. Premiere," 10 February 1917, p. 675.

"Topical, Devoted Exclusively to American War News, to Be Offered State
    Rights by New Company," 14 April 1917, p. 1302.

"Motion Pictures and the War," Editorial, 28 April 1917, p. 1433.

b) Motion Picture Magazine:

Dench, Ernest A. "Preserving the Great War for Posterity by the Movies,"
    July 1915, pp. 89-91, 169.

Everets, John Allen. "How I Got to Przemysl and Filmed the Bombardment,"
    February 1916, pp. 56-65.

Sibley, Hi. "That Dam Film," October 1916, pp. 121-2.

Sibley, Hi. "The Why of the Tankless Film," August 1917, pp. 59-63.

Van Loan, H.H. "Shooting the War: The Camera as a Modern Weapon of
    War," March 1918, pp. 63-8, 121-2.

c) Motion Picture News (previously Moving Picture News):

"Disgraceful Fake Pictures," 16 December 1911, p. 5.

"Ramo Rushes to Launch European War Film," 15 August 1914, p. 24.

"The War Cloud and Its Silver Lining," Editorial, 15 August 1914, p. 43.

"Drama That Thrills With War Spirit," 15 August 1914, p. 61.

Milne, Peter. "With Serb and Austrian," Review, 22 August 1914, p. 70.

"Cincinnatians Flock to War Pictures," 5 September 1914, p. 22.

"Real War Pictures Will Be Rarities," 12 September 1914, p. 22.

Franklin, Theodore. "Reaction in Capital Against War Films," 19 Sep-
    tember 1914, p. 20.

"New York and Los Angeles Authorities Open Campaign Against War Films,"
26 September 1914, p. 19.

"Los Angeles Censors Object to "Fake" War Films," 26 September 1914,
p. 19.

Pangburn, Clifford H. "The War Of Wars," Review, 24 October 1914, p. 48.

Lang, Arthur J. "Cashing in on Europe's War," 28 November 1914, p. 25.

"Picture Playhouse Offers Genuine War Pictures," 6 March 1915, p. 69.

"Pathe "News" Scores Two Scoops on Live Events," 10 April 1915, p. 40.

"Pathe Camera Man Decorated for Work at Przemysl," 17 April 1915, p. 38.

"First Authentic Pictures of Vosges Battle," 15 May 1915, p. 57.

"Prepare Against Invasion, Is Vitagraph Film Lesson," 31 July 1915, p. 49.

Andrews, W.R. "The Battle Cry of Peace Is Epic of Patriotism," Review,
21 August 1915, p. 82.

"Cameraman Thompson Off to War for Paramount," 6 November 1915, p. 46.

"German Side of the War Makes Record Run," 13 November 1915, p. 75.

"On the German Firing Line Packs Western Houses," 18 December 1915, p. 48.

"Universal Weekly Gets Shipment of War Films," 18 December 1915, p. 54.

"Kane Gets War Films from Man in 38 Battles," 8 January 1916, p. 77.

"Fighting for France a Special Feature for Mutual," 8 January 1916, p. 80.

"First Selig-Tribune News Pictorial Makes Hit," 15 January 1916, p. 247.

"Kane-Thompson War Films Get Page in Leslie's," 15 January 1916, p. 247.

"Horrors of War from Pathe Freres on January 24," 22 January 1916,
p. 352.

"Germany On Firing Line Officially Approved," 22 January 1916, p. 413.

"Newspaper Promotion for The Fighting Germans," 20 May 1916, p. 3042.

"Cameramen Swarm Like Bees at Pennsylvania Militia Camp," 15 July 1916,
p. 228.

"Urban Tells How 'Battle of the Somme' Was Obtained," 14 October 1916,
p. 2393.

"War Films on State Rights from Thompson Company," 2 December 1916, p. 3453.

"Pathe and International Weeklies Combine," 20 January 1917, p. 386.

"W.K. Vanderbilt Heads War Films Company," 27 January 1917, p. 607.

Shorey, George N. "Germany and Its Armies of Today," Review, 3 February 1917, p. 758.

"Government will Censor Films Showing Ships of War," 14 April 1917, p. 2343.

"Independent Producer to Put Out American War News Weekly," 21 April 1917, p. 2498.

"Gaumont Company Is Covering War in Its Single Reels," 28 April 1917, p. 2665.

"Apportion Country on British War Film Prints," 19 May 1917, p. 3132.

"British Commission at Benefit War Film Showing," 26 May 1917, p. 3267.

"Appropriate War 'Specialties' from Pathe--Fine Scenics," 2 June 1917, p. 3434.

"Mutual Releases 'Heroic France' June 4," 16 June 1917, p. 3770.

"Creel Confers with N.A.M.P.I. for Giant Film Drive," 21 July 1917, p. 371.

"Pathe's New War Film Escapes Submarine," 25 August 1917, p. 1264.

"Government Rules for Film Men During the War," 1 September 1917, p. 1436.

"Life in Cantonments in Hearst-Pathe News," 8 September 1917, p. 1615.

"Italian Pictures Showing to Packed Houses," 8 September 1917, p. 1656.

"Italian War Pictures Pack Chicago House," 15 September 1917, p. 1802.

"Shell-Wrecked Villages in Pathe Pictures," 15 September 1917, p. 1844.

"Lawrence J. Darmour Is Appointed Lieutenant," 20 October 1917, p. 2746.

"Pathe Booms Forth with New French War Film," 3 November 1917, p. 3090.

"Pathe Shows Good War Films," 29 December 1917, p. 4535.

"Cameraman Writes from War Front," 12 January 1918, p. 264.

"Travis Returns with Red Cross Films," 2 February 1918, p. 716.

"Pathe Releases Big War Series May 12," 4 May 1918, p. 2686.

"Timely Subjects in Gaumont News Reels," 11 May 1918, p. 2853.

"Official War Film at Lyric," 1 June 1918, p. 3245.

"U.S. Film Division Makes Vast Plans," 29 June 1818, p. 3863.

"Truce in the Universal-Creel Row," 6 July 1918, pp. 57, 62.

"Explanations Clear War-films Row," 13 July 1918, p. 201.

"Second Official War Film at Cohan," 27 July 1918, p. 594.

"Outline Pathe War Review," 27 July 1918, p. 599.

"Lift Ban on Aeroplane Scenes," 24 August 1918, p. 1209.

Rothapfel, Samuel L. "Rothapfel Gives Some Hints on Weeklies,"
      24 August 1918, pp. 1220, 1228.

Rothapfel, Samuel L. "Rothapfel Tells of Advance of Weeklies,"
      31 August 1918, pp. 1374, 1377.

"Italian Picture in Six Reels," 31 August 1918, p. 1399.

"Hearst-Universal-Mutual in Big Deal," 16 November 1918, p. 2929.

"Under Four Flags," Review, 30 November 1918, p. 3269.

d) Motion Picture Classic:

Dench, Ernest A. "The President as a Movie Fan," July 1917, p. 64.

Blakeslee, Fred Gilbert. "Movie Battles That Make Mars Blush,"
      August 1917, pp. 16-18.

Desmond, William. "Home Bayonet Practice," September 1917, pp. 44-5.

"Uncle Sam's Official War Pictures," September 1918, pp. 56-7.

e) Moving Picture World:

"The Topical Picture," 16 July 1910, p. 132.

Henry, "The Historian of the Future," 8 July 1911, p. 1565.

"A Weekly Film of the World's Events," 29 July 1911, p. 187.

"Advent of the Topical Picture--Vitagraph to Release News Film," 5 August 1911, p. 283.

"The Pathe Journal," 12 August 1911, p. 359.

"The Camera Press Man," 23 September 1911, p. 868.

"The Pathe Weekly," 23 September 1911, p. 871.

"A Combination of Interesting Subjects," 13 April 1912, p. 118.

"Gaumont Weekly for Film Supply Company," 3 August 1912, p. 431.

Bush, W. Stephen. "Camera on the Firing Line," 31 January 1913, p. 522.

Bush, W. Stephen. "Mexican War Pictures," 7 February 1914, p. 657.

"Universal War Service," 2 May 1914, p. 681.

"Pathe Opens Exchanges," 16 May 1914, p. 975.

"Pathe Putting Out News Daily," 13 June 1914, p. 1524.

"Wagner in Mexico," 18 July 1914, p. 440.

"No Cameras Going to the Front," 12 September 1914, p. 1487.

Bush, W. Stephen, "War Films," 19 September 1914, p. 1617.

"All War Pictures Fakes," 3 October 1914, p. 50.

Sinn, Clarence E. "Music for the Picture," 17 October 1914, pp. 339-40.

"Local 'War' Scenes," 17 October 1914, p. 352.

"Close Calls of American Cameraman," 24 October 1914, p. 498.

Sinn, Clarence E. "Music for the Picture," 7 November 1914, p. 776.

"Siege of Antwerp Shown in Pictures," 28 November 1914, p. 1218.

"Faking War Pictures," 28 November 1914, p. 1249.

Bush, W. Stephen. "Genuine War Films," 14 August 1915, pp. 1134-5.

Denig, Lynde. "The Battle of Przemysl," Review, 14 August 1915, p. 1175.

"Paramount Photo-News Man," 6 November 1915, p. 1114.

"Real Thrills in Battle Pictures," 11 November 1916, p. 857.

Blaisdell, George. "War on Three Fronts," Review, 21 April 1917, pp. 447-8.

"The Weekly News Reel," 21 July 1917, pp. 419-20.

Reynolds, Captain Bob (Robert R.). "Filming a News Event for the Screen," 21 July 1917, p. 421.

MacMahon, Henry. "Uplifters Boss War Films: Secret Events Revealed Showing How and Why the Government Failed to Accept the Film Industry's Offer of Hearty Aid," 26 January 1918, pp. 482-4.

"Official War Review No. 4 Is A Stirring Release," 3 August 1918, p. 698.

f) Photoplay Magazine:

Carr, Harry C. "Capturing The Kaiser," March 1916, pp. 111-2.

Cohn, Alfred A. "A Film Newspaper in the Making," April 1916, p. 44.

Shorey, Jerome. "The Romance of the News Reel," February 1919, p. 74.

Croy, Homer. "Handing It Down to Posterity," September 1919, pp. 70-2, 132.

g) Picture-Play Magazine:

Dench, Ernest A. "Camera Men At The Front," January 1916, pp. 91-3.

Cushing, Lieutenant Charles P. "What Movies Mean to the Marines," September 1917, pp. 55-7.

Packard, Roger. "The Movie Machine Gunner," September 1917, pp. 61-2.

Carter, Charles. "Making American History," November 1917, p. 31.

Tenny, Louis. "Filming the Trail of the Serpent," March 1918, pp. 111-5.

Gatchell, Charles. "Filming the Fighting Front," January 1919, pp. 19-24.

h) Reel Life:

Rothapfel, Samuel L. "Dramatizing Music for the Pictures," 5 September 1914, p. 23.

"Facts and Figures and Such," 8 May 1915, p. 6.

i) Variety:

"War Film's Big Draw," 2 June 1917, p. 20.

"Government War Pictures," 13 July 1917, p. 22.

"Picture Engineers Devise War Camera for Government," 12 October 1917, p. 30.

"Lieut. Von Hoffman in Service," 7 December 1917, p. 49.

"Official War Pictures will go on Tour as Shows," 19 April 1918, p. 49.

"War Film Bureaus Confuse Industry as to Exact Duty," 31 May 1918, p. 37.

"America's Answer," Review, 2 August 1918, p. 38.

"Hearst Buys Universal News; Will Issue Daily Service," 8 November 1918, p. 36.

The following articles in magazines of general interest---as distinct from trade publications--are listed in normal bibliographic style:

Anon., "Capturing Mexico with a Camera," Literary Digest, 6 June 1914, p. 1390.

Anon., "Fake War-Movies," Literary Digest, 13 November 1915, p. 1079.

Anon., "Tragedy and Comedy in Making Pictures of the Russian Chaos," Current Opinion, February 1918, pp. 106-7.

Dench, Ernest A. "Methods by Which the European War Has been Filmed," Scientific American, 20 March 1915, p. 277.

Reid, Charles I. "The Adventures of the 'Movie' Camera Man," The Photographic Times, June 1915, pp. 235-7.

Steene, E. Burton. "'Shooting' the Generals with the Movie Camera," Literary Digest, 8 December 1917, pp. 78-81.

As with the trade press articles, I have grouped the newspaper stories chronologically under the name of the paper.

a) New York Times:

"Villa To War For 'Movies'," 7 January 1914, p. 1.

"More Film Men for Villa," and "Ojinaga Federals Defy Villa," 8 January 1914, p. 2.

"Warfare is Waged for the Movies," 8 January 1914, p. 10.

"New Russian War Film--Donald Thompson's Pictures Show Regiment of Women in Training," 10 December 1917, p. 15.

"'America's Answer' Stirs War Spirit," 30 July 1918, p. 9.

b) <u>Topeka Daily Capital</u>:

"Capital Secures Don Thompson's Great War Film," 19 December 1915,
        pp. 1-2.

"'Somewhere in France' Tells Real Story of War," 21 December 1915, p. 14.

"War, Awful, Terrifying, Shown by Don Thompson's Pictures," 23 December
        1915, p. 11.

"War Film will Show Christmas in Trenches," 25 December 1915, p. 16.

"Thompson is Here Ready to Describe War to Topekans," 26 December 1915,
        p. 2B.

"Thompson Movies Bring War Close," 27 December 1915, p. 6.

"Thompson Shows Topeka the War," 28 December 1915, p. 10.

"Thompson Tells Tales of Battle," 30 December 1915, p. 12.

        Contemporary books are listed in normal bibliographic style:

Collins, Francis. <u>The Camera Man</u>. New York: Century, 1916.

Committee on Public Information. <u>Information Concerning the Making
        and Distribution of Pictures that show the Activities of the
        Army and Navy</u>. Washington, D.C.: Government Printing Office,
        1917.

Creel, George. <u>How We Advertised America</u>. New York: Harper and
        Brothers, 1920.

Croy, Homer. <u>How Motion Pictures Are Made</u>. New York: Harper and
        Brothers, 1918.

Dench, Ernest A. <u>Making The Movies</u>. New York: Macmillan, 1915.

Dickson, William Kennedy Laurie. <u>The Biograph in Battle</u>. London:
        Unwin, 1901.

Dyer, Frank Lewis, and Martin, Thomas Commerford. <u>Edison--His Life and
        Inventions</u>. New York: Harper and Brothers, 1910.

Lescaboura, Austin C. <u>Behind the Motion-Picture Screen</u>. New York:
        Scientific American Publishing Co., 1919.

Malins, Lieutenant Geoffrey H. <u>How I Filmed The War</u>. London: Herbert
        Jenkins Ltd., 1920.

Powell, Edward Alexander. <u>Fighting in Flanders</u>. New York: Charles Scribner and Sons, 1916.

<u>The Times History of the War</u>, vol. 21. London: The Times, 1920.

3) <u>OTHER PRIMARY SOURCES--OFFICIAL RECORDS, CORRESPONDENCE AND PAPERS</u>:

"Records of the Adjutant General's Office." Navy and Old Army Branch, National Archives, Washington, D.C.

"Correspondence of Signal Corps Laboratory," Records of American Expeditionary Force General Headquarters. Navy and Old Army Branch, National Archives, Washington, D.C.

"Correspondence of the Chief Signal Officer." Records of American Expeditionary Force General Headquarters. Navy and Old Army Branch, National Archives, Washington, D.C.

"Correspondence of the Office of the Chief Signal Officer, 1917-1940." General Archives Division, National Archives, Washington, D.C.

"Correspondence of the Division of Films." Judicial and Fiscal Branch, National Archives, Washington, D.C.

"Papers of George Creel." Manuscripts Division, Library of Congress, Washington, D.C.

4) <u>SECONDARY SOURCES--BOOKS AND PERIODICAL ARTICLES</u>:

a) <u>Books</u>:

Baechlin, Peter, and Muller-Strauss, Maurice. <u>Newsreels Across the World</u>. Paris: UNESCO, 1952.

Bardèche, Maurice, and Brasillach, Robert. <u>The History of Motion Pictures</u>. New York: W.W. Norton, 1938.

Barnouw, Erik. <u>Documentary: A History of the Non-Fiction Film</u>. New York: Oxford University Press, 1974.

Bauer, K. Jack. <u>List of World War I Signal Corps Films</u>. Washington, D.C.: National Archives, 1957.

Brownlow, Kevin. <u>The Parade's Gone By</u>. New York: Albert A. Knopf, 1968.

Brownlow, Kevin. <u>The War, The West And The Wilderness</u>. New York: Albert A. Knopf, 1979.

Butler, Ivan. <u>The War Film</u>. South Brunswick and New York: A.S. Barnes and Co., 1974.

Crozier, Emmet. _American Reporters on the Western Front_, 1914-1918. New York, Oxford University Press, 1959.

DeWeerd, Harvey A. _President Wilson Fights His War: World War I and the American Intervention_. New York: Macmillan, 1968.

Fielding, Raymond. _The American Newsreel, 1911-1967_. Norman, Okla.: University of Oklahoma Press, 1972.

Furhammer, Lief, and Isaksson, Folke. _Politics And Film_. New York: Praeger, 1971.

Hall, Ben. _The Best Remaining Seats: The Story of the Golden Age of the Movie Palace_. New York: Clarkson N. Potter, 1961.

Jacobs, Lewis. _The Rise of the American Film_. New York: Harcourt, Brace, 1939.

Jowett, Garth. _Film: The Democratic Art_. Boston: Little, Brown and Co., 1976.

Leuchtenberg, William. _Perils of Prosperity_. Chicago: University of Chicago Press, 1958.

Low, Rachael. _The History of the British Film, 1914-1918_. London: George Allen and Unwin, 1950.

Millis, Walter. _Road To War: America 1914-1918_. Boston: Houghton-Miflin, 1935.

Mock, James R., and Larson, Cedric. _Words That Won The War: The Story of the Committee on Public Information, 1917-1919_. Princeton: Princeton University Press, 1939.

Niver, Kemp. _Motion Pictures from the Library of Congress Paper Print Collection, 1894-1912_. Berkeley: University of California Press, 1967.

Palmer, Frederick. _Newton D. Baker: America at War_. New York: Dodd, Mead and Co., 1931.

Peterson, Horace C. _Propaganda For War: The Campaign Against American Neutrality, 1914-1917_. Norman, Okla.: University of Oklahoma Press, 1939.

Ramsaye, Terry. _A Million And One Nights_, 2 vols. New York: Simon and Schuster, 1926.

Scott, James Brown. _A Survey of International Relations between the United States and Germany_. New York: Oxford University Press, 1917.

Smith, Albert E. Two Reels and a Crank. Garden City, N.Y.: Doubleday,
    1952.

Smith, D.M. The Great Departure: The United States in World War I,
    1914-1920. New York: Wiley, 1965.

Staples, Donald E., ed. The American Cinema. Washington, D.C.: Voice
    of America, 1973.

Terrett, Dulany. The Signal Corps: The Emergency. Washington, D.C.:
    Government Printing Office, 1956.

Waldrop, Frank C. McCormick of Chicago. Eaglewood Cliffs, N.J.:
    Prentice-Hall, 1966.

Wood, Leslie. The Miracle of the Movies. London: Burke, 1947.

b) Articles in journals and periodicals:

Anon. "Speaking of Pictures . . . Library of Congress Unearths First
    Newsreels." Life, 20 September, 1943, p. 18.

Cornwell, Elmer E., Jr. "Wilson, Creel and the Presidency." Public
    Opinion Quarterly (Summer 1959): 189-220.

Goldsmith, L.C. "Grinding Out History." Sunset Magazine, July 1925,
    pp. 32-3.

Gordon, Kenneth. "The Early Days of News-Reels." British Kinematography.
    (August 1940): 47-50.

Isenberg, Michael T. "The Mirror of Democracy: Reflections of the War
    Films of World War I, 1917-1919." Journal of Popular Culture 9
    (Spring 1976): 878-85.

Lyons, Timothy J. "Hollywood and World War I, 1914-1918." The Journal
    of Popular Film 1 (Winter 1972): 15-30.

Mackenzie, Stuart. "How the Movie News Man Gets Pictures of World
    Events." American Magazine, January 1924, pp. 38-40, 119-20.

Peet, Creighton. "Hollywood at War, 1915-1918." Esquire, September
    1936, pp. 60, 109.

Pratt, George. "No Magic, No Mystery, No Sleight of Hand." Image,
    December 1959, p. 207.

Sugrue, Thomas. "The Newsreels." Scribner's Magazine, April 1937, p. 9.

Thiesen, Earl. "Story of the Newsreel." The International Photographer,
    September 1933, pp. 3-4, 24-5.

Thiesen, Earl. "The Photographer in the World War." <u>The International Photographer</u>, November 1933, pp. 4-6, 24.

Varges, Ariel. "Ace Newsreeler Gives Light on How He Films News of the World." <u>American Cinematographer</u>, July 1938, p. 275.